The legendary inv
to help humanity

MW00325512

Tesla & me

Didier van Cauwelaert
Translated by Regan Kramer

First published in 2016 under the title Au-delá de l'impossible
by Editions Plon, a branch of Place des Editeurs
12, avenue d'Italie
75013 Paris

KAMP Books (English Edition)
2020 Alameda Padre Serra, Suite 135 Santa Barbara CA 93103
Phone: (415) 595-6451
www.teslaandme.com

Ordering Information
Quantity sales. Special discounts are available on quantity purchases by corporations, associations, and others. For details, contact KAMP Books at the address above. Orders for college textbook/course adoption use. Please contact KAMP Books at the address above.

Library of Congress Cataloging-in-Publication Data
ISBN: 978-0-9779472-0-1
ISBN for EPUB: 978-0-578-41915-2

Cover design: Carl de Vaal
Interior design: Rick Greer
Production service: Rick Greer

"People like us, who believe in physics, know that the distinction between past, present, and future is only a stubbornly persistent illusion."

—Albert Einstein

Letter to the widow of his childhood friend
Michele Besso, 1955.

"The present is theirs; the future, for which I really worked, is mine."

—Nikola Tesla

Statement to a New York Court in front of
his creditors, 1916.

Contents

6|TESLA AND ME

A note from the publisher

This is an extraordinary book. It is a book about innovation written by a novelist, and the sources for the technological breakthroughs don't live in the world that we know. When it was first published, in French, in 2016, it quickly became a bestseller in France, despite the fact the lead character in the book had lived most of his life in the United States. Today, more people know Tesla as a car than as the last name of an inventor who made astonishing discoveries in the early parts of the past century.

Nikola Tesla experimented with creating electricity literally out of thin air. Some of his experiments seemed to show that free energy may not be a strange dream. Tesla has hundreds of patents in his name, and many people have attempted in vain to replicate his most daring trials.

There are stories, anecdotes and mysteries surrounding this amazing inventor who fought "the war of the currents" with Thomas Edison.

One thread is clear throughout Tesla's life: his mission was not to generate a fortune for himself. His inventions could have made him a wealthy man, but he repeatedly chose to value science, discovery, and innovation above business. Tesla's mission was to serve humanity with cheaper energy and better communication. It is fair to state that Tesla wanted to change the world.

This unfinished business is what brought me to this unusual book. As hard as this may be to believe for the Western mind, Tesla himself may be the source of this story about his life and the unaccomplished parts of his mission. Didier van Cauwelaert, who has made a name for himself as a leading novelist in France, has done a remarkable job following and writing this unbelievable story. Through his ability to be open to the unknown yet keep his distance as a reliable observer, that which is hard to believe may become credible.

We know that physicists are only able to document four percent of our existence—we have no clue about the remaining 96 percent that has conveniently been set aside as "dark matter." Whatever happens in that dimension, we don't know—yet. Maybe this story can help us open our eyes to get a better understanding of the world in which we live. While you read this book, you may conclude that Nikola Tesla is the perfect guide on that journey.

Whether you read this book as a work of fiction or non-fiction, you will enjoy it either way. Van Cauwelaert's fine writing is a pleasure to experience. You will probably feel as I did—sometimes the inspiration of the story lies in the challenge to believe it, and sometimes it is the other way around. Even if only a small part of this story is true, it is clear to me this book should not remain—as is the case with too many great French books—confined within the borders of the French-speaking world. That is why you hold this copy in the English language in your hand.

Jurriaan Kamp
Santa Barbara, February 2018

1
Opening

What if we had proof that after death, our consciousnesses were still able to transmit emotions and information? And what if that proof turned our view of time, the universe, and humanity upside down?

Losing your usual points of reference isn't necessarily a bad thing; it could mean your horizons are expanding, but your capacity for critical thinking would have to adapt to the new context. That is why, when people ask me if I believe in the paranormal, I say no—I observe, examine, consider and share information, that's all. I believe that systematic conviction in the face of an unexplained phenomenon is every bit as pernicious as rejecting it out of hand, but the existence of unexplained incidents doesn't bother me in and of itself. Which may be why they sometimes happen to me.

The facts I'm going to describe in this book are—I might as well make it clear, right from the start—absolutely genuine. Yet if you go by the laws that are supposed to govern reality, they can't have happened. Having said that, are the rules that define credibility still applicable? Not really. Like stars, ideas often continue to shine after they have died out, and most of the old laws that used to decree what was or wasn't possible or what was or wasn't scientific have been laid to rest by science itself.

In light of recent medical discoveries, academic proofs, military disclosures, and legal decisions, it would seem the very concept of the "paranormal" is no longer up-to-date. Official recognition has already replaced suspicions of gullibility, illusion, or fraud in a great many fields.

While some scientists are still mourning what they see as a decline in rationalism, many others publicly applaud this new opening. From among the many cases laid out in detail in the two tomes of my book, *The Dictionary of the Impossible*,[1] I will provide just one example from each category of the startling phenomena that have now been recognized by physics, biology, medicine, the army, and the law: phenomena that until recently had been placed in the realm of the "paranormal" (i.e. "outside of or beyond the norm").

Of course, "the norm" depends on the progress of knowledge, which has undergone unprecedented acceleration over the past century. In the early 1900s, for instance, the French Academy of Science was still refusing publications relative to atoms and molecules, whose existence was believed to be irrational superstition.

Let's start our overview with psychokinesis, or the mind's effect on matter. In 1986, at the University of Nantes (France), it was the subject of a medical student's doctoral thesis: *Demonstrating a Psychophysical Effect in Humans and Chicks*.[2] The jury unanimously approved Dr. René Peoc'h's thesis, which showed both why and how a chick behind a pane of glass could draw a randomly moving robot toward itself through mental effort alone.

Why? Because the wheeled machine was the first moving thing the chick saw upon emerging from its shell. Therefore, the chick believed that the machine was its mother. So if a pane of glass keeps the chick from following the machine when it moves, the chick will *get the machine to come to it.*

How? By broadcasting an *intention* in the shape of brainwaves that affect the wheels' movements, whether the robot's propulsion system is located within its structure, in the next room, or even outside the building.

Peoc'h's statistical research shows that as far as mental remote-control goes, humans are infinitely less skillful than chicks. That is because the humans aren't nearly as motivated as the chicks are. Since they don't think the robot is their mother, they have less faith in their psycho-physical abilities, and their thoughts soon turn to something else. In fact, it turns out that humans do best at mental remote control when they're asleep, and their unconscious shoos the robot as far away as possible because it's so noisy.

When real motivation is present—dictated by the survival instinct, a sense of duty, or the need to escape from suffering—it sometimes happens that unknown powers in the mind win out over the skepticism that usually overwhelms them. At that point, anything becomes possible.

In 1905, for instance, the British Parliament witnessed the presence of MP Frederick Carne Rasch during a vote he cared about deeply, even though he was bedridden due to illness at the time. Both his family and the doctor at his bedside certified to that in writing. The MP, who was as white as a sheet, followed the debate in the House of Commons, then evaporated without replying to his fellow MPs' questions about his health. No witnesses mentioned having any physical contact with the fierce opponent of parliamentary absenteeism.

Although it has been forgotten today, the thought-provoking event was front-page news in Britain at the time.[3] It is not an isolated incident, however. The mental projection of a convincing double can even lead to a veritable ubiquity called "bilocation," which includes corporeal materialization and words and actions in *both places*. That was the case—as confirmed by a large number of historians and eyewitnesses—with Yvonne-Aimée de Malestroit, an Augustine nun who led a Resistance cell during World War II.

In 1943, while she was being tortured by the Gestapo in Cherche-Midi prison in Paris, she appeared in the flesh before her friend, Father Paul Labutte, to get him to help keep her from being deported. *At the very same moment*, she materialized aboard *H.M.S. Eridan*, a Royal Navy hospital ship, to urge the sailors on during a sea battle with cries of *"Courage, vive la France!"* The crew was composed essentially of sailors from Brittany, and the engineer, Officer Edouard Le Corre, recognized the nun.

When he inducted her into the Legion of Honor on July 22, 1945, General de Gaulle doffed his uniform cap to the already highly-decorated military heroine. With his *kepi* over his heart, he declared, "I thank you in the name of France," and stage-whispered in a gruffly ironic tone of voice, "I hope you're not in London getting decorated by Churchill right now, too!"

De Gaulle was well aware of the bilocations with which the partisan nun was credited during the war, one of which helped save a submarine in distress.[4] Yvonne-Aimée's feats may defy comprehension, but they were no surprise to the nun herself. Historian Jean-Christian Petitfils points out that she had written detailed predictions of them during her childhood, in notebooks whose authenticity has been established.[5]

Still, you don't always have to project your body to a remote location to get what you want. Some people prefer more discreet means of action. American Army officer Joe McMoneagle received the Legion of Merit, which was awarded for exceptionally meritorious conduct in performing "over 200 mediumship espionage missions for the CIA."[6]

Among other things, McMoneagle, a "remote viewer," was able, based on a satellite photo of a hangar sealed inside an envelope, to draw the prototype of a double-hulled, Typhoon-class submarine that the Soviets were secretly building in the middle of the Cold War. He even managed to predict the exact date it would be launched. President Jimmy Carter made the telepathic espionage practices public in a press conference in September 2005, just before the files were declassified.

Can the existence of phenomena like clairvoyance and pre-cognition be scientifically proven? In 2002, at the University of Illinois, neurologists McDonough, Don, and Warren studied how brains react at the instant intuition is solicited.

The experiment itself was very simple: playing cards were randomly displayed on a computer screen, and "ordinary people" wearing electrode helmets were asked to state out loud what they thought the next card would be. As a result of the experiments, the three neurologists revealed a fascinating fact: when the person had guessed the right answer, the encephalogram line was different just *before* the card flashed onto the screen. In other words, our brains know they're right even before they have been shown proof of it.[7]

Cases of remote healing by magnetizers have been attested to through strict protocols in hospitals. They have become more and more common since Dr. Elisabeth Targ's well-known 1988 double-blind test. It can be summed up as follows: "The California-based psychiatrist came up with two clever, strictly controlled studies in which some 40 distant healers scattered throughout the United States, proved to be capable of improving the health of terminally ill AIDS patients, even when the healers had not met them."[8]

In addition, researchers now believe they have identified the type of brainwaves healers emit. Their therapeutic effects have been measured on patients who were not aware of the time of the treatment. They were placed inside Faraday cages, which block electromagnetic waves. The brainwaves must, therefore, be longitudinal waves moving in a vortex, the famous scalar waves detected by Nikola Tesla, which, as it happens, will come up quite a bit in this book.

Thanks to these discoveries, in order to relieve patients' pain and improve their overall health, a growing number of hospitals is providing magnetizers' on-call schedules in addition to offering anesthesia through hypnosis. In France, this revolution in clinical practice had its start in burn units, at the initiative of surgeons like Dr. Patrick Lacroix, at Besançon University Hospital Center.

Lacroix was one of the first to officially communicate the exceptional results obtained by magnetizers, even when their "subjects" were babies with second-degree burns. "On a 10-day-old baby," Dr. Lacroix pointed out, "you can hardly attribute improvement to the placebo effect or whatnot."[9]

In response to achievements impossible to obtain through traditional methods—such as the sudden disappearance of pain or the spectacular acceleration of healing—neuro-psychiatrist David Servan-Schreiber concluded, "I don't know if magnetism is scientific or not, but considering its success rate, it is definitely rational."[10]

Let's have a brief word about UFOs, shall we? Everyone is free to have their own opinion about their existence and nature, but the fact is that they are now an officially recognized reality for every army in the world. This has been the case for the French high command, for instance, since the 1995 disclosure of the COMETA report.

Published under the aegis of the Institute for Advanced National Defense Studies, the 120-page document contains astounding observations described by both civilian and military personnel, including harassment maneuvers performed by a UFO against Commander Giraud and Captain Abraham.

On March 7, 1977, the two officers were at the helm of a Mirage IV carrying an atomic bomb. Both men described a "white sphere flying at a speed of nearly 4,000 m.p.h." At first it would loom up randomly, sometimes to their left, sometimes their right, but then it began to anticipate the Mirage's changes in direction, as though it were plugged into the pilot's brain, and he were unwittingly remote-controlling it.[11]

General Denis Letty, who supervised the COMETA report, concluded that, "The extra-terrestrial hypothesis is far and away the best and most scientific one. It is the one that best matches the phenomena observed."[12]

Considering the above mentioned examples, you might legitimately wonder if the remote realization of an intention is a faculty inherent to animals, humans, and extra-terrestrials. Plants are capable of it, too, as botanist Jean-Marie Pelt has shown.

When subjected to a massive invasion of caterpillars, for example, trees send an ethylene-based gaseous alert to their fellow trees. In response, the others trees render their leaves toxic for the caterpillars *before they are even under attack.*[13]

Cleve Backster, an American engineer, invented an extremely efficient lie detector for the CIA. A major scientific journal also published the stunning results of his work on how plants perceive mental images emitted by humans.[14] When someone *conjures up a mental picture* of themselves burning one of a tree's leaves with a lighter, the intention triggers stress in the tree that can be measured with an electroencephalograph (EEG).[15]

Fortunately, a form of "plant joy" can also be detected with an EEG. Following a protocol similar to the one established by biologist Rupert Sheldrake to prove the telepathic connection between a dog and its owner,[16] Backster discovered that office plants react remotely at the precise moment that he decided to go back and water them, even though his return was dictated by the random ringing of a timer in his pocket.

What's even more extraordinary is that the same researcher revealed the "emotional" connection existing between people and samples of their blood drawn for testing. In an absolutely scientific—i.e., measurable, quantifiable, and reproducible—way, Backster showed that, among other things, the fear a subject feels while watching a horror film is also "felt" by the subject's blood cells in a test tube stored several miles away.

An EEG connected to the blood sample displays an identical peak at the exact same time as one measuring the blood donor's reactions to watching a scene from a horror film. "I have been shown, in a scientific demonstration, the reality of conscious, non-local, instantaneous communication between my thoughts and my cells," Dr. Myra Crawford wrote after this had been demonstrated to her, research director at the University of Alabama at Birmingham.

In 2002, Crawford founded the UAB Human Energetics Assessment Laboratory. There she reproduced and furthered the fabulous experiments first performed by Backster, a selfless genius who died in 2013 at the age of 89, a virtual unknown, despite having transformed our understanding of biology as radically as Albert Einstein did theoretical physics and Nikola Tesla energy.

Backster's discoveries did lead to one crucial question, however: do the emotions' capacity for remote resonance only work for cells that have belonged to the same body at some point? Apparently not.

In the late 1980s, in the middle of the war between Israel and Lebanon, a group of American scientists (Orme-Johnson, Alexander, Davies, and Chandler) carried out an unprecedented experiment called the "International Peace Project in the Middle East." The idea was to send a "commando" of trained Transcendental Meditation participants into combat zones. Their mission was to delight in feelings of peace and joy as if the war were already over.

This wide-scale application of the power of positive thinking produced such spectacular results that they were described, analyzed, and statistically modeled in *The Journal of Conflict Resolution*, a highly respected, peer-reviewed academic journal.

As incredible as it may seem, the peace the "Pink Helmet" squads congratulated each other for became a reality in every combat zone they visited. Terrorist actions stopped, a significant drop in both offensive and retaliatory actions was recorded, ceasefires were spontaneously and unexpectedly respected, rival factions fraternized, and more.[17]

Based on those concrete results, a theoretical formula was drawn up, and psychologists and statisticians from Princeton University worked out how many people it would take to end a war through the power of thought. According to their calculations, all it would take is for the square root of 1% of the affected population (i.e. in the year 2007, just 7,746 volunteers around the world) to sense peace in order for it to become a reality.[18]

Let's take that even further.

If thought can have a remote effect on movement, matter, our health and emotions, is it capable of manifesting itself when the brain is not functioning? This leads us to the problem of NDEs—Near Death Experiences— first revealed by Dr. Raymond Moody in the late 1970s.[19]

For years, accounts of out-of-body experiences with hyper-perception after patients have been declared clinically dead have been pooh-poohed by the medical establishment. Doctors have explained NDEs away as hallucinations caused by a lack of oxygen to the brain. The stress supposedly causes the brain to release a "dissociative anesthesia," along the lines of ketamine. The anesthesia, they say, explains the famous tunnel of light in which angels, departed friends, relatives, and/or strangers welcome you briefly to the afterlife before sending you back to your body—if the intensive-care staff manages to get your heartbeat going again, that is. But as Dr. Pim van Lommel, a Dutch cardiologist who in 2001 published the first scientific study of that type of experience in the medical journal *The Lancet*, says, "Such a brain would be roughly analogous to a computer with its power source unplugged and its circuits detached. It couldn't hallucinate; it couldn't do anything at all."

In that case, we can only surmise the work of a relocated consciousness acting as a relay for the unavailable brain. Picture a kind of external hard drive: not only does it back-up data memory, but it also continues to perceive and generate information. That information can be "recovered" by the brain once it is able to function again, i.e., when the heart is back in working order. That explanation has been proposed by several scientists, including both Dr. Jean-Jacques Charbonier,[20] an intensive-care anesthesiologist in France, and Dr. Eben Alexander,[21] a renowned American neurosurgeon.

In early 2008, Dr. Alexander, a materialist who was hostile to "paranormal nonsense," was pronounced clinically dead, having been struck down by bacterial meningitis that was destroying his brain. Resuscitated despite the odds, he immediately began to transcribe his memories of an extraordinary psychic journey. During his NDE, instantaneous and unlimited knowledge of quantic universes had been engraved within him, while his relocated consciousness had "discovered" a sister whose existence had always been kept hidden from him.

Once back on his feet, Dr. Alexander decided to study his own case file. Scanner and other test results, as well as neurological examinations, all pointed to the same inescapable conclusion: the part of his brain that deals with perceptions, analysis and memorization "was no longer in existence" while he had been performing those mental operations.

Proven untenable, the hallucination postulate has finally been laid to rest after four decades of accumulated evidence. Much of it is as edifying as the evidence provided by Dr. Alexander, but his story attracted more media coverage due to his status as a surgeon. I will cite just one other incident, to my eyes the most thought-provoking one: the case of Irène Badini.

After she was resuscitated, Badini, a blind woman who had undergone an NDE, was able to provide a precise description (hair and skin color, names on their badges) of the hospital employees who had stolen her jewelry while she was brain dead. Stunned by the accusations of a blind woman who "saw" them plundering her "remains," the guilty parties confessed their crimes, and the jewelry was found exactly where Badini had said it would be.[22] Should we conclude that, when it is functioning outside of the brain, the consciousness is freed from certain physical handicaps?

Nowadays, academia offers de facto recognition of the existence of the NDE phenomenon that it denied for so long. On December 15, 2014, François Lallier obtained a doctorate in medicine with the highest honors for a thesis devoted to the reality of near-death experiences.[23]

This revolution in mindset is even picking up speed in courts of law. That same year, Jimi Fritze, a 43-year-old Swede, surprised everyone when he emerged from an "irreversible" coma, after which he sued the hospital in Göteborg where he had been on life support.

Completely paralyzed after a stroke, classified as clinically dead, he had, in fact, heard *everything* that had been said around him. He was able to quote the conversations that had traumatized him the most while trapped deep inside his slumbering consciousness—word for word. The most upsetting of those was when the doctors had tried to convince his girlfriend it was urgent, in the name of the common good, to allow them to begin organ retrieval. "The surgeons were talking about doing tests on my liver and kidneys in order to transplant them into other patients. I was terrified of being subjected to a horrific death."[24]

The survivor explains that he didn't sue the doctors for his own sake, but so that what had happened to him wouldn't happen again. He also wants everyone to know that a human being in a coma is neither a vegetable, nor a future corpse on life support, nor an insensitive organ bank.

Duly noted.

But what about when someone dies for good?

That brings us to the crux of the question underpinning this whole book: is communication with the deceased possible at a high enough level that posthumous intelligence, memory, and sensitivity could lead to real dialogue, whether written, oral, or visual? In 2011, 64% of French people surveyed believed in some form of life after death (compared to 35% in 1981), and over 50% thought that a dialogue of that type was within the realm of the possible.[25] But how can we go about establishing it, and in what way should we study its manifestations?

Lacking instruments capable of conclusively analyzing the automatic-writing process, scientists have trained their attention on the audiovisual evidence arriving from the hereafter, grouped under the acronym ITC (instrumental trans-communication).

In France, the acknowledged pioneer in the field is Monique Simonet. A former grade-school teacher who died in June 2016 at the age of 93, Simonet spent her nights holding a microphone up to the dead in order to offer comfort to the living.[26] Over 20,000 audio messages—ranging from "I'm fine, I love you," to philosophical, puckish, or religious considerations—fill the tapes she mailed to the four corners of the globe, never once charging for her services. The messages are pronounced by voices that, in many cases, trained ears or sound-analyzing software have recognized as belonging to a given departed person.

The "little old recording lady from Reims"—as the sound engineer who introduced us in 1988 called her with polite deference—was a hotline, a painstaking relay transmitter, a bridge between two worlds unto herself. The sound material she and her acolytes around the world have gathered has been subjected to numerous electro-acoustic analyses.

To date, the most thorough studies are the ones carried out in Frankfurt, Germany by Dr. Ernst Senkowski,[27] and in Bologna, Italy by sound engineer Paolo Presi.[28] In France, very few researchers have been brave enough to publish their results. There is just one hitch, but it rubs "serious" scientists the wrong way: for any given message, the radio-wave frequencies change from one analysis to the next. As though the scientists were dealing with living matter. As though rather than analyzing a sound sample, they were analyzing a blood sample whose statistics depended on the person's overall condition at a given moment.[29]

That being said, bogus recordings made with synthetic voices—those that can be explained away by "normal" interference—are easy to spot. As for the other cases, sound measurements have come up with two interesting facts. One is that the voices analyzed frequently surpass 1,400 Hz, whereas human voices range from 80 to 400 Hz. The other is that the voices do not possess the fundamental frequencies, i.e., ones corresponding to air passing from the lungs over the vocal cords. Still, that doesn't prove they come from the afterlife.

In the presence of Brian Josephson, Nobel Prize-winner in Physics, the University of Toronto used an electroencephalogram to display the brain projection of British medium Matthew Manning at the exact moment that a "paranormal" voice was being recorded. Austrian Franz Seidl, an electrical engineer and winner of the Getty Prize for his work on energy, was also able to materialize a sentence on magnetic tape by focusing his mind on it. This is comparable to the way in which a man named Ted Serios has produced psychic photos in a lab, "imprinting" on a Polaroid the image of a prehistoric man he had been asked to think about.[30]

Professor Rémy Chauvin (1913-2009) was one of the best-known scientists to publicly endorse the study of these phenomena, applying critical analysis to them during his classes at La Sorbonne. In reaction to some of the many instances described, he wrote:

If that isn't the dead speaking, then we have been confronted with a troublesome problem. Our brains are much more than just our brains: they seem to have at their disposal an all-encompassing super-power, which, until now had exerted itself only over our own bodies.[31]

Analyses of images of unknown origins appearing in "snow" on TV or computer screens reveal one constant: they come from *pre-existing images* (photos, film stills, TV shows, etc.) that have been reworked by unidentified means.

That is the case, for instance, of the famous photo of Romy Schneider "received" by engineer Klaus Schreiber via his television screen in Aix-la-Chapelle in 1987.[32] The photo comes from a feature film the actress had starred in, *Max and the Junkmen*, except for one small detail.

When specialists in Vienna undertook a meticulous comparison of the photo and the film material (final cut, out-takes, rushes, publicity stills, etc.), they discovered that the "trans-image" emerging from a shifting white mass on Schreiber's screen is unlike any shot in which the actress ever appeared. The angle of her face, the location of the shadows or the placement of her hair relative to the background of the shot—some detail is always off. The photo seems to have been touched up, but by whom?

"It seems quite likely that Romy Schneider herself drew on remnant waves from the era when she made the movie," Rémy Chauvin has suggested, "in order to send us an image of herself that she was particularly pleased with."

Another, even more curious example that would seem to support that hypothesis involves Friedrich Jürgenson (1903-1987), founding father of ITC, ornithologist, and filmmaker who captured over 100,000 voices believed to be paranormal.

After his death, his followers received an image of him on a small screen that turned out to be an excerpt from a program on which he had been a guest during his lifetime. The only difference was that the tie he was wearing in the post-mortem picture was not the same one he is wearing in images from the original show.

Karine Dray, a young woman who died in Mexico at the age of 21, "sent" a sort of photomontage to an *unplugged* computer in the CETL lab in Luxembourg in 1997.[33] The image combined a photo of herself and her cat, Magna, which had been taken two years before she died, with an unidentified background. Moreover, a caption under the image says, "keyword: Magna." The recipient—who knew Karine's parents—forwarded the mail to them in Mexico.

Along with computer specialists, I have personally compared the original document on the hard drive of the Luxembourg computer with the e-mail the Drays received. Over the course of its transfer through the ether, Karine's parents' dog had been inexplicably added to the image.

Sometimes, as we will see in the following chapters, sound and image come together to express something more than just a wink and a nod, a posthumous medical bulletin or a sign of affection. But how reliable is the information contained in those messages? The American judicial system has spoken: In 1978, a spirit's statement was found admissible by a Chicago court.[34] For the first time in investigative history, the victim of a murder disguised as an accident accused her killer *post-mortem*, backing her accusations up with hard evidence.

Yet nothing had led detectives to suspect foul play until the late Teresita Basa appeared to a former fellow nurse, indicating her murderer's name and address. The revenant also explained where the killer had hidden her jewelry, although the police hadn't even been aware of the theft. The combination of the discovery of the loot where the ghost had said it would be and the guilty party's confession led to jurisprudence that ipso facto acknowledged the existence of ghosts and the validity of their testimony in court.[35]

One unexpected consequence: nowadays, in some American states, as with termite or asbestos issues, property sales can be voided if hauntings or other ghostly phenomena take place in a house…as long as the seller provided ghost-free certification,

A decision about intellectual-property rights has also been handed down regarding texts that seem to have been dictated from the hereafter via automatic writing, offering legal recognition of the "incorporeal" author.

Following suits brought by Frederic W.H. Myers' heirs, the Geraldine Cummins case, among others, brought a critical question to legislators' attention: who gets the royalties on a work composed and dictated by a revenant or ghost and transcribed by a medium?[36] Barring conclusive expertise, Anglo-Saxon law comes down on the side of the deceased.[37]

First let's find out a little more about Miss Cummins (1890-1969). A celebrated playwright, poet, medium, and champion hockey player, in 1925, the Irishwoman unintentionally became the "exclusive importer" of the ideas of Mr. Myers. Known as the father of the psychology of the subliminal self, in addition to being an eminent scientist, Myers, a tireless explorer of the soul, was also a poet and professor of literature at Cambridge.

According to both eyewitnesses to her trances and specialists in his work, 24 years after his death, the flamboyant author admired by Nietzsche, Bergson, and Jung dictated—at the impressive speed of 1,600 words an hour—over a thousand pages of text to the young woman. In them, he describes his death and the different stages of his evolution in the afterlife.[38]

Skeptics immediately accused Cummins of having deliberately plagiarized Myers and faking their posthumous collaboration for the sake of publicity, which seems unlikely, considering how well-known she already was. Before choosing literary exclusivity via Cummins's plume, Myers had already provided supreme proof of large-scale, post-mortem communication for which he had searched, in vain, during his lifetime.

When he wasn't teaching, Myers, the founder of the Society for Psychical Research, spent his time testing—and often debunking—hundreds of mediums. Yet even when the information provided was confirmed, he was never able to exclude the possibility that the subject in a trance state might in fact have been communicating with another living person. He died, frustrated, at the age of 58, after promising his colleagues to do "everything in his power to provide them with the proof he lacked" once he was on "the other side."

Three months after his death, a dozen mediums in England, the United States, and India began receiving automatic-writing messages signed Frederic Myers. The mediums could make neither heads nor tails of the phrases, which were often in Greek or Latin. Each correspondent, however, was asked to get in touch with another person—one they usually didn't know—who had also just received a scrap of incomprehensible text, with the name of yet another medium with whom to get in touch.

Assembled in the order indicated, the bits of text began, like the pieces of a jigsaw puzzle, to shape themselves into a text of tremendous literary distinction. Over 3,000 correlated communications were collected via these "human relay stations" over the span of 20 years. The outcome of this posthumous protocol has been preserved by the Society for Psychical Research. For historians who have studied the case, it constitutes the most irrefutable example known of actual communication between the dead and the living.

*

Of course, you've probably never heard about any of this in the mainstream media. They prefer to keep the public on a steady drip of anxiety-inducing news that clips their wings and shrinks their horizons. And yet, no matter how amazing or disorienting the examples I have just mentioned might be, this is where we actually stand today in terms of how science, medicine, history, justice, and society see these "impossible" phenomena.

So, what are we sure of, in an experimental context, at this point in time? At least the following: thought influences matter and circumstance; it can act, soothe, or heal remotely; consciousness can, in certain cases, function independently of the brain; animals and vegetables can communicate with each other (and us) via a kind of telepathy; unidentified phenomena challenge our technologies; and the invisible can leave actual audio and/or visual "footprints" that come either from the afterlife or the intention of a living person.

Nevertheless, in my opinion, we shouldn't try to interpret these events as infringements on natural laws ruling the universe and objective reality. When anomalies and exceptions become that numerous, it is time to acknowledge that the laws are inaccurate, or at the very least, perfectible. Still, it would be a shame to stop there. Once the existence of a phenomenon has been established, what matters is to try to understand the reason behind it, to find its meaning or purpose, and to look for what it can teach us.

As I see it, the signs are food for thought, leading us to reconsider what we think we know, rather than simply submit to powers beyond our grasp. Everything I have just shared has one thing in common, which seems glaringly obvious to me: no matter who or what the source or the receiver is, every episode involves the *circulation of information*. A necessary, pressing circulation, for which the end justifies the means, even if those means violate scientific principles established by humans.

Despite the fact the transmission methods have not been properly elucidated yet, this active information (telepathic, via a medium, curative, or disconnected from brain activity) can no longer be cast into doubt, short of elevating deliberate ignorance of all advances to the rank of rational method.

On the other hand, the proofs and confirmations we have just reviewed—particularly the ones involving dialogue between the living and the dead—do not automatically guarantee the veracity or relevance of information received through these channels, nor do we know their true origins or source.

We should bear in mind that a medium is just as likely to channel lies, nonsense, or manipulative information as is a television set or website. Constant vigilance and methodical doubt—taken as tools rather than ends in and of themselves—summarize, I believe, the approach I remain faithful to, despite the stunning strength of the facts I have just been personally confronted with.

And "confronted" really is the word. The incredible tale you are about to read actually took place in real life, no matter how similar it may seem to a piece of fiction I had been working on at the time.

In 1983, Frédéric Dard, the immortal creator of police commissioner San -Antonio, dreamt up a kidnapping plot for a novel he was working on that would turn out to be *exactly like* the one his daughter Josephine would fall victim to in real life just a few days later.[39] The details included her abductor scouting the location by slipping in with a film crew, the sum demanded as ransom, the happy ending, and more.

Like Frédéric, I too found myself—although luckily without having to worry about my loved ones—in the position of an author whose life imitates their art. I had the same type of questions that my friend—in a far more worrisome situation—shared with me at the time: had his mind simply captured something, or had he somehow actually caused or inspired the kidnapper's *modus operandi*?

Before those dramatic events took place in real life, Dard had not shown the manuscript that would wind up "tempting fate" (as he put it) to anyone. When he wasn't working on it, he kept it locked inside a desk drawer.

As for me, although I had shown several people the prophetic manuscript, I hadn't submitted it for publication yet. Something was stopping me. Even though the plot was taut and exciting and I had poured my heart and soul into it, something was telling me it just "wasn't quite ready" yet. It seemed to require another rewrite, which I gave it, again and again.

But that wasn't the problem. I kept postponing the publication date, and the start of production for the film version. I knew I had to wait, although I didn't know what for. Now I know.

I had to wait for the story to actually happen to me just as I had imagined it on paper. I had been equipped to live through the experience by the very fact of having dwelled on and written about it beforehand. That preparation allowed me to better accept, deal with, and describe what actually happened. Then and only then could the feelings the events had inspired in me be poured into the fiction that reality had "copied."

The story I'm talking about relates how a deceased, obsessive, and mischievous scientist psychically harasses two mediums who are unalike in every way. It was the very situation I would find myself in the midst of, starting on December 19, 2015.

*

I do, of course, realize just how extraordinary, unlikely, and surreal the account that follows may seem. But aside from the evidence that supports it, it is not unprecedented in my line of work. It is part—if not of a long tradition, exactly—then at least of a fairly logical continuity when an author realizes it is his passion, profession, and obligation to transmit to his contemporaries the feelings that affect, assault, intrigue, or gnaw at him.

In a nutshell, I am hardly the first novelist to relay feelings and information he believes to be arriving from the afterlife. Honoré de Balzac, Alexandre Dumas, Victor Hugo, Arthur Conan Doyle, and Jean Cocteau—to name but the best-known and most outspoken—usually did it through table-turning or automatic writing, which is not my case.

It is well known, for instance, that while Victor Hugo was in exile on the Channel Islands, he divided his time between his own work and that of some of his most esteemed fellow authors (Dante, Shakespeare, Châteaubriand, and others) who, he claimed, wanted to complete manuscripts posthumously through his pen.[40] There is nothing that direct or deliberate where I am concerned.

I was perfectly content to make do with receiving and following up on stunningly precise messages received via the intermediary of two women renowned for both their mediumship and their reliability. Unlike my illustrious predecessors, who were methodically obsessed with spiritualism, I didn't try to provoke anything. I wasn't expecting answers; I hadn't solicited contact with the hereafter to ask for news of my dearly departed—I had already received some, thank you very much. That was enough for me, and I was happy to leave them in peace. I had decided, as the saying goes, to "Let the dead bury the dead," meaning, in a nutshell, that I would rather worry about the living.

Apparently, the dead were having none of that.

Suddenly I was being called upon to bear witness, get involved, and investigate. I was pointed in the direction of scientists I didn't know, as well as of breathtaking—and sometimes, mind-blowing—discoveries. I was shuttled between terrifying secrets buried in the past and the radiant future the fossil-fuel and other energy lobbies have done their best to prevent.

No, I hadn't asked for any of it. But how could I refuse the humanitarian aid a revenant seemed to be requesting? How could I remain deaf to the pleas of a man who had been broken during his lifetime by the scope and scale of his own discoveries, the apocalyptic use some of his inventions had been put to, and the way in which the others—the ones that could have brought peace and well-being to the world while reducing inequality—had been sabotaged or tossed on the junk pile of history?

I answered the call, but I do still wonder about it all. In response to the ideas that came to me, the clues that were transmitted, and the events that occurred, was I being "guided," manipulated, or was I simply following my own free will for all those months? I honestly don't know. At this point, it's up to you, the reader, to judge.

My sincerity and lucidity, as well as the honesty and integrity of the key players in my tale, the witnesses to these staggering phenomena, are absolute. Despite all the proof that has been accumulated as I write these lines, that is the only thing I know for sure.

Yes, I still wonder if all that information really did originate in the hereafter, but I have complete faith in the living beings who channeled and incarnated it. Why would I want to destroy both their good reputations and my own by presenting what I know to be fraudulent as real, by lending credence to a scam through my negligence, by affirming the truthfulness of facts that had not been confirmed by eyewitnesses, specialists, documentation, and/or expertise?

Nevertheless, I do still have my doubts about the actual source and purpose of the revelations that targeted me over the winter of 2015-2016; or let's say I maintain a certain critical distance from it all.

I have one last thing to add before I open my Pandora's Box. For the sake of argument, let's assume the deceased actually do have the faculty of deliberately appearing to us in the shape of phantoms that have kept their identity. Taking that as my starting point, what I wonder about the most— aside from the phenomenon in and of itself—is just what it is in their past, in their emotions or ours, that justifies the effort it takes to assemble their thoughts, former physical appearance, and earthbound concerns. It is a great leap back that may represent a great leap forward for them, a kind of evolution they are trying to connect to our own.

I'm not sure what the answer is, but I do know it is time to explore the question.

1. Plon, 2013, and J'ai Lu, 2014. *Le Nouveau Dictionnaire de l'impossible*, Plon, 2015, and J'ai Lu, 2016.
2. The thesis can be consulted (in French) at the following URL: http://psiland.free.fr/savoirplus/theses/

peoch.pdf

3. *Daily Express, Evening News* etc., 17 May 1905.
4. Dr. Patrick Mahéo and René Laurentin, *Bilocations de Mère Yvonne- Aimée*, F.-X. de Guibert, 1990.
5. Jean-Christian Petitfils, *Jésus*, Fayard, 2011.
6. www.inrees.com; and *Enquêtes extraordinaires, Sixième sens* ("Extraordinary Investigations (EI): Sixth Sense") (DVD), Ed. Montparnasse
7. *Le Monde des Religions*, May 2008.
8. *Western Journal of Medicine*, December 1988.
9. *Enquêtes extraordinaires. Les Guerisseurs* ("EI: The Healers" DVD), by Thierry Machado, Ed. Montparnasse, 2011.
10. David Servan-Schreiber, *Guerir*, Robert Laffont, 2003; interview with Stéphane Allix in *Les Guerisseurs* (*"The Healers"*), above.
11. COMETA report, www.cnes-geipan.fr
12. General Denis Letty, in *EI* by Natacha Calestrémé and Stéphane Allix (DVD) *Les Ovnis* (*"UFOs"*), Ed. Montparnasse, 2014.
13. Jean-Marie Pelt, *Les Langages secrets de la nature*, Fayard, 1999.
14. "Plant Primary Reception," in *Science*, vol. 189, n° 4201, 8 August 1975.
15. Cleve Backster, *Primary Perception: Biocommunication with Plants, Living Foods and Human Cells*, White Rose Millennium Press, 2003.
16. Rupert Sheldrake, *Dogs that Know when Their Owners Are Coming Home*, Crown Publishers, 1999.
17. *Journal of Conflict Resolution*, vol. 32, 1988.
18. www.youtube.com/watch?v=65cizkTTrig
19. Dr. Raymond Moody, *Life After Life*, Mockingbird Books, 1977, HarperCollins, 2015.
20. Dr. Jean-Jacques Charbonier, *La Medecine face à l'Au-delà* (*"The Medical Establishment and the Hereafter"*), Guy Tredaniel, 2011.
21. Dr. Eben Alexander, *Proof of Heaven*, Simon & Schuster, 2012.
22. Sonia Barkallah, *Faux depart* (*"Not Really Gone"*), S17 Production, 2010.
23. François Lallier, "Facteurs associes aux experiences de mort imminente dans les arrêts cardiorespiratoires reanimes," (Factors Associated with NDE in Cases of Reanimated Cardio-respiratory Arrest) doctoral thesis defended at the Medical School of Reims (France), 2014, www.sudoc.abes.fr
24. *The Telegraph*, April 6, 2014.
25. *Ça m'interesse*, April 2001.
26. Monique Simonet, *Realite de l'au-delà et transcommunication* (*"The Reality of the Hereafter and Trans-communciation"*), Editions du Rocher, 2004.
27. *Instrumentelle Transkommunication*, RG Fischer, Frankfurt, 1989.
28. laboratorio26@hotmail.com
29. François Brune, *Les morts nous parlent* (*"The Dead Are Talking to Us"*), Philippe Lebaud, 1993.
30. Marie-Monique Robin and Mario Varvoglis, *Le Sixième Sens* (*"The Sixth Sense"*), Le Chêne, 2002.
31. Rémy Chauvin, *L'Autre science, in A l'ecoute de l'au-delà* (*"The Other Science" in "Listening to the Beyond"*), Philippe Lebeau, 1999.
32. Rainer Holbe, *Bilder aus dem Reich der Toten*, Knaur, Munich, 1987.
33. Maryvonne and Yvon Dray, *Karine après la vie* (*"Karine After Life"*), Albin Michel, 2002; Le Livre de Poche, 2004.
34. "Accused of Murder by a Voice from the Grave," *Ebony*, June 1978.
35. "A Chicago Murder Solved by a Ghost," *The Chicago Tribune*, April 9, 1992.
36. Cummins versus Bond, 1927.
37. "Communication spirituelle et droit d'auteur : à qui les droits d'une œuvre litteraire dictee depuis l'au-delà?" ("Spiritual Communication and Intellectual Property Rights: Who Gets the Rights to a Work Dictated from Beyond the Grave?") by Laurence Bich-Carrière, in *Les Cahiers de la propriete intellectuelle*, Vol. 19, n° 3, October 2007.
38. Geraldine Cummins (& Frederic Myers), *The Road to Immortality*, Pilgrims Book, 1984.
39. San-Antonio, *Faut-il tuer les petits garçons qui ont les mains sur les hanches?* (*"Should Little Boys who Put their Hands on their Hips Be Killed?"*), Fleuve Noir, 1984.
40. Victor Hugo, *Transcripts of this Table Turning Sessions in Jersey*, presented and annotated by Gustave Simon, Stock, 1980.

2
Visiting Hours

December 19, 2015, 6 a.m.: An artist wakes up to find a man standing at the foot of her bed—not just any man, but probably the greatest scientist the world has ever known. He will return several times. He has, it seems, some information to share with me, as does one of his friends.

There's just one small problem: one of them died in 1955, the other in 1943.

What's the point of the impossible? Are phenomena that surpass our understanding meant to disorient us, to reveal our limits, or to encourage us to overcome them? That is a question that crops up a lot in my books. It is both their wellspring and their byproduct. I think that's because over time, I have become more and more convinced that the events that make the greatest impact on us are those that resonate with our hopes, desires and fears, and the imaginings that stem from them.

For me, what most people call fate is just a tool of my trade, a rough draft that can be modified as long as we take the trouble to do so. I see the world as a scenario being endlessly written and rewritten, a playing field on which fact and fiction are constantly battling to outdo each other, whether to the benefit of our dreams or at the expense of them. The trick is in figuring out how to interpret the causes and effects of what happens to us.

On December 19, when I received what would turn out to be the first in a long series of messages, and again, at each new stage of the incredible "dialogue" that would ensue, an expression popped into my mind. It resonated in my brain with the precise insistence of a tuning fork. I had heard it for the first time in 2001, spoken by a gruffly smiling Professor Rémy Chauvin.

A world-renowned bee specialist, Chauvin had been showing me how scout bees dance along an axis representing the sun to inform the rest of the colony where a new source of nectar or pollen is located. If their dance lingers on due to the forager bees' skepticism, the scouts take the sun's change of position into account in the flight plan they tirelessly repeat.[1] But how?

"Well," Chauvin mumbled with a sort of cautious pleasure, "that's where we begin to find ourselves *beyond the impossible.*"

"Which is?"

"In a conception of the world where everything becomes possible once again."

"Meaning?"

"Natural."

It's true that in my long experience with unexplained phenomena, the thing that has impressed me the most—what I have felt more intensely than surprise, knee-jerk incredulity or amazement—is the realization that the human spirit can adapt to an apparently supernatural situation with incredible ease, provided that situation is flagrant, shareable and long-lasting, and that it occurs repeatedly.

And that is exactly what would happen over the next few months in response to information that was apparently coming from a pair of geniuses who had relocated to the hereafter.

*

But let's get back to that December morning. The artist is Geneviève, the wife of Michel Delpech, a well-known French singer who is spending his last weeks on Earth in hospice care. A painter and writer who has also been a medium since she was a teen, Geneviève has always refused to be paid for her gift. She woke up that morning to find a man standing in front of her bed. A bit pale and fuzzy, with a density comparable to a hologram, but expressive nevertheless.

For Geneviève, there's nothing particularly unusual about the incident—it's her usual mode of reception when a departed person wants to contact with her. This particular deceased person is surprisingly easy to identify. His bushy mustache, disheveled hair, and scruffy appearance are world-renowned. He is, she writes, "a dead ringer for the Nobel Laureate Albert Einstein."

The text message I've been scrolling through comes to a screeching halt beneath my fingers. Einstein? Although I've met Geneviève twice, I have never mentioned his name to her, nor referred to the film I'm supposed to be making in 2017 about the deceased physicist and the pair of mediums he pesters.

Holding my breath, I read the rest of the text. The Einstein-like hologram spoke, too. He shared a detail about "his" personal life that meant nothing to the medium and that very few people would recognize as proof of his identity. For me, however, the allusion is as clear as the emotional charge underpinning it.

At this point in my story, I should give a bit of background. I want to shed some light on my reaction, approach, and implication. I also want to explain what my state of mind was when I received that information and perhaps even "triggered" the situation in which I would soon find myself so deeply entrenched.

In November 2015, a month before that first appearance took place, Geneviève Delpech, whom I knew nothing about at the time, had sent me a copy of her book, *The Gift from Elsewhere*.[2] Sub-titled *Autobiography of a Medium*, my copy was autographed with a hand-written note: "We should get together someday to talk about all this."

"*All this*" referred to a long series of contacts with the hereafter, precise episodes of clairvoyance that had been confirmed, inexplicable manifestations and signs that had been peppering her life since she was a teen.

Having opened the book out of idle curiosity, I couldn't put it down, struck by the extent to which it resonated with the phenomena I myself had experienced, studied, and documented in the two volumes of my *Dictionary of the Impossible*.[3] There were some very striking testimonials confirming her skill as a medium—police detectives from the Versailles division of the National Police force had requested her help on several missing-person cases, as had investigative journalists, victims' families, and others.

But the chapter about Pauline Lafont, a young actress I had met in 1987 and who had been set to star in the screen adaptation of my second novel, was the one that affected me the most. I'd been very impressed by her talent, the vulnerable strength she projected, and her sensual humor enhanced by rare kindness.

Her disappearance at the age of 25, while she was out hiking alone, had profoundly upset me. Her body wasn't found until three months later, in a ravine below the family's home in the Lozère region. It was, her mother later told me, precisely where a medium had "sensed" she would be.

The family had chosen to ignore the medium because at the time, they were convinced Pauline had been kidnapped or had chosen to leave home. I have never forgotten what Pauline's mother, the actress Bernadette Lafont, told me a year after the tragedy:

> If only I had listened to Geneviève... from 200 miles away, she had a vision, and she came down to beg us to send a helicopter, because the spot she had seen was inaccessible. Geneviève even had some internal bleeding, she was feeling my daughter's wounds so deeply.

The instant I closed the book by "Geneviève"—whose full identity I had finally learned, all these years later—I called her press agent to ask for her phone number. Within minutes, we agreed to meet.

With her surprising blend of cheerfulness and rigor, lightheartedness and acuity, Geneviève Delpech is a sunny person whose natural enthusiasm softens her distress as she sips her hot chocolate. A straightforward woman, her extraordinary abilities surprise everyone, though she never uses them to impress people. Unfortunately, her skills bring her no comfort in the stressful situation she has been in since her husband was diagnosed with cancer.

A loving wife and mother, she is both "inconsolable and gay," as the title of the Guy Bedos song would have it. Although the phrase is generally attributed to Blaise Pascal, we actually owe it to Jean Anouilh. That's the kind of crucial detail that would never escape Geneviève, a book lover who happily flaunts her total lack of interest in and ignorance of anything but literature, song, and art.

Einstein is hardly her cup of chocolate, but that doesn't bother her—she's happy to transmit whatever floats into her mind when it goes into medium mode, even if she doesn't understand a word of it. Fortunately, she's in the habit of writing it all down.

To my surprise, the very first time we meet I find myself practically ordering her to do more with her gift. In a scolding tone of voice, I say that waiting for the police to ask her to help locate bodies, advising her nearest and dearest, shedding light on cold cases for TV shows, and telling her friend Francis Basset what horses to bet on isn't enough. (Speaking of Francis, could the fact that he wagers only trifling sums that won't change his life partially explain why he wins every time he follows her advice?)

She listens to me without batting an eye as she stirs her hot chocolate. Then she objects, with the disarming, eternally youthful smile of someone for whom living in the extraordinary is both natural and gratuitous, "But

Didier, I've never wanted to turn this into a profession!"

"That's not what I meant, but... isn't there any way you can *solicit* information? Not just human interest stuff or predicting the future." I have no idea why I just asked her that.

She, on the other hand, seems to know. "That's why I sent you the copy of my book. I've been reading your work for years, and I've always known that we'd meet and work together someday, I just don't know what we're going to work on. We shall see."

The confident, cheerfully fatalistic tone of her sentence vanishes the moment her eye falls on the screen of her cell phone, which is vibrating with alarming news from the hospice.

For the past three years, the rhythm of her life has been dictated by Michel's cancer. The fact that she "saw" the tumor a year before the doctors did, as he has stated in public, doesn't change a thing. She is a loving spouse facing the ineluctable, which she is doing her best to cope with, one day at a time.

Even though Michel had witnessed many proofs of her clairvoyance, he had refused to go for a check-up when she expressed concern about his throat. Was it fear of finding out what was already happening, a desire to continue exercising his free will, or an intuition that this ordeal was necessary for his spiritual development—something he owed it to himself to accept?

"If you had come to me a year ago," declared the specialist he finally saw when the pain had become unbearable, "we could have removed it in under an hour. But at this point, there's nothing to be done." Actually, there was: all of the inner work, the mystical elevation with which Michel, with Geneviève's support, would react to his incurable disease.[4]

As Geneviève was taking her leave, she promised to stay in touch.

The following week, when we get back together, she has a personal message for me. Around dawn, she explains, a revenant came to talk to her about me. She reads me her notes without seeming to have guessed her visitor's identity, which is almost instantly obvious to me.

There isn't the shadow of a doubt as to the content or style of the information transmitted, nor is there any as to the origin of the details, some of which I am the only living person who knows. There are some that even I myself have forgotten about until she mentions them, which would tend to undermine the telepathic-communication-of-my-own memories hypothesis.

"I saw a man dressed in black," she tells me, "a judge, or a freemason—

I'm not sure which. A very nice guy. He told me you had been wrong to get upset by 'Green Cabbage'—it was just a joke.

"Does that ring a bell with you or did I misunderstand him? It can happen. In any case, talking about 'Green Cabbage' gave him a good laugh."

A chill runs down my back. When I was a schoolboy in Nice, the other boys pronounced my Flemish last name with a Niçois accent: "Cao-lay-ver-tay." They loved to taunt me with my name's meaning, too, shouting it across the playground during recreation. Hearing them snickering stupidly as they chanted "Green Cabbage, Green Cabbage" would make me see red. Trying to shove the dreaded nickname down their throats, I would start fights against ten of them at once... fights I inevitably lost, of course.

The day my father finally asked me about the black-and-blue marks and torn clothes, I explained that I had been trying to defend our family name. I'd expected him to share my indignation over the affront, but all I got was a burst of amused laughter. It was an insignificant anecdote from my childhood, and I had only told it to a few close friends.

Still, since my instinct is always to look for a rational explanation before I allow myself to be amazed, I discreetly googled Cauwelaert/*Green Cabbage* on my cell phone, and got exactly two hits: a 2002 article in a Belgian newspaper, *La Libre Belgique*; and an interview for an annex to the school edition of my novel *Cheyenne*.[5] But when I casually ask the medium a question about the novel, she says she hasn't read it.

In fact, aside from what she'd gleaned from four or five of my novels, she didn't know a thing about me. Besides, why would she lie to me? What could motivate her to go to the trouble of offering a bogus display of her powers, when they have already been attested to by police officers, judges, and celebrities?

She doesn't need anything from me; her books sell quite well, and she already gets more media hype than she cares for. Moreover, at this precise moment, the only thing that matters to her is her husband's failing health.

Even if we set aside the idea of deliberate cheating, there is still the possibility of telepathy. Could it be that my unconscious channeled the Green Cabbage story to her? Has she managed to serve it back to me in the shape of a spectral apparition of my father in his lawyer's robe?

When I explain to her that she has just related one of my childhood memories, she is stunned. She candidly admits that she hadn't identified either the revenant's profession or the nature of our ties—elements that are clearly unnecessary to the transmission of information.

She does, however, add that based on what she sensed during the brief visit, I am lucky to have had a father like him. I know that. As a living person, he was great. And even as a departed one, he still rocks. Although I'm forcing myself to cling to a certain prudent skepticism, it's hard to ignore what I've already acquired from earlier experiences.

Because this wasn't the first time René has pleaded his case through a medium. After he died (and with my mother's somewhat strained benediction), he started an out-of-body relationship with a friend of mine, Marie-France Cazeaux.

On September 30, 2005, three hours after his death—which none of us was aware of yet—Marie-France, a retired nurse, called me at dawn to reassure me that he was fine, and that his death had been as peaceful as possible. She also casually mentioned the title of the Georges Brassens song I'd been singing to him the day before, while we were alone and he was in a coma.

Still, the two of them had at least met while René was alive. Feeling his soul vibrating through the voice of a woman he had never met, but who had been instantly charmed by his posthumous humor and kindness was a unique thrill. Geneviève Delpech has more to say though: "In any case, he said that you still make him laugh, especially when you're working at your almond-green desk."

This time, her comment doesn't ring any bells. I mentally scan through all the desks I use for my writing: an oak one from a monastery, hazelnut from a farm, English mahogany... nothing that could be described as "almond green," three syllables that conjure up Ikea-style molded plastic furniture in my mind. But then she went on, "He says that Marcel thinks it's funny when you work at that desk, too, because your buttocks are shaped just like his."

That leaves me truly flabbergasted. In a flash, I understood the unflattering connection between the first name and my buttocks. In 2006, I purchased the late, great Marcel Aymé's worktable at auction. It's a Louis XVI desk inlaid with... almond-green leather.

To be fair, I never think of it in those terms because the color is so faded from decades of sunlight: the author of *Passe-Muraille* (*"The Man Who Walked through Walls"*) had written his entire body of work with his back to a window. And the black leatherette seat of the armchair—a curious Scandinavian piece from the 50s with Viking-style armrests—has sagged so low on the right side that to avoid lumbago, I have to sit in it cross-legged, just as its previous occupant had.

Mrs. Delpech has truly blown me away. Granted, generous critics have occasionally compared me to my favorite novelist, but it has never been in terms of our hindquarters before!

"Oh, that's right," she adds, deciphering her notes. "This Marcel person also told him that he liked the little two-tone car that's always in the same place, over the big one. I can't say I understood what all that's about."

I did. The two-tone Dinky Toys car placed beneath my desk lamp is a miniature replica of my 1963 Rover P4 110. The full-sized one is parked in the garage a floor below. The incredible precision of the extra details leaves me speechless.

"Aside from that, your father says to tell you he's been feeling no pain since he lay his body down. His bones have stopped making beaks... I must have misunderstood something there."

I shake my head. As far back as I can remember, he had been wracked with pain, particularly from his "parrot beaks," the calcium deposits in the tendons that are characteristic of Forestier disease.

The pain was treated with incurable cheerfulness and ironclad *joie de vivre*. "When I lay my body down," was an expression he used to use when he was still alive. Counting on the "power of the spirit" to project himself beyond the grave, the soothing words helped downplay the metastases overwhelming his organism at age 91, while sparing his lucidity, sense of humor, and generous faith to the very end. I spoke about René a great deal in my book *The Adopted Father*,[6] but none of the details the medium mentions appear in it (I've checked).

What meaning should I impart to the identifying clues raining down on me so intensely? This first contact, obtained without my having asked for it, is so personal, confirmable, and invigorating that it puts me in the right frame of mind for what will come next. That doesn't mean my critical faculties are impaired. I have simply taken note that two of my dearest references in the afterlife—Marcel and René—seem to be joining forces to confirm this woman's abilities.

What a lot of people might have experienced as an impossible dream come true—receiving news and proof of life after death from the dearly departed—is just the starting point for me. As it turns out, my father, ever the conscientious lawyer, seems to have been "prepping the jury" before putting the witness on the stand. And what a witness he will turn out to be!

1. Rémy Chauvin, *L'Enigme des abeilles* (*"The Bee Enigma"*), Editions du Rocher, 1999.
2. Geneviève Delpech, *Le Don d'ailleurs* (*"The Gift from Elsewhere"*), Pygmalion, 2015.

3. Plon, 2013, and J'ai Lu, 2014. *Le Nouveau Dictionnaire de l'impossible*, Plon, 2015, and J'ai Lu, 2016.
4. Michel Delpech, *J'ai osé Dieu* (*"I Dared to Follow God"*), Presses de la Renaissance, 2013.
5. Magnard, coll. "Classiques Et Contemporains," 2001, interview with Jeanne Dupuy.
6. Albin Michel, 2007; Le Livre de poche, 2009.

3

Unfaithful Einstein

The next day, December 19, 2015, at 7:12 A.M., I received the text message that would set everything off:

Around 6 a.m., I saw someone very luminous, who looked just like Albert Einstein, standing at the foot of my bed, right where your father had been the day before. He materialized before me in high spirits, looking about 50 years old, and wearing a gray jacket. He said, 'I'm everywhere at once, it's marvelous. Plus, my compass is 132 years old today. That's how you'll know it's really me.'

The last phrase may seem odd, but the detail is actually quite meaningful to me. It refers to the gift Hermann Einstein gave his son Albert when he was five. The compass, with its magnetic needle stubbornly pointing north, dramatically changed how the boy related to the world. Until that time, he had been a quiet, borderline-autistic child who stared glumly into space a lot, emerging only to listen to music or burst into fits of anger. He later wrote that the compass had been the key to his vocation: decades later, that "irrefutable proof of the remote effect of something hidden" would become the basis for his theory of gravity.[1]

I immediately check the dates in the book by Laurent Seksik, one of Einstein's best biographers.[2] Albert did indeed receive the compass 132 years ago.

That type of revealing detail—meaningless to the medium who transmits it but with great sentimental value for both the entity mentioning it and the recipient—is a recurring element in the most reliable communications received in this manner. My father is proof of that – "living proof," I almost wrote. In any case, the fact that his appearance the night before matched his earthly character so perfectly had a decisive impact on how I would react to this new user of Mrs. Delpech's psychic channel.

With subjects like green cabbage, authors' buttocks, and Dinky Toys, there was absolutely nothing the least bit urgent or profound about his message from the day before. It was no more than a teaser, a kind of "signature" in the shape of a wink and a nod. I believe it was intended to instill confidence and establish an atmosphere of whimsical precision, which is exactly the sort of thing it takes to pique my interest in that sort of phenomena. I have always been more than willing to leave the morbid, the emphatically occult, the stress-inducing prophecies, and acute spirituality to their hucksters.

"What's the point of an afterlife without a sense of humor?" the amazing Delphine de Girardin (1804-1855) once asked. Thanks to her skill, character, and beauty, the journalist, novelist, poet, and salon hostess had a huge influence on the greatest writers of her day. De Girardin initiated Hugo, Balzac, Dumas, Gautier, Lamartine, and many others into spiritualism. I should point out that she asked the above question 34 years after her death.

At least, that's what the medium Henry Lacroix claimed.[3] He was one of the many admirers of Mme. de Girardin who perpetuated her memory through automatic writing, dictated either by psychic connection or loving mimicry. Sometimes very enjoyably, too, like when the presumptive erstwhile Delphine describes the posthumous peregrinations of one of her fellow writers in the sparkling style of her best books:[4] "That darling Eugène Scribe showed up spellbound by his latest tepid successes. He thinks we should form an Academy up here. He misses his ribbons and medals. He was so happy there on Earth that he is still hesitating about settling down to his new place."[5]

Like the great stylist Frederic Myers, the ravishing Delphine de Girardin brings us back to the byword dictated to Victor Hugo by one of his tapping tables in Jersey: "All great minds create two bodies of work: one as living beings, and one as phantoms of the night."[6]

All that is very well and good, but let's get back to that compass. Skeptics will object that the detail about its age doesn't prove a thing: the medium could have checked Seksik's biography to learn the date of young Albert's present as easily as I did. Granted. For the moment, I can only trust in her references, her good faith, and my own instincts. Objective proof will come later. For the moment, there's nothing more than affective resonance, but that moves me more than irrefutable proof would.

So let's follow the compass. As proof of identity, it feels all the more acceptable in that, due to its apparent insignificance, it could only serve to convince someone like me, who had been reading up on Albert Einstein and featuring him in my work for over a decade. And his way of using it to "introduce" himself to a medium who had never channeled scientists until he showed up doesn't surprise me in the least.

In fact, it was the exact opposite of a random act. In all modesty, I could call it a continuation conjured up by my imagination. Because the impossible adventure I am just starting to experience in real life is starting to look a lot like the culmination of a work of fiction—without my having anything to do with it, or at least not consciously.

*

Albert Einstein first entered my life for the needs of a novel around the time of my father's death. The famous physicist was:

- An iconoclastic genius who hated socks and bourgeois morals.
- A hedonistic hermit who adored women, sailing, and the violin.
- An unrepentant scatterbrain whose professors said he'd never accomplish anything in physics.
- An obsessive, intuitive thinker whose famous formula $E = mc2$ demonstrated that not only can matter be turned into energy, but that light can create matter.
- A non-believer who was illuminated by a mathematical conception of God.
- A stateless person who had to flee the Nazi persecution of Jews.
- An immigrant who became an American citizen and was persecuted by the FBI for his supposed Communist sympathies.
- A humanitarian activist who, back in the 1930s, became one of the first public figures to defend the Civil Rights Movement (by, among other things, opening his Princeton home to a pretty black singer who had been refused a room in nearby hotels).
- A tireless pacifist who, to this day, is still being blamed for the atomic bomb, even though the United States built it without informing him.
- An eccentric, raggedy old man who is best remembered by many for sticking his tongue out at a photographer on his 72nd birthday, when we should actually think of him gratefully whenever we listen to a CD, watch a DVD, or use a GPS—all inventions directly descended from his theories of relativity and his research into lasers.
- The 1921 Nobel Laureate in physics, who was relegated just six years

later to the status of has-been by the triumph of quantum physics, despite the fact that he had been the first to define the theoretical basis for that field.

- A lucid idealist who said, "It's easier to smash an atom than a prejudice."
- A philandering spouse and hopeless father who inspired both love and resentment in exchange for a few brief moments of intense happiness.
- A neurotic prankster whose anger over injustice and humiliation gave him ulcers.

Between his invulnerable intelligence and his wounded humanity, his consistency and his contradictions, his loving heart and his cruelty to his loved ones, behind all those distracting façades, he is one of the most complex beings who has ever walked the earth. I find his radiance as fascinating as the darker sides that we have been finding out about over the past few years. Could it be that even now, some form of active consciousness of his still remains—independent of his ashes, whose location has never been revealed, and his brain, which was sliced up in order to allow other scientists to attempt to discover the secret of his genius? I had already explored the possible consequences in fictional form before life decided to confront me with the issue for real.

In 2005, I welcomed Einstein into one of my novels for the first time. Published eight years later, *The Woman of Our Lives*[7] tells the story of David, a seemingly dim-witted farm boy who is saved from the gas chambers by a German resistance fighter. She runs a school for gifted children, and she passes him off as a precocious genius who could be useful to the Third Reich. In 1942, the teen arrives in the United States on a mission to deliver a message to Einstein from anti-Nazis in the Wehrmacht: Hitler is going to be assassinated by his generals any day now. The generals will then join the Allies, so the Americans really shouldn't drop the atomic bomb the physicist is finalizing for them.

In my novel, David's message is how Albert learns, to his shock and horror, that he has been deceived by his closest friends. The atomic scientists Oppenheimer, Bohr, Szilárd and Wigner had been ordered by the FBI to keep Albert in the dark about the fact that they were working on a nuclear weapon based on his calculations of nuclear chain reactions' release of energy. In Hoover's opinion, Einstein was a potential Soviet spy.

According to most historians, in real life, Albert didn't learn the truth until 1944, and he begged the authorities in vain not to drop the bomb on Japan. Unfairly, posterity still seems to hold him accountable for the bomb's devastating effects.

Einstein's complex, misunderstood, ecstatic, and despairing personality has haunted me ever since. In the wake of *The Woman of Our Lives*, I decided to devote myself to a huge project about him, one that I'm still working on at the present time. It encompasses both a novel and a film in which I dream up an afterlife for him.

I Lost Albert describes how a gifted young medium has been living with the physicist's spirit ever since she was a child. It is constantly swamping her with information meant for the greater good, contributing to the progress of science, peace, and the overall mental atmosphere. But there is such demand for what the medium knows that she gives in to the temptation to try to become rich and powerful, which so upsets Albert's soul that one day he packs up and "moves" into the mind of a waiter who doesn't believe in anything. In early 2012, I had been writing dialogue for precisely that scene when my creation suddenly "stepped off the page."

At that time, I had been waking up as fresh as a daisy every morning at 4 a.m., and getting straight to work on the plot, whose twists and turns often seemed to come to me in my sleep. But on that particular Tuesday, I decided to ignore the call of the blank page. I was going to the theater that night, and I didn't want to nod off in the middle of the first act. So I went back to bed and slept in 'til 7.

I had barely finished breakfast when I got a phone call from Marie-France Cazeaux. A tall, striking redhead from Brittany who now lives in Nice, Marie-France can only be described as warm-hearted. Talkative, with a contagious laugh, she radiates energy in a way that can be soothing, annoying or invigorating, depending on the circumstances. A former head nurse, she devotes her retirement to bringing comfort to both the living and the dead. With an open hand, a keen ear, and eyes constantly solicited by the invisible, she spends all her time transmitting messages from the hereafter to everyone who needs to hear them.

We first met in 2003, at the Monaco International Cinema and Literature Forum. That very day, while I was signing her copy of my book, she announced right from the get-go that a man called Eugène had indeed received his wife's letter informing him that she was pregnant before he died in the trenches. The question had gnawed at my grandmother her whole life: had her man at least known he was going to be a father?

The two volumes of my *Dictionary of the Impossible* describe a few of the many astonishing feats Marie-France has achieved, all the while remaining both down-to-earth and modest. On July 28, 2015, on the radio station RTL, the wife of a pediatrician from Nice found the courage to describe how Mme. Cazeaux, a medium she had never met, had spoken to her for three hours about her 18-year-old daughter who had been run over by a garbage truck. Only Marie-France could see and hear young Clémence—who looked as alive as you or me—sharing all sorts of detailed anecdotes and information about herself and her loved ones, all of which were later confirmed.[8]

The deceased pop up all over the place in Marie-France's daily life: at the supermarket, on the train, at the hairdresser's, and anywhere in between. They drop in to say hi or to offer a helpful warning to people near her: shopping-cart handlers, cashiers, ticket collectors, or the woman who shampoos customers' hair. The last time I saw her, at Nice Airport, she stopped in front of a young soldier who was standing guard with a machine gun. As though she were picking up the thread of an earlier conversation with someone she knew well, she commented, "Gee, you really hated having to quit judo, didn't you? Your grandfather's so sorry. He did his best, but your parents just wouldn't have it. He's showing me how he used to drive you there in his little old Citroën 2CV. So, who is Jean-Pierre?"

"Uh… that's my grandfather," the soldier managed to choke out, looking stunned. "Do I know you?"

"No, but he says, 'Jean-Paul has to make his mind up about Charlotte; things can't go on like this much longer. He's showing me that the relationship is like a message in a bottle. Are you Jean-Paul?'"

"Yes," the soldier answered, choking back tears. "She's in the United States; she wants me to go live with her there."

"Well, that's all clear then. Have a nice day."

We left that soldier dumbstruck, machine gun lowered, torn between a childhood sorrow and an urgent life decision. From hard-core skeptics to the undecided, from nobodies to grieving celebrities who share her contact info, from artists, doctors and entrepreneurs to politicians, everyone who knows Marie-France has, like me, witnessed her public, improvised, clairvoyance sessions. Anyone else can get a sense of them by reading her autobiography.[9]

I'd just like to add the incredible coincidence we discovered when I was working on the entry about Yvonne-Aimée de Malestroit for my *Dictionary of the Impossible*.[10] One day I told Marie-France about the amazing bilocations of the nun and partisan I had just found out about. To my surprise, she replied:

> Oh, I met her when I was a little girl! In 1945, she came to the Augustine convent in Tréguier where my mother and I had gone into hiding when my father went to join de Gaulle. We hadn't seen or heard from him since he left for England. I was five years old, and she gave me a big hug and said, 'When he gets back, your daddy will tell you all about how he saw me on the H.M.S. Eridan.'

It turned out that Marie-France's father was none other than Edouard Le Corre, the second-class engineer who had described the Augustine nun's spectral appearance on board his ship on February 16, 1943, at the exact moment she was being tortured in a Gestapo detention center in Paris.

That morning in 2012, when I went back to sleep instead of getting up and setting to work, Marie-France called to scold me gently. She had been awakened at 4 a.m. by a tall, skinny, disheveled-looking ghost with a mustache and tousled hair.

"You don't think it could be Einstein, do you?"

I was speechless. I hadn't said a word to her about the screenplay I was working on about the physicist's spectral apparitions.

> He told me to tell you that you have to get straight to work when you wake up at 4—that's when it flows best. And there was something else, too. Hold on…what was it again? Oh, yes. 'If you don't convey this message to him, I'll take away your gifts as a medium and give them to that waiter instead!' That doesn't make any sense, does it?

I had to take a few seconds to swallow hard before I could reply, "Well, actually…"

That was the starting point for a friendly, episodic relationship with my "character," not unlike the humorous ties that have bonded her to my father since his death.

It was a relationship free of stunning revelations, a revenant's running monologue that played more like background music, filled with pleasant memories of the violin, happy times sailing, social commentary, and a father's nostalgia for his children's childhood. Then in 2014, their relationship began to sour. Einstein was getting more and more "technical" as she put it. He had started complaining that she was too flighty, and would insist that she note down equations when she didn't have a pen handy.

"Your Albert's been pretty grouchy lately," she told me. "He says that I don't remember what he tells me, but it's his fault—I can't understand a word he's saying!"

I stuck up for "my" Albert for a while, but then, focused as I was on my fictional character, I gave up mediating between the real life clairvoyant and her revenant. It hardly mattered anyway, because he'd stopped appearing to her.

"He's being unfaithful," she sighed with resignation the last time I checked in to see how she was doing.

That was when Geneviève Delpech appeared in my life, and the 1921 Nobel Prizewinner showed up with his childhood compass as a calling card.

So in December 2015, my scenario, which is already at the casting stage, suddenly seems to be inspired by (or inspiring?) real life. For reasons of occasional incompatibility, and with the same sudden brutality, implacable logic, and casual off-handedness as my fictional version, the presumptive erstwhile Einstein has changed mediums.

What had never crossed my mind though, was that he might bring someone with him… and that his friend would do most of the talking from then on.

1. Albert Einstein, *The World As I See It*, Citadel Press, 1956, 1984.
2. Laurent Seksik, *Albert Einstein, Folio*, 2008.
3. Henry Lacroix, *Mes experiences avec les esprits* (*"My Experiences with Spirits"*), De Monroe, Michigan, 1889.
4. Delphine de Girardin, La Joie fait peur ("Joy Is Frightening"), Calmann-Levy, 1855.
5. *La Revue spirite*, 1861.
6. Victor Hugo, *Le Livre des Tables*, Les séances spirites de Jersey, Edition de Patrice Boivin, Folio classique, 2014 (for the English version: adapted from John Chambers, *Victor Hugo's Conversations with the Spirit World* Destiny Books, 2008").
7. *La Femme de Nos Vies*, Albin Michel, 2013; Le Livre de Poche, 2015.
8. *Les aventuriers de l'impossible*, RTL, 28 July 2015.
9. Marie-France Cazeaux, *L'Invisible, ça saute aux yeux* (*The Invisible Is Blindingly Obvious*), First Publishing Co. (in French), 2017.
10. See Chapter 1.

4
Of soccer players and battles for ashes

Let's get back to that text message on December 19, 2015. After the bit about the Einstein look-alike that took shape before Mrs. Delpech's eyes, this is what appears on my phone:

Then another man materialized behind him. He was thin, fairly good-looking and cheerful enough, but not in high spirits like the first one. He was very tall and dark-haired, and he seemed quite mild-mannered, shy and gentle. Long nose, small moustache, stiff collar. Unlike Einstein, I didn't recognize him; I really don't have a clue who it was. All he said was, "Young lady, ask Didier to tell Marco Metrovic I said thank you."

I reread the message, and a face starts to take shape in my mind: Nikola Tesla. I call the medium to suggest his name, but she doesn't know who he is. "Coincidentally," the very next day, she happens to stumble across a TV program about the Tesla electric-car company. When a picture of the cars' namesake appears on screen, she realizes that the man she saw at the foot of her bed the night before was indeed Tesla.

On the other hand, even if she is in contact with the inventor's memory, I still don't have the slightest idea who I'm supposed to express his gratitude to. This early in the adventure, in late 2015, I don't know that much about the great Serbian-American engineer yet. It pretty much boils down to the inventions he'd either gotten credit for or had stolen from him: an AC engine, radar, X-rays, a semi-autonomous electric car, radio, television broadcasting, robotics, drones, computers and more.[1]

I do, however, know that some of his discoveries are still being kept under wraps by the authorities for economic, medical or military reasons. Especially anything related to the detection or use of scalar waves, which offer a bottomless supply of both domestic energy and remote therapy, as well as secret weapons of mass destruction. But more about that later.

Back to Marco Metrovic, the person the master of electricity seems to want to put in the spotlight. Is he a former assistant, an inventor perpetuating Tesla's work, an admirer defending his memory? The name doesn't ring any bells. Why has Tesla brought him up? While Albert Einstein's compass struck an immediate chord with me, I don't see how his ectoplasmic traveling companion's asking me to thank an unknown person constitutes proof of his posthumous identity.

So I google it. But when I type "Marco Metrovic" in the search box, *nothing* comes up. Paradoxically, this first discrepancy is terribly disorienting for me. Reader, please don't say I didn't warn you. After a while, the impossible generates its own logic, its own space-time, and its own rules. Once you get used to them, the irrational doesn't seem disturbing anymore—only the incongruous does.

Why couldn't a Tesla from beyond the grave have chosen to offer me an obscure clue that I would still have managed to decipher, like Einstein's compass? The Serbian's compulsive habit of disposing of his kid gloves after wearing them just once, for instance; his phobias about microbes and jewelry, or his passion for pigeons. Or any of the many peculiar character traits I would soon learn about from his biographers.

I go back online, giving "Marco Metrovic" another try. Still nothing, not even in the Yellow Pages. It bothers me because it isn't *normal*. The details the medium picked up concerning my father and the writer Marcel Aymé—the first of my dearly departed to communicate via her—were immediately and luminously meaningful for me. But my search for the object of the "favor" the inventor of AC current is asking me to do is drawing a complete blank. Which means I can't do it. Why, oh, why doesn't Marco Metrovic have the slightest on-line presence?

No matter how I phrase it, the search engine systematically redirects me to "Marko Mitrovic," a 23-year-old Swedish soccer player currently playing in the Netherlands. Reality check: maybe the go-between misheard or misspelled the name, because what connection could there possibly be between our brilliant, unfairly-forgotten inventor and the up-and-coming star of the FC Eindhoven soccer team?

I decide to call a players' agent who helped me out years ago, when I was researching pro-soccer secrets for my novel *Anonymous Encounter*. I leave him a voicemail asking how to contact the Dutch team's star forward. "What's it about?" he texts back. Hmm....I can't really see myself replying, "I need to pass on the undying gratitude of an inventive genius who passed away in 1943." I figure I'll have to improvise something more palatable. Maybe "Working on a follow-up to *Anonymous Encounter*. I'd like to know how Mitrovic felt about being traded from Chelsea to Eindhoven" would do the trick...

Just then, the medium gives me a call that stops me in my tracks. Tesla, she informs me, came back to reiterate that he had indeed said *Metrovic*, not *Mitrovic*. So there's no point in pestering the soccer player. "That's all he said?" I ask.

"That's all, Didier. I'm sorry."

So am I. As long as Tesla was bothering, couldn't he have given me a clue about the elusive Metrovic? Maybe he's trying to respect my free will. Or maybe he's challenging me to find him with strictly earthbound means. The only problem is that it's not as though that's all I have to do right now! Over the next few days, totally taken up with putting the finishing touches on my latest novel, the message the wraith asked me to transmit totally slips my mind.

So on January 9, he comes back to his spokeswoman's bedside to clarify things. To hell with free will; since I have proven myself incapable of finding the person on my own—have in fact forgotten all about it—he points me in the right direction.

"I saw Nikola Tesla again last night. He told me the person he'd mentioned previously is one of three Serbians demanding respect for his ashes. And he added, 'Leave me in peace!'"

Was that last phrase meant for us?

I go back on line. This time, I google, "Serbia/Tesla/ashes/Metrovic," and I land on a blog in Serbian that Google translates into robotic-sounding French for me. Amazement isn't exactly the word for what I'm feeling. It's more like a calm excitement, a composed euphoria tempered by a kind of deep humility. That's how I often feel when a bit of the veil is lifted from one of life's great mysteries, affording a glimpse behind what we like to call reality...

In 2014, the Serbian government decided to remove their national hero's ashes from the Tesla Museum in Belgrade. For political purposes, they wanted to put the ashes on display in the Church of Saint Sava, the largest Orthodox church in the Balkans. Three students immediately launched a protest on Facebook. Their movement's slogan: *Ostavite Teslu na miru,* or "Leave Tesla in peace." Their leader? The photo shows a friendly-looking 24-year-old giant with the fashion sense of a geek and a bemused look on his face. He's an economy major, and his name is…Marco Metrovic.[2]

The Facebook page describes moving the ashes to a church as an affront to the memory of the inventor, who had described God as "the aspiration toward knowledge" and who had never expressed a preference for one religion over any other. The online movement has attracted over 40,000 members. A single click on the Tesla Museum site informs me the protest has succeeded: the inventor's urn is still in the museum's catalog.

Magnanimously, or prudently, the three on-line crusaders who stood up to the authorities in Belgrade have said that their victory was not over the government or the Church. "This is not a spiritual issue, but a civic one. We contest that anyone can appropriate a public figure belonging to all of humanity and not just to the Serbian nation. Apolitical and non-denominational, our movement is based first and foremost on common sense," Marco Metrovic wrote on Facebook.

When this book is translated into Serbian, may he find here a testimonial to the gratitude Nikola Tesla asked me to express. That is not the only reason for this book's existence, but I do think the discovery of the object of his posthumous indebtedness was the triggering factor. Over the weeks that followed, I came to understand why that information had chosen me. Accepting it, opening myself to its source, responding to its appeal for help soon led, as we shall see, to a host of other requests from the presumptive Einstein and Tesla, along with revelations with untold consequences.

Most of the revelations went way over my head. But for the sake of this narrative, I did what I could to confirm them. My tools were reflexive rationality, rigorous investigation methods, and, above all, the aid and assistance of scientists in a position to understand and explain the raw data that would soon be coming my way, and which was far beyond my ken.

The thing is, if, for the sake of argument, we accept the idea that I am indeed in touch with geniuses in the hereafter, it is still perfectly legitimate to wonder why me. Why had I been *chosen*? Please don't think that my italicizing that term for the second time reflects the slightest pretention to cast myself as an "initiate" or a "chosen one." Both my nearest and dearest, and my readers alike, all know how far that kind of ego trip is from my true nature.

To put it another way, if Einstein and Tesla have decided to "use" me, I can only suppose that it's because of my experience as a popularizer of scientific mysteries clouded by religious conflict. The first time I addressed them was in 2005, in my book *Cloning Christ?*[3] and in the documentary film Yves Boisset and I then based on that book.[4] All that was long before the two volumes of my *Dictionary of the Impossible*. If I am indeed being called upon as a spokesman, perhaps it is also for my literary credentials, or at least the sympathy they inspire among a number of scientists. It often surprises them that a Goncourt Prize[5] winner with no more than a high-school degree is so interested in their work.

Or perhaps it's just because of what some people call my bravery—others my foolishness—or my taste for the off-the-wall. I personally believe that those character traits of mine stem from one key flaw: my native incapacity to place caution before curiosity, risk-avoidance before enthusiasm, or propriety before altruism. Besides, transmitting information that may contribute to "un-wrinkling the desert," as Jacques Brel was wont to say, is one of my greatest pleasures as an author.

Without false modesty, it cannot be excluded that *they* have chosen to correspond with me because of my "connections." Over the past twenty years or more, I have established ties with several cutting-edge researchers whose work is inspired by, or in the same fields as, the discoveries and ideals of Albert Einstein and Nikola Tesla, a stubborn genius who spent eight decades attempting to harness the universe's hidden resources for the sake of humanity's well-being and progress.

Like those two geniuses, I believe that the point is not necessarily to convince people today, but to enable progress rather than to stand in its way. I do what I can at my modest level, but my attraction may also reside in the huge gaps in my knowledge, which my presumptive "recruiters" from the hereafter will soon undertake to fill in.

To do so, the consciousness of Einstein—or the unknown entity transmitting information in his name—will offer me a sneak preview of the confirmation of one of the physicist's most brilliant postulates. It was one his peers had laughed at a century before, and his well-meaning biographers had "forgotten" so thoroughly that I had never read a word about it. As for Tesla, not only will he point me toward his own "disappeared" discoveries, but also toward the fascinating work of living scientists and inventors who are pursuing that work, none of whom I had ever heard of: De Palma, Inomata, Searl, Moray, et al.

And let's not forget that all the information will be transmitted via a medium with absolutely no scientific background. She is the first to apologize for the "utter nonsense" she might utter without realizing it. Nevertheless, well-respected scientists like Jean-Pierre Garnier Malet, Christophe Galfard, and Gaston Ciais, to whom I will submit messages strewn with equations and diagrams, will find data that is usually comprehensible and sometimes complementary to their own research.

Let me add that all the statements "signed" by Einstein or Tesla reproduced in this book were received by text message on my phone. The detail matters, because it offers proof of when I received them, particularly as regards a major scientific discovery that was revealed to me shortly *before* its surprise announcement in the press.

As a precautionary measure—and out of respect for the skeptics whose reservations I understand all the better for having shared them myself—I had a man of law take pictures of all the text messages, including the date. Allergic to proselytism, I don't think of the photos as aces I'm keeping up my sleeve, but rather, as additional exhibits in the record I'm providing for assessment by specialists and the general public alike. The photos generally establish only the factual and psychological exactitude of the information received through a channel whose mode of operation does not allow us to exclude any hypothesis, aside from a hoax. Or not one that can be pinned on the living, at any rate. Circulating decoded and confirmed information is my one and only motivation for writing this book. It is the only mission "they" assigned me. I accepted the burden, and I am conscious that what I am revealing may expose me to certain risks. But danger is the one thing I disdain.

For now, let's get to know the exceptional human being Nikola Tesla was before becoming—as appearances would seem to suggest—a mass of potential energy in search of transformers in the hereafter. For my money, the best picture we have of him is the one where he's holding in his bare hand a glowing light bulb that's not plugged in to anything. The bulb is lit thanks to the current running through his body only. That body, which has since been reduced to ashes, hardly seems to matter to him now: the effect lives on.

One last thing on that subject—in the New Year's Day message that I'll get back to later, the presumptive Nikola interrupted his mind-boggling explanation of the Big Bang with a heartfelt cry that seemed to come out of nowhere: "My God, how I hated when women wore pearl necklaces! Ugh, those horrible round things." Since I had learned about his jewelry phobia by then, I chalked his outburst up to it and didn't think any more about it.

Ten days later, after a treasure hunt that led me to the website of his museum in Belgrade, I learned that his ashes were kept in a round urn with a surface that shimmered like a pearl!

1. His patent No 725 605 concerning computing systems was approved on April 14, 1903!
2. www.mondeacinter.blog.lemonde.fr/2014/03/28/en-serbie-vive-contestation-autour-des-cendres-du-scientifique-nikola-tesla
3. Albin Michel, 2005; Le Livre de Poche, 2007.
4. *Ils veulent cloner le Christ* (*They Want to Clone Christ*), Special Investigation, Canal+, December 12, 2005; DVD Editions Montparnasse.
5. Translator's note: The Goncourt Prize is France's most prestigious literary award, the equivalent of the Pulitzer Prize for literature or the National Book Critics' Circle Award.

5
The sky engineer

One consequence of those first contacts with an active memory claiming to be Nikola Tesla is that I delved into his life to confirm the things he'd mentioned. Because the truth is, before being pointed toward his urn, the only thing I really knew about Tesla was his set of wheels. A real "clunker," as an old mechanic I knew affectionately referred to the imposing Pierce-Arrow sedan car that had been provided to the inventor.

In 1931, Tesla reconfigured the sedan, equipping it with an alternating-current electric motor with an available speed of 1,800 revolutions per minute. The summer he turned 75, Tesla performed road trials around Buffalo, New York. The car was driven over 600 miles in one week, with a top speed of 90 miles per hour.

Tesla rode in the passenger seat for every mile, and the man behind the prototype's wheel was a Yugoslav named Petar Savo. A former pilot in the Austrian Army, he is often referred to as one of Tesla's nephews. It is actually Savo's account, published 30 years after the fact, which revealed the experiment that had previously not been widely known.

According to Savo, under the hood there was a 40-inch-long by 30-inches-in-diameter engine, a torque converter, a fan, and 12 corrective electron-beam tubes... and that's it. No battery.

So where did the electricity that made the car run come from?

An antenna. A six-foot-tall antenna, pointing at the sky—or, to be more precise—at what is known as the Schumann Cavity (or resonances), located between the Earth and the ionosphere, at an altitude of about 50 miles. That's where Tesla drew what his patent applications called "free energy," "electricity from the ether," or even "vibrations from the quantic void."

All you had to do (as it were) was to capture, convert, and distribute those seven-to-eight-hertz low-frequency waves through a wireless transmission system.[1] Not only did the Pierce-Arrow's electrical engine recharge itself in contact with the air, but its torque converter was so powerful it could even supply current to the house the car was parked in front of.

"Tesla's Wireless Power Dream Nears Reality," read the headline in the New York Daily News on April 2, 1934. Three years after the test drive in Buffalo, the article announced the imminent production of a car using "wireless transmission of electric energy."

And then: nothing.

One can easily imagine the pressure the elderly man must have been subjected to in order to keep him from upending the world with his invention: an automobile that produced more energy than it needed to drive! Was there a technical glitch, financial blockage, political intervention, withdrawal of sponsorship… or was it something else?

The American press of the day unanimously portrayed Tesla as a fallen hero, a senile nutcase, a scientific well that had gone dry and was now willing to say any crazy thing to attract attention and subsidies. The announcement in the *New York Daily News* never came to anything… other than to confirm his senility in the eyes of his detractors.

Nine years after the *Daily News* article, Tesla died without ever having alluded to his sky-powered Pierce-Arrow again. Then posterity did its utmost to erase every trace of that motoring legend. Arguing that Tesla never had a nephew named Petar Savo (in fact, he was simply a fellow Serb who affectionately referred to the inventor 40 years his senior as "Uncle"), rationalists and the gas and oil lobbies decreed that the gas-less, battery-less car had never existed. Based on the same genealogical argument, even such popular sources as Wikipedia relay the same information. But…

In 1986, while searching for spare parts for my 1963 Rover in the want ads in *Autoretro*, I actually met an old mechanic who, in his youth, had participated in transforming the Pierce-Arrow with the free-energy engine designed by Tesla. The adventure of a lifetime, he called it, with photos to back his story up.

That anecdote popped back into my mind twenty-seven years later. While working on an entry on scalar-wave therapy for my *New Dictionary of the Impossible*, I again stumbled across the name of Nikola Tesla, the man who had first detected them. At the time, I resolved to learn more about that interesting character someday... but not even in my wildest dreams had I ever imagined that he himself might be the one to finally get me to do it.

*

"I never accomplished the great things I set out to do," the holographic apparition of Tesla acknowledged on March 24, 2016. "I was defeated. I had hoped to light up the whole planet." Instead he himself was extinguished.

How did a utopic inventor who dreamed of becoming a benefactor to the human race turn into Public Enemy Number 1? Why did the leaders and media of the United States, his adopted country, first flaunt him as a hero then taunt him as a zero? Toward the end of his life, they tried to isolate, neutralize, and short-circuit the inventor of alternating current.

Discrediting and eradicating Tesla, and rendering him harmless to the interests of the global economy became the FBI's goal, as dictated by its all-powerful director, J. Edgar Hoover. Around the same time, Hoover—in his opportunistic lunacy—also had it in for Einstein, whom he believed to be a Soviet spy. In Hoover's paranoid eyes, however, Tesla represented a tribe that was even worse: swarthy, dangerous immigrants he suspected of trying to destroy American industry in favor of foreigners and the poor.

And it is true that the unmanageable immigrant really was obsessively intent on—and capable of, or so it seemed—supplying the entire human race with free and unlimited wireless energy. Consequently, obliterating techniques were used against him on every level, from his private life to his public image, as well as his access to financial backing. They even sicced Superman on him!

A cartoon from 1941 shows the superhero grappling with "mad scientist" Nikola Tesla, the inventor of an "electric earthquake" that humanity needs to be protected from.[2] We will examine the potency of that infamous "death ray" a little later. But while many people insist that the USSR, the Third Reich, and the United States stole the "ultimate weapon" from him in order to enhance their military arsenals, their real motivation was to remove the very notion of "free energy" from the view and curiosity of both the general public and independent scientists.

The grandiose dream that brought Tesla to America to light up the planet was ending in a pathetic nightmare. Even Superman, sent to overcome him when he was 84 years old, was nothing compared to the humiliation he'd been subjected to for the previous three decades.

The lowest blow? At age 60, he was taken to court for $935 in unpaid property taxes... when he had never even owned a home! Before the judge and the press, the man who had been the most famous scientist of the late 19th century was obliged to plead guilty to avoid going to jail. He was forced to repent to the tax administration and to publicly confess that he was living on credit in ever-less-luxurious hotel rooms; that he was penniless, burdened with debt, and, therefore, no longer worthy of the American citizenship that had been bestowed upon him.[3]

After having outed him, his enemies had expected him to hang himself in shame. But Tesla refused to oblige—he was too busy inventing the detection system that would be known as radar 30 years later. Having sacrificed everything to pay for his experiments, deprived of his laboratory and getting no credit—for either his work or his bank account, living off the meager earnings of the few patents that hadn't been stolen from him, he kept on with his research until the day he died. But aside from his persecutors and creditors, who was paying attention to the bankrupt, painfully gaunt old man any more anyway?

His generosity had been limited to feeding the pigeons... and the press, at his annual birthday luncheon. Without touching a bite of food, he would ceremoniously present his latest inventions to science journalists who, enjoyed the free lunch without bothering to listen to their "lunatic" host. Alone, laughed at, with neither scientific credibility nor social life, old man Tesla had turned back into the "alien" he had seen reflected in adults' eyes throughout his childhood.

*

Having appeared on Earth on July 10, 1856 in Smiljan, a modest village at the foot of the Velebit Range, little Nikola was born Serbian in a Croatian region of the Austrian Empire—which is why both Croatia and Serbia now claim him as their own. Austria, on the other hand, couldn't give a damn. And yet, on the documents he filled in when he applied for American citizenship 35 years later, Tesla declared his nationality as Austrian. But to him, his homeland was never a question of geography, whether by birth or by choice. He belonged to all of humanity, to the cosmos, the atoms, the waves of energy that ran through him, and the mental images that sparked his inventions.

"I am the Sky Engineer!" he would exclaim at the tender young age of five, when he would go out in the midst of a thunderstorm to direct the thunder and lightning like an orchestra conductor. Needless to say, the neighbors weren't terribly amused by that sort of precocious eccentricity.

Having his mental gymnastics and visualizations interrupted to attend his father's church services only led to phobias. Allergic to women's finery and the hypocrisy of falsely pious women who used church as an excuse to flaunt their charms, he would sometimes rip their jewelry from them with as much violence as Jesus driving merchants from the temple. Once, during Mass, when everyone went to the altar to take communion, he deliberately stepped on the train of a bourgeois woman's dress, tearing it to teach her a lesson in humility.

Displaying aristocratic manners in all other situations, the asocial farm boy and general pain-in-the-butt irritated, annoyed, and scared people, foreshadowing the high-voltage old man they would later try in vain to short-circuit through deprivation, indifference, and sarcasm.

In a nutshell, except for his mother, Đuka Tesla, everyone felt uncomfortable around the gifted little boy. She, however, admired him, and the feeling was mutual. It should be pointed out that in addition to her work on the farm and at home, Đuka was also a household inventor. Illiterate, but with a passion for Serbian poetry, she had memorized thousands of verses she would recite as she built automated irons, heat recuperators, salad spinners, and more. His father, Milutin Tesla, who had become an Orthodox priest late in life, expected Nikola to go into the priesthood, but the child chose his mother's "camp."

At age five, he designed and built his first invention: an insect-powered engine in which four June bugs were chased by a predator. All five of them were attached to small spokes arranged around a spindle with a pulley that transmitted their energy to a larger disk. Adjusted for size, his infinite-pursuit system generated about as much energy as a watermill.[4] With stubborn yet vain vigilance, the terribly pious Milutin fought against the mechanical perversions distracting his offspring from Orthodox spirituality. To hell with June bug energy: you will be a priest, my son.

As Nikola put it in his notebooks, cholera saved him from the priesthood. Bedridden for nine months at the age of 15, he wrenched a promise from his father: if the teen survived his illness, he would enter the Engineering Institute of Graz rather than a religious order. The promise was the key to both his recovery and his fate.

There were not many other significant events in his childhood, except perhaps the accidental death of his infinitely handsome brother, Danilo, whose innate grace enchanted all who knew him. Was the rigid elegance Tesla cultivated throughout his life an attempt to artificially extend the memory and natural charm of his lost elder sibling?

Faithful to the dead but distrustful of the living, Nikola always kept his distance from women. In fact, when he got his heart broken for the first time—at the ripe old age of eight—he realized how much harm could come from falling in love. And, more to the point, how hard it was to concentrate in that state, whether floating on the waves of the first flush of happiness, tossed by the tempest of jealousy, or becalmed by lonely nostalgia. Nothing, he reluctantly decided, should distract him from his work. "An inventor," he wrote in his notebooks, "must not have a wife: he would give her everything."

Systematically dissuading the many ladies attracted to his almost 6'6" frame, baselessly accused of homosexuality by J. Edgar Hoover, the director-for-life of the FBI (who donned dresses to pleasure his right-hand-man, Clyde Tolson), Tesla lived alone and died in the company of the pigeons he'd fed with his last pennies. To further his work and his humanitarian goals, Tesla made a point of pride of disincarnating himself in his own lifetime. If whoever is talking to the medium and me really is Tesla, could it be some kind of compensation phenomenon that's now granting his posthumous conscience such density?

*

As a child, Tesla's absolute priorities were controlling his thoughts and coping with his many obsessions and phobias as well as possible. Intense flashes of light, followed by scenes or objects that seemed to pour from his brain to take shape in front of him sometimes disturbed his vision.

Since doctors couldn't explain what was wrong with him, he decided to think of the visions as a gift. In his opinion, the 3-D images that rotated slowly before his eyes were the result of a reflex action of his brain on his retina. On a practical level, he thought of them as virtual sketches that allowed him to build his inventions without having to draw them first.

On a more theoretical level, as Tesla wrote in his autobiography, "If my explanation is correct, it should be possible to project on a screen the image of any object one conceives. Such an advance would revolutionize all human relations. I am convinced that this wonder can and will be accomplished in time to come; I may add that I have devoted much thought to the solution of the problem."[5]

Could the conscious hologram now appearing in the medium's bedroom be one of the applications of the "solution" he sought? Might he, like Einstein, be using their hostess's brain as a re-transmitter?

But for the moment, let's get back to Tesla's childhood. In 1875, at age 19, his dream came true: he was accepted into the Engineering Institute of Graz. Studying unceasingly, 20 hours a day, he absorbed the first two years' curriculum in just a few months. But upon returning home with exceptional grades at the end of the first semester, he got a terrible shock. Rather than congratulating him, his father informed the young man that he would not be going back to school after the holidays. Nikola's parents had decided he would have to take a sort of gap year instead.

Nikola was aghast, but he couldn't afford to go against his parents' will. He wouldn't discover the real reason for their incomprehensible attitude until years later: "After my father's death, it pained me to find a stack of letters my professors had sent to warn him that if he didn't take me out of school, I would die of exhaustion."[6]

Sent away for several months to the mountains for the fresh air and wholesome environment, the young man developed his capacity for creative visualization at the same time as his body was recuperating. While rock-climbing or spelunking, he would build futuristic machines, like flying cars, household robots and geo-stationary satellites, in his head. Other people would patent them in his place. During that time, he perfected a work method that depended on an asceticism he would stick to for the rest of his life.

Our essentially self-taught inventor first earned a living in telecommunications, where he developed an amplifier that would become the ancestor to the loudspeaker. Thanks to both his innovations and his incredible work ethic, in 1882, he was hired by Edison General Electric, who sent him to galvanize their Paris office. Amazed by the visionary yet pragmatic skills of the prodigy (who swam over half a mile in the Seine to get to the office every morning) his supervisor recommended him directly to Thomas Edison, the head of the company, who was in the process of developing the first electrical-power distribution network for the city of New York. Perfect timing: Tesla had plenty to say on the subject. The great Edison had chosen direct current, or DC. The young Serb believed that DC was dangerous, costly, and ill-suited to long distances—in a nutshell, obsolete before it had even been implemented.

At age 27, Tesla had just built his first alternating-current-based induction motor. "I have almost never achieved such happiness in my life," he wrote at the time. "Ideas flow continuously; the only problem is not letting any slip away. The pieces of the devices I am picturing appear to be perfectly real and tangible in every detail, even to the point of showing signs of wear and tear." He knew in his bones that alternating current (AC) was the only safe, practical solution for large-scale distribution of electricity.

Not only did DC cause frequent fires, it also lost power over distance, meaning that delivering it required installing relay stations every 300 yards. So Tesla crossed the Atlantic in an attempt to persuade his esteemed boss—the inventor of the phonograph and the incandescent light bulb— that he was making a mistake and should switch to AC. His journey was a complete failure, on that score anyway.

When the two men first met, however, they recognized each other's talent in a flash. Still, it seems inevitable that sparks would soon fly between two such high-voltage minds. Tesla started out by improving Edison's unreliable dynamos. He installed automatic-regulation systems protecting power plants from short circuits, while at the same time multiplying their output, and the profits they generated.

Initially skeptical about the breadth of the task his employee had assigned himself, Edison promised Tesla a $50,000 bonus if he succeeded. When the young engineer showed his boss his results and tried to claim his bonus, Edison burst out laughing and added with a little jab that Serbs clearly didn't understand Americans' sense of humor. Humiliated, Tesla resigned after having refused the consolation prize of a raise from twelve to eighteen dollars a week. And so began the AC-DC war.

Hired by Edison's direct competitor, the impetuous George Westinghouse, Nikola was given carte blanche to install his AC motors in all of the corporation's power plants. Then Edison launched an absolutely outrageous anti-Tesla lobbying campaign. To demonstrate the dangers of the alternating current the Serb was promoting, Edison electrocuted hundreds of animals—from poodles to circus elephants—in public.

It was pure propaganda—bearing in mind that direct current would have had the exact same effect under similar circumstances. But Edison's goal was for consumers to instinctively associate Tesla's system with sudden death by electrocution. The unexpected outcome? The "clean" execution technique appealed to the newly elected president, Calvin Coolidge. Wanting to replace hanging with the more "humane" electric chair in death-penalty cases, he decided the chairs should be equipped with alternating current.

The federal administration followed suit, and Edison lost the battle.

Tesla, however, was mortified. A philanthropist who opposed the death penalty in any form, he became an overnight celebrity thanks to the execution of William Kemmler, the first person in history to have been "Westinghoused." The term was coined by a furious Edison to describe those who were executed by what actually should be known as *Teslasation*.

Edison, however, was no more successful in imposing his new word than he has been in imposing his direct current. In 1898, based on patents filed by Tesla, Westinghouse won the contract to install the electrical infrastructure for the whole of the USA. At age 32, the formerly obscure Serbian immigrant was about to light up the world.

*

Without meaning to offend his memory, it is flagrantly obvious that Nikola was a pure genius, except where money was concerned. Westinghouse had bought all 40 of his patents for the ridiculously low sum of $5,000 plus 150 shares in his company, which added up to the bonus Edison had refused to pay. Thus the Serbian engineer made peace with Americans and their odd sense of humor.

Without holding a grudge, he graciously thanked his munificent boss when Westinghouse offered him two dollars and fifty cents for every horsepower of electricity sold. Then, entirely absorbed by his colossal tasks, he forgot all about that trivial detail. The firm gave him enough to pay for his research materials, his hotel room and—obsessed as he was with the idea of being contaminated by microbes—the eighteen cloth napkins he required twice a day in order to meticulously clean the silverware in the hotel's dining room where he took all of his meals. What more could he have asked for?

Then came the day to settle accounts. Four years after they had signed their contract, George Westinghouse showed up one evening at dinnertime looking despondent. His bankers had pointed out that between the $2.50 per horsepower clause and the incredible output of Tesla's electrical equipment system, Westinghouse already owed him over $12 million. Tesla, his employer sighed, was going to be one of the richest people in the world.

The lucky beneficiary listened to the news without raising an eyebrow, finished wiping his silverware, and with his mind on the invention he had been working on night and day, asked with polite distraction, "What can I do for you?"

"Our contract is going to ruin me," the industrialist glumly replied, as he dug into the first course. "If you insist on my paying up, I'll go bankrupt."

"And if I don't, would you save your company and retain control of it?"

"Yes."

"And would you keep offering the world the safety of AC through my poly-phase system?"

"Of course—it's the most spectacular electrical system ever invented!"

Uninterested in numbers as soon as they were disconnected from calculations and represented nothing but filthy lucre, Tesla was in no position to judge how accurate his employer's financial woes really were. Even if he did suspect an element of bluff, Westinghouse was the first person to have given him both a chance and the means to carry out his research.

That very evening, Nikola tore up the contract. Foregoing not only the $12 million of accumulated debt but also the billions his patents would have earned him over the course of his lifetime, he gave away all of his rights for a definitive lump sum of $216,600. And he picked up the tab for dinner, too.

Due to his suicidal generosity, eight years later, when he was barely more than forty years old, Tesla, having been abandoned by Westinghouse, no longer had a penny to his name. There was nothing left to finance his inventions or their construction. As his biographer Margaret Cheney points out, the number of discoveries lost to humanity is incalculable.

Westinghouse's savior would live another 40 years with the same brilliant mind, the same brutal work schedule, and the same indifference to financial details. Nothing mattered to him except the fruit of his labor, the quality of his shirts, the well-being of the pigeons in Bryant Park, and the possibility of improving the human condition through electricity, which he had decided to make available for free. The only thing that would change in the second half of his life was how other people would perceive him. Their self-serving interest would soon give way to the pseudo-pity that gifted people who don't know how to sell themselves often inspire.

Yet although they saw him as someone who was all washed up, at 40, Tesla had in fact barely scratched the surface of his many inventions that would change the world—for better or for worse. Radio, radar, X-rays, robots, the Internet (a patent from 1893): all of them familiar elements in our daily lives. As well as artificial lightning created in a laboratory, particle-beam weapons, remote-controlled missiles, anti-missile shield waves, climate-changing systems: all more-or-less secretive innovations available almost exclusively to the military, which pounced on them as soon as he died, if not before, according to some of his biographers.

It does seem to be more than enough to keep a tormented soul from getting any peace, to make it feel enraged over the lack of recognition, truth, and success in achieving its goals. The very soul, perhaps, who, as I write these lines, has been hanging out once or twice a week in the bedroom of a medium swamped with information and requests intended for me. A soul seeking light; a form of consciousness that has remained attached to life here on Earth in order to demand, if not reparation, then increased awareness, greater justice, improvements to society, protection for the planet, and as long as we're at it, making the dreams his contemporaries' stole from him come true.

It's one thing not to believe in ghosts. But at this point, it's starting to feel like ignoring his messages would be shirking my moral duty to rescue a soul in distress.

1. "Running on Empty," The New Scientist, 25 April 1998.
2. Superman vs Nikola Tesla (The Mad Scientist), Max Fleischer, 1941 (YouTube).
3. The New York Times, March 18, 1916.
4. Margaret Cheney, Tesla: Man Out of Time, Touchstone (Simon & Schuster) 2001.
5. Nikola Tesla, "My Inventions," Electrical Experimenter, 1919.
6. Ibid.

6
Back to Earth

"I was defeated," Tesla's posthumous appearance repeatedly stated. You can definitely detect some bitterness in the 40-odd messages dictated between December 2015 and June 2016, but there is very little blame. Although Lord knows there would have been more than enough to go around!

The first people who tried to extinguish the inventor's genius and renown were his sponsors, the very people he had made rich, believing they were his friends. They began to distance themselves from him as early as 1899, when he set up an experimental station in Colorado Springs to build his famous "magnifying-transmitter": his greatest invention, in some people's eyes; his worst, in others. The one which, according to a handful of scientists and throngs of conspiracy theorists, was diverted for military purposes and recuperated by HAARP[1] and its Russian counterpart, and has led to global climate change (sanctimoniously camouflaged as the "greenhouse effect"), let alone the wave war and all its attendant psychological manipulation.

Myth or reality? We'll get back to that later.

It all started with two metal towers: one 80 feet tall, the other 120. They descended to a depth of 100 feet belowground and were topped by copper balls three feet in diameter. Able to discharge up to 100 million volts, they produced artificial lightning at will. As long as Tesla had the transmitter on, lightning rods for 20 miles around were linked by sparkling bolts of non-stop lightning. You can imagine how thrilled the neighbors were. One of those artificial thunderstorms took out the generator in Colorado Springs, blacking out the whole city. The local populace demanded the electrical mischief-maker be run out of town, but Tesla offered to pay for repairs, spending a fortune in damages to be able to continue his experiments in Rockies, which he said were highly "conductive."

George Westinghouse was beginning to feel glum. How could he make any money out of artificial lightning? Or lighting 200 incandescent bulbs stuck directly into the soil up to 25 miles away, as Tesla had done in 1899? Or out of pumping and desalinating ocean water to irrigate poor regions?[2] Or perhaps even adapting ball lightning along the principles of nuclear fusion?

For his contemporaries, Tesla's ideas seemed like science fiction, and Tesla himself like a mad scientist. It wasn't until 1978 that engineer Robert Golka was able to reproduce the Colorado Springs results relatively successfully, at Wendover Air Force Base, in Utah. Results which were confirmed in a lab by Dutch astrophysicist Gerard Dijkhuis in 1995.[3]

For the time being, however, the only thing Tesla's backers saw in all those costly experiments was an ever-growing financial hole, which all those spectacular—but hard to monetize—phenomena did little to justify. Artificial lightning was starting to get on their nerves. Free electricity from the sky for all? He's got to be kidding!

And that wasn't all. "The discovery of these new properties…opened up the possibility of transmitting, without wires, energy in large amounts… very economically, whether at a distance of a few miles or of a few thousand miles."[4] Presented that way, his discovery of scalar waves— which he said came from the sun's neutrinos—considerably cooled his backers' ardor. Freezing his credit was the first step in the new Ice Age.

Heeding the warning, Tesla pretended to be more reasonable. Was his lab in Colorado Springs too costly? Fine, he would move back to New York… but his concession to budgetary restrictions was purely geographical. On Long Island in 1900, he undertook the construction of gigantic Wardenclyffe Tower. He intended to use the tower to broadcast radio programs around the world, to reply to the signals from extraterrestrials he said he'd received in Colorado Springs, and to transmit wireless electricity around the world.

That was the turning point. From then on, even those who had supported him until then began to turn against him. His friend George Westinghouse, who owed his fortune and his corporation's survival to

Tesla, refused to lend him the money he needed to finish construction of his tower. Later, Westinghouse went so far as to sue Tesla for non-payment of delivered materials. "The transmission of power without wires will very soon create an industrial revolution and such as the world has never seen before. Who is to be more helpful in this great development, and who will derive from it greater benefits than yourself?"[5] Thanks, but no thanks, Westinghouse replied, in essence.

It was incomprehensible. Only governmental or military pressure could explain such an attitude from a billionaire known for his audacity and sixth sense when it came to investment opportunities. It is, on the other hand, somewhat easier to understand the withdrawal of his other sponsor, the fabulously wealthy J.P. Morgan, who had bought up all the copper mines in order to enjoy a monopoly on electrical wire. Wireless wave transmission? Was Tesla out of his mind? "But where would I put the meters?" Morgan snapped back.

As for Thomas Edison, who had never forgiven his former employee for the defeat he suffered over direct current, he finished his former employee's reputation off by informing the press—in a statement filled with sarcastic mockery—that Tesla hoped to communicate with aliens. You almost have to laugh when you consider that, three years later, the author of those gibes would announce that he was working on a device for conversing with the dead.

"The apparatus," Edison said in an interview, "will at least give them (i.e. the deceased) a better opportunity to express themselves than the tilting tables and raps and Ouija boards and mediums and other crude methods now purported to be their only means of communication."[6] Fortunately, Tesla had had plenty of time to get used to the American sense of humor by then.

Seized by his creditors, Wardenclyffe Tower was converted into a pickle factory at first. Later, they blew it up and sold the remains as scrap metal. Tesla's dreams went up in smoke for a fistful of dollars.

In retrospect, whatever reasons they claimed to have, it seems hard to believe that backers would have withdrawn voluntarily from a project that, among other things, would have provided them with exclusive worldwide rights to transmit information by radio. But at the time, Marconi was the officially recognized inventor of wireless telegraphy, and it must have seemed more sensible to deal with a man who would settle for transmitting human voices over long distances, without dragging communicating with extraterrestrials, let alone supplying free energy, into the mix.

It wasn't until a few months after Tesla's death that the U.S. Supreme Court upheld his patent, thereby annulling Marconi's, which was nothing more than a blatant copy of ones filed earlier by the deceased. Tesla was posthumously awarded complete intellectual property of his invention. It should be mentioned that the decision came in 1943, while the world was at war, and that the U.S. government had nationalized the radio-broadcasting company founded by the despoiled inventor. So at the end of the day, after having deprived Tesla of the profits he deserved and granting them to Marconi instead, the government wound up robbing the profits from Marconi as well!

The solitary old man in the New Yorker Hotel lived out the last three decades of his life in crushing poverty. To his detractors' and despoilers' dismay, that situation only served to multiply his inventiveness. But then the military started making trouble for him. The last patent he could afford to file, in 1928, concerned an airplane with vertical take-off and landing.

The only traces we still have of the abundant unpatented research and discoveries that followed that patent come from his annual birthday press conferences. They include a blend of sensational announcements and subtle allusions reserved for members of the secret services who had infiltrated the press corps: the only people still taking him seriously.

His later work included research into interstellar energy transmission, controlling the weather, and cosmic rays, both for the purpose of military deterrence and for their therapeutic effects. He presented those discoveries to "a hostile, mocking audience, knowing full well that he would be making a spectacle of himself."[7]

As for Albert Einstein, at the outbreak of World War II he wrote a letter to President Roosevelt to which he never received a reply. Nevertheless, though Einstein hadn't realized it at the time, his letter convinced the president that the Nazis' advance in terms of developing an atomic bomb was alarming. The White House decided it was time to overtake them, and the Manhattan Project was born.

The nation's top physicists were all secretly mobilized in Los Alamos—except for Einstein himself, who, as we have seen, had been classified as a

Soviet spy by the unsinkable J. Edgar Hoover—still the head of the FBI.

Meanwhile, old man Tesla went on with his work on anti-gravity, parallel universes, and directed-energy weapons meant to prevent war—spectacular advances that he informed the military authorities about without asking for anything in return. They, on the other hand, waited for Tesla's death to use the inventions their spies had been keeping track of in ways he would never have allowed.

On January 8, 1943, a chambermaid at the New Yorker Hotel found Tesla dead in his bed. The coroner's official report gave the cause of death as cardiac arrest due to coronary thrombosis. The opaque, dubious way in which the FBI handled Tesla's estate would soon give rise to all sorts of crazy rumors.

Had the 86-year-old man been assassinated, whether to put an end to his annual media frenzy or to steal his final discoveries? Some people believe so. In Erik Orion's conspiratorial book, *The Bush Connection*, a former SS commando leader, Otto Skorzeny, boasts of having suffocated the inventor in his hotel room with his pillow before emptying all of the papers from Tesla's safe to provide Hitler with preliminary sketches of the inventor's secret weapons.

Insofar as it provided a credible explanation to the general public for the extraordinary disappearance of Tesla's notes and projects—about which more later—the targeted-assassination story has never been formally denied by the FBI. But that's not what the victim had to say for himself. "They didn't need to get rid of me physically," the presumptive Tesla stated on January 10, 2016. "They settled for destroying me morally, financially, scientifically, and in the media. But I'm not done yet. I haven't finished. It's time to stop ignoring my struggles! It's time to break the silence surrounding me!"

And that is precisely the purpose of this book: transmitting Tesla's energy as I receive it and understand it, and attempting to analyze it. The selfsame energy that various lobbies of his day got the better of, but which death, apparently, has been unable to contain. The Sky Engineer never surrendered. He may have been forcibly removed from circulation, but no one has ever been able to muzzle him.

If the historical record can be believed, Geneviève Delpech is not the first medium to have been solicited by the inventor as he wanders through the hereafter. As is the case among the living, the astral world has its charlatans, compulsive liars, and posthumous imposters who pass themselves off as "ascended masters" or cosmic prophets—but their wordy, fuzzy, New Age messages, often with an apocalyptic cast, fool only the most gullible or sectarian followers.

On the other hand, towards the end of their lives, such illustrious "intermediaries," known in their day for their reliability, people like the mystic Edgar Cayce (1877-1945)[8] and the oh-so polyvalent Madame Fraya (1871-1954)—advisor to the French Chiefs of Staff during World War I and fortune-teller to the stars, from Sarah Bernhardt, Sacha Guitry and Marcel Proust to statesmen, philosophers, and political activists like Georges Clemenceau, Jean Jaurès and others[9]—are said to have received requests from the late Tesla relating to the transmission of his free, wireless electricity.

To this day, many free-energy activists swear they are connected to that "ghost on stand-by" who knocks on so many doors; that inexhaustible source of information which infiltrates all available channels to pursue its battle against the opacity, amnesia, censorship, regression, short-sighted selfishness, and fatality that are leading humanity to its own doom. This perpetually trusting, immoderately brilliant genius who knew how to attract thunder—both literally and figuratively—managed to have all sorts of roadblocks thrown in his way, in vain. Even the way he was hastened to his grave was a failure. Believing they had "grounded" him for good, it seems like the only thing they actually accomplished was to make him even more conductive than before!

In his lifetime, Albert Einstein, whose intuitions have so often turned out to be true, said, "I believe in life after death, simply because energy can't die; it circulates, is transformed and never stops." Tesla and he certainly seem to be doing everything they can to convince us of that. But what is the hidden purpose of all their efforts?

1. High Frequency Active Auroral Research Program. See Chapter 19.
2. Nikola Tesla, *Colorado Springs Notes*, 1899, Nikola Tesla Museum, Belgrade; and BN Publishing, 2010.
3. www.criticalpast.com, www.orage-et-foudre.pagesperso-orange.fr
4. "The Problem of Increasing Human Energy" *The Century Magazine*, June 1900.
5. Letter from Nikola Tesla to George Westinghouse, January 11, 1906 (as quoted in *Tesla: Man Out of Time*, by Margaret Cheney. Simon & Schuster, 1981).
6. Thomas Edison, in *Scientific American*, October 1920.
7. Martine Le Coz, *L'Homme électrique*, Michalon, 2009.
8. Dorothée Koechlin de Bizemont, *L'Univers d'Edgar Cayce*, 3 tomes, Robert Laffont, 1985, 1987, 1992.
9. Simone de Tervagne, *Une voyante à l'Elysée: Madame Fraya*, Pygmalion, 1975.

7
The light-beam riders

People with the least similar biographies can have the most revealing things in common. Albert Einstein's fate—which might, at first glance, seem infinitely more glorious than Nikola Tesla's—actually followed a remarkably similar pattern.

They both showed precocious inventiveness and enjoyed fleeting fame followed by a long decline in reputation. They both displayed eccentric, marginalized behavior, and both men's relentless productivity inspired jealousy in the "scientific community" and suspicion from the powers that be. Definitive exile to the USA had been imposed upon them both by circumstances in their respective homelands, and both of their American dreams acquired nightmarish overtones because of the paranoid, racist persecution of the FBI's unmovable boss. Finally, they were both hyperactive virtually up to their deathbeds, despite the shameless criticism and calumny aimed at them, which tried to change their public personas from men of infinite creativity to doddering old fools who wouldn't admit that their silly tinkering had fallen drastically behind the times.

At age 76, on the eve of his death from a ruptured abdominal aneurysm, racked by pain on his hospital bed, Einstein was still demanding pen and paper from his faithful secretary, Helen Dukas. He still hoped to convincingly present his Unified Field Theory, a.k.a. the "Theory of Everything," which would reconcile gravity and quantum mechanics, the infinitely small and the infinitely large, while laying the foundations for a worldwide government that would ban the atomic bomb.

As for the 86-year-old Tesla, in the midst of a world war he wore himself out trying to communicate the secrets of international peace, the energy revolution, and free electricity to President Roosevelt via his wife, Eleanor.

The dynamics of their old age were analogous: both men reconnected with the youthful intensity that had led to their earliest discoveries. While Tesla had nicknamed himself the "Sky Engineer" as a child, Einstein had proclaimed himself a "Light-Beam Rider" at a similarly tender young age. He later explained that he'd first developed his theory of special relativity by imagining himself sitting astride a beam of light, traveling at a speed that depended on whether the observer was accelerating or not.[1]

When Tesla adopted the nickname for himself, in a 1917 speech criticizing Einstein, he specified that as a rider, he would not let himself be unseated by the speed of light (which he refused to assert could not be exceeded). The barb didn't prevent him from acknowledging common ground with the physicist later that same evening: "The greatest mysteries of our being are still to be fathomed, and all the evidence of the senses and the teachings of exact and dry sciences to the contrary notwithstanding, death itself may not be the termination of the wonderful metamorphoses we witness."[2]

What were those wonderful metamorphoses? Well, to begin with, surely the ones that start with an intuition and become a concept, a general law, or a technical achievement. Both men explained—repeatedly and in great depth—that they were in the habit of performing "thought experiments." It was during those modified states of consciousness that the creative visualization of their calculations and discoveries occured.[3]

For instance, referring to his general theory of relativity, Einstein declared that he had a "physical intuition" of it by picturing himself in an elevator in free fall.[4] For his part, Tesla described his inventions as being revealed in visions that came to him like flashes of lightning: "the images I saw were wonderfully sharp and clear and had the solidity of metal and stone."[5]

While the two extrovert hermits are often seen in opposition—one as a pure theoretician, the other as "just" an inventor—that dichotomy is inaccurate. In his notes, Tesla analyzed his thought processes regarding the cosmos with the abstract rigor of a fundamental physics researcher. While Einstein, a former patent officer, also held many patents, including ones for an extremely precise voltmeter; a safe, noiseless refrigerator; a camera; and a hearing aid that was free from the Larsen effect.[6]

Those practical efforts must have inspired admiration for the Serbian inventor's technical mastery. When a journalist asked him how it felt to be the smartest man alive, Einstein quipped, "I don't know, you'll have to ask Nikola Tesla."

While their relationships with women were radically opposed, their conceptions of God were virtually the same. They both saw God as a sort of mathematical principle that could be deduced by observing nature and evolution, studying both the infinitely large and the infinitely small, and searching for the laws that ruled them.

When Einstein declared, at the 1927 Solvay Congress, that "God does not play dice with the universe," he was insisting more on his refusal of randomness than on his belief in the divine. When looking at a clock mechanism, he was far more interested in how the cogs and gears turned than in the clockmaker's personality.

Einstein's obsession with theory ("It is the theory that decides what we can observe") represented no more than the need to establish a framework, a playground with rules that could always be adjusted or relaxed as needed. That is exactly what he did with his theory of general relativity, stunning all of his peers. No one had been attacking him, everyone had accepted his theory as sound—except for Einstein himself. Acting on a sort of precautionary principle, he wanted to defend his theory against an objection that no one but he suspected, one that would have invalidated his theory if he hadn't protected it with an addition.

During World War I, when he first published the theory, at a time when the existence of other galaxies was as yet unknown, no one before him had dared to attempt a mathematical conception of the cosmos. The experimental data of his day (and not a "retrograde" personal conviction, as some people still insist) continued to suggest a stable, stationary and finite universe, which his general relativity belied. So he added an element: the cosmological constant, or vacuum energy, which would explain the accelerated expansion of the universe, if that should turn out to be so. Disapproval of that addition was so intense—among both friends and foes—that he was obliged to publicly retract it in order to preserve his credibility. On top of all that, now that the existence of vacuum energy has been recently confirmed by astrophysicists,[7] it is his forced retraction that is currently held against him!

But the worst injustice perpetrated against Einstein concerns quantum physics. How cruelly ironic to have had his reputation assassinated by the triumph of a theory that he himself gave rise to! For as far back as 1905, it was Einstein who first introduced the concept of a light quantum (now known as a photon), the founding principle of quantum mechanics. Alas, it was unanimously rejected by physicists at the time. Einstein—who had clearly been ahead of his time—was treated like a heretic for over 20 years.

Yet in 1927, the young "quantums" at the Solvay Congress made a complete about-face, treating him like a has-been instead, and burying his reputation in all due respect. In other words, in deference to his international prestige, they made it a first-class burial. The future was theirs; they honored him for the impact he'd had on the past. The work they were doing, they claimed, would advance and conclude Einstein's theories. They had sincerely intended to pay tribute to him, but for Albert, it was the basest of affronts. He was only 47 years old, and there they were, putting him on a shelf with the archives. Profoundly affected, he endured the barrage of compliments with dry wit and perfect manners, but the wound never truly healed.

I believe that what he shared most deeply with Tesla was that sense of betrayal. They had both been discriminated against because of their backgrounds—Jewish for the one, Serbo-Croatian for the other—and both men suffered at the hands of those who wished to neutralize them. Einstein's books were burned; Tesla's lab was burned down. Each of them stood up to his foes with intelligence, courage, and lucidity, but both of them were most deeply wounded by their friends. For Albert, it was his beloved disciples, Niels Bohr and Werner Heisenberg, whose quantum studies he had inspired; for Nikola, the sponsors who owed him everything, along with his fellow inventors, who spared no low blow.

Despite the flattering façade of an official tribute, Einstein experienced the 1927 Congress as a public humiliation. For him, it was every bit as cruel as it had been for Tesla ten years earlier, when his peers awarded him with the only real distinction he ever received: a medal struck with the profile of his worst enemy, Thomas Alva Edison. Did those parallel blows to their pride bring the two diehard outcasts closer together? No, or at least not in their lifetimes, anyway.

Toward the end of his life, Tesla trained the last beams of his humanity on pigeons, while Einstein dedicated his final bursts of activism to bees. Guided by the guardians of the temple, posterity has reduced one of them to his bird fantasies, and sworn that the other never actually pronounced the famous phrase that has, unfortunately, become so topical since: "If bees disappear from the face of the earth, then mankind would have only four years of life left." Despite those who would deny him even that statement, in the year 2000,

Rémy Chauvin explained to me that a few months before Einstein died, he'd made that prediction to their mutual friend, Nobel laureate Karl von Frisch, the man who had deciphered bees' dance-based communication tactics. Einstein based his calculation on the fact that 80% of the world's fruit and vegetables require pollination. Their survival depends, therefore, upon bees.

As for the behavior that the wilfully blind J. Edgar Hoover described as Tesla's perverse love of birds, it was simply mutual appreciation. Throughout his life, his prodigious genius enriched others, yet only the pigeons ever showed him the slightest gratitude.

*

Can a friendship that never had time to develop on Earth come to fruition in the afterlife? After your own funeral, are you free to hang out with whomever you please, whenever you please? That's the impression one gets from most messages from the hereafter. Is it a reassuring reality or false advertising aimed at the living?

If we choose to recognize the identities they have presented themselves with, we see that the ebullient, celebrated Albert has acted as a trailblazer for the overlooked, discreet Nikola, "introducing" him to me via the medium's bedroom. This role as a sort of sponsor might surprise anyone who is familiar with their relationship on Earth, but might it not be seen as a sort of rehabilitation or compensation in the afterlife?

As we have seen, at first glance, everything would seem to pit the celebrated champion of relativity and seeker of the absolute, the scruffy, disheveled and sockless ladies' man against the elegantly attired gentleman who avoided women like the plague. And the divide between them didn't stop there. In Tesla's eyes, in any case, there was a skeleton in the closet, in a manner of speaking.

While the Nobel Prize for Physics was awarded to Albert Einstein in 1921 (for his discoveries about light's dual wave-particle nature), it had been awarded to Nikola Tesla six years earlier... but only for a week. On November 6, 1915, based on a dispatch from Reuters, The New York Times announced the news and interviewed the laureate-to-be. Anyone can imagine Tesla's joy, particularly at a time when his name was being dragged through the mud by jealous enemies, and his beloved Wardenclyffe Tower had recently been turned into a pickle warehouse.

He learned about the unexpected honor from the press before receiving official notification from the prestigious jury in Stockholm. But the supreme irony was that he would be sharing the prize with Thomas Alva Edison, the very man who had sworn to destroy him! When the journalists asked him how he felt about it, Nikola magnanimously replied, "Edison deserves a dozen Nobel prizes."

Convinced he was being rewarded for his discovery of wireless energy transmission, the inventor struck an impassioned tone throughout the interview. As millions of soldiers were being blown to bits in the hellish trenches of World War I, Tesla promised mankind a radiant future in which war would be waged with electric waves, rather than explosives. The international press spread the news of Tesla's newfound glory and gratitude, while his co-laureate, Einstein, refused all interviews.

On November 14, a new dispatch arrived from Reuters: the Nobel Prize for Physics had just been awarded—not to Tesla and Einstein, but to William Henry Bragg and his son for the use of X-rays (invented by Tesla) in determining the structure of crystals.

What had gone wrong?

Absent an official statement from the Nobel Foundation, in all likelihood, Edison did it. Already overwhelmed with both honors and dollars, Edison most likely informed the Committee that he would sooner refuse the prize than share it with "the Serb." In this way, Edison deprived Tesla of his $20,000 share of the prize money, which would have enabled him to buy Wardenclyffe Tower back from his creditors.

The following year, as the tower was being demolished and sold for scrap, the American Institute of Electrical Engineers awarded Tesla their highest honor as a sort of consolation prize. Adding insult to injury, the honor in question was called the Edison Medal. Ruined and defeated, a heavy-hearted Nikola had to praise his persecutor during his acceptance of the award that bore his arch-enemy's name.

Afterward, he had a few somewhat bitter words to say about Albert Einstein, whose glory, according to Tesla, was founded on erroneous calculations and incomplete conclusions. The worst part, in Tesla's eyes, was that the ideas had grown from accurate intuitions, but the muddled perfectionist seemed to have done his best to undermine them! It was disappointed admiration, rather than jealousy, that fueled his resentment.

The star-crossed engineer also believed that the famous physicist's theory of special relativity had done him considerable damage. When Einstein had first published it, in 1905, he hadn't mentioned ether—that "substance incarnating the vacuum" and "mediator of gravitational force," according to Isaac Newton. For Tesla, ether was the reservoir of inexhaustible energy from which he said he drew his wireless electricity. Einstein's oversight led the scientific community to conclude that ether didn't exist and, therefore, that Tesla was selling snake oil.

Eleven years later, however, Einstein reintroduced ether into his theory of general relativity as a deciding element in electromagnetic phenomena. "Space without ether is inconceivable," he wrote to Tesla, "because the propagation of light would be impossible."[8] He publicly confirmed that position during an address at the University of Leiden (Netherlands) whose topic was Ether and the *Theory of Relativity.*[9]

For his 75th birthday, a discredited, humiliated, and destitute Tesla, alone in the New Yorker Hotel room he had turned into a pigeon clinic, received a telegram from Einstein. Amends in the shape of birthday wishes. Might it have been that unexpected gesture, that un-hoped for recognition from the most admired scientist of his era that gave Tesla the strength to finish that same summer speeding around Niagara Falls at 90 miles an hour, performing road trials in his battery-less electric car?

Not only did the Nobel Prize winner validate Tesla's ether theory; he shared the Serb's utopic dream of seeing science become the key to world peace. Einstein outspokenly defended a worldwide government born of a balance of terror and based on an equal distribution of wealth. As for Tesla, his plan was to eliminate poverty and social inequality altogether, by freely distributing the inexhaustible energy he would draw from the vacuum. At present, if their minds are indeed still active, we can see that while Einstein's political ardors are somewhat calmed, Tesla is still strongly attached to his revolutionary ideals.

While they were alive, the two notoriously misunderstood geniuses had a curious relationship, composed of a blend of mutual sympathy and aversion. Even as Nikola attacked Albert in public, Albert defended Nikola in private. The German Jew and the Serbo-Croatian never really had a chance to hash out their disagreements, which, when you get right down to it, were no more than superficial differences in approach and style in response to the prevailing hostility to their ideas.

Although they were as dissimilar in physical appearance as they were in their senses of humor, PR skills and attitudes toward the pleasures of the flesh, the two geniuses were subjected to the same attacks and the same xenophobic jealousy, and they shared similar sensibilities. All in all, they seemed fated to meet again...

*

And here they—or their holographic doppelgangers, anyway—are, reunited in a bedroom in Neuilly sur Seine, on the outskirts of Paris, in this winter of 2015. The question is, why? To chat about a compass and an urn? To confirm their identities and convince us that their consciousness goes on? As we will soon see, they are there to lead us across their old stomping grounds and battlefields.

After first arguing over ether, they later crossed swords again over quantum mechanics and space-time. At the age of 81, Tesla had even shouted from the rooftops that he was in the process of elaborating the new theory of relativity. It was one that would include both gravitational waves and the cosmological constant, two of Einstein's intuitive ideas that had been laughed at by his peers and which he had been obliged to publicly renounce in order to avoid becoming as discredited as Tesla.

Einstein's renunciations weren't just about clinging to fame. They were dictated by a combination of financial imperatives and a kind of academic blackmail. Having given his ex-wife, Mileva, the money from his Nobel in lieu of alimony, the Princeton professor needed the fees he received as a conference speaker to pay for the psychiatric ward in Zurich where their son Eduard was committed for schizophrenia for over 30 years.[10]

Caught up in their respective work and problems, the two brilliant men never actually spent much time together. As far as anyone knows, the only project they ever worked on together was the incredible, and incredibly controversial, Philadelphia Experiment, which took place during World War II, just a few months before Nikola passed away. In the experiment, Nikola's discoveries related to space-time combined with Albert's Unified Field Theory led, according to a range of more or less farfetched eyewitness accounts, to the momentary dematerialization (a.k.a. illusory invisibility) of the destroyer *U.S.S. Eldridge* and its crew.[11]

Pure nonsense, in some people's eyes (officially, it was simply a strategy to prevent enemy torpedoes from detecting the ship), the complicated affair was, by all accounts, badly bungled. Both of our scientists blamed themselves for letting the U.S. Navy convince them to participate.

Nevertheless, alongside the occasional differences their common foes did their best to magnify, Einstein and Tesla shared the same dreams, lived through the same nightmare, and been subjected to the same persecution by the FBI, economic titans, and more "traditional" academics.

Einstein has come back into favor in our day: all the predictions that inspired incredulity in his peers—from the cosmological constant to the recent detection of gravitational waves—have turned out to be true. Perhaps now it is Tesla's turn to break the fetters of censorship and disdain that have been used in an attempt to hush up his work. May this book contribute to that.

Alas, the moral and physical violence that scientists and artists are subjected to is a subject that won't let my pen run dry any time soon. As I delve into the events that inspired me to write this book, I have to wonder if its real purpose was simply to create a posthumous playground, a place where those kindred spirits who never "connected" while they were alive—and whom, to my knowledge, no other biographer has ever brought together—could make up for lost time and finally get to know each other well.

1. *Le Monde*, Special issue: *La Révolution Einstein*, July 2015.
2. Tesla's Edison Medal acceptance speech, from the *Minutes of the Annual Meeting of the American Institute of Electrical Engineers*, May 18, 1917, Smithsonian Institution.
3. Thibault Damour, *Si Einstein m'etait conté*, Le Cherche-Midi, 2005.
4. *Le Monde*, Special issue, art. cit.
5. Nikola Tesla, *My Inventions*, op. cit.
6. *Le Monde*, Special issue, art. cit.
7. *La Constante cosmologique*, www.cnrs.fr/publications.
8. Martine Le Coz, *L'Homme électrique*, op. cit.
9. Roland Clark, *Einstein. His Life and Universe*, Simon & Schuster, 2007.
10. Laurent Seksik, *Le Cas Eduard Einstein*, Flammarion, 2013.
11. William Moore, with Charles Berlitz, *The Philadelphia Experiment: Project Invisibility*, Ballantine Books, 1979

8
Via her left ear

"Do ghosts arise from their own earthly memories or from an existence that we lend to them?" Sir Arthur Conan Doyle wondered in 1925. The creator of Sherlock Holmes, who was familiar with all sorts of spectral apparitions, organized an international congress on spiritualism in Paris that year.[1] He was referring in particular to the case of Estelle Livermore, a lovely young New Yorker who was madly in love with her husband, Charles, a well-known banker.

In 1860, when she fell ill, she promised him that if the need arose, she would send him proof of her love from the hereafter. Neither one of them really believed it would come to that, however, and the banker fell apart when his wife died. True to her word, a few months later, Estelle began appearing to him before witnesses. She made a total of 388 appearances over a period of five years.

"I am in training," was the first public statement the revenant made through the medium Kate Fox, in the presence of both her widowed spouse and the man who had treated her during her final illness, Dr. Gray. Later, she appeared more directly. She would be more or less luminous and her body more or less complete from one séance to the next. Levitating, sitting down, dancing, changing from a holographic state one moment to the density of flesh the next, she would allow her widowed husband to stroke her hair and take her picture. She also spoke French as elegantly as she had while alive and even wrote some hundred or more love letters while everyone watched. Family members and graphologists alike confirmed it was indeed her handwriting.[2]

At the time, many people dismissed the sightings as "collective hallucinations," but they left actual physical traces. In addition, the participants' maturity and social status make it extremely unlikely they would have kept a practical joke running over the course of five years. The long series of weekly or twice-weekly séances, which was subjected to a rigorous protocol checked by various skeptics, was revealed to the public by the famous social reformer Robert Dale Owen (1801-1877), member of the U.S. House of Representatives, drafter of the bill founding the Smithsonian Institution, and advocate for birth control.

As a witness to these amazing phenomena, I would suggest, in all modesty, that in his time he played a role not unlike my own today, writing both a book and several articles in scientific journals about what he had seen.[3] His style, however, is considerably more categorical and activist than my own—as is often the case with former materialists who become determined to convert those whose disbelief they once shared.

Aside from the fact that the contacts with Estelle's ectoplasm seem more like spiritualist trysts than information-sharing sessions, the main difference with what I am currently experiencing stems from their very conception, not to say their staging. Those ghostly manifestations in New York were *brought about* by such a powerful longing they would seem to confirm Conan Doyle's second proposition: Estelle's appearances may have been literally *caused* by her loving husband's need to reestablish contact, and by the energy he put at the phenomenon's disposition. For that matter, the materializations ceased when Charles Livermore had worked through his grief.

There's no point in accusing the medium Kate Fox however. Although she originally responded to a request from Estelle's doctor to facilitate the reunion by supplying the necessary "psychic fluid," there's a simple reason she can't be accused of performing hypnosis-based hoaxes. The deceased, as several witnesses and photographs attest, materialized in exactly the same way whether Miss Fox, her original "source of energy," was present or not. So are ghostly apparitions nothing more than the materialization of our hopes and desires, as Conan Doyle suggested?

"After death, consciousness continues in a parallel universe," Tesla's avatar replied in his second message. That was on December 21, 2015, two days after setting me on the trail of Marco Metrovic, the student defending his ashes. Before going any further on that score, I would like to describe the way in which Geneviève Delpech receives her visits.

First of all, she's alone—there are no witnesses and no cameras. The only evidence I have is the dated text messages, and, as we will see, some photos. A study protocol can be established later if she so desires (particularly to determine if "her" Einstein and Tesla can be seen by anyone else). Respecting the intimacy of both the substance and the style of the contacts seemed more important to me, at least to begin with, than an external demonstration of the reality of the phenomenon per se. That type of demonstration took place so often in the 19th and 20th centuries... all too often with a focus on spectacle over meaning, which can be seen clearly in the archives of both the Society for Psychical Research, founded by Frederic Myers, and the International Metapsychical Institute, presided for several years by Physiology Nobel Prize winner Charles Richet.[4]

In concrete, practical terms, Geneviève Delpech doesn't solicit anything. She neither concentrates nor deliberately puts herself into a trance-like state or auto-hypnosis, as the illustrious and controversial Kate Fox did, nor does she make any effort to tune in to a particular frequency. No, she simply goes to sleep, and a presence awakens her. Her night visitor's image, whether head-to-toe or from the waist up only, is standing in front of her or sitting on her bed.

The sort of gray or sepia, hologram-like image of variable luminosity and density has often been described and photographed over the course of psycho-physical experiments in earlier centuries.[5] Nevertheless, in all of the literature available about "speaking apparitions," I can find just one parallel to the materializations of Einstein and Tesla accepted or generated by the medium from Neuilly. Only one other example of equally recurrent appearances by a famous deceased person concerned with both the past identity it claims as its own and events that are contemporary to its appearances. Oddly enough, that example is yet another philanthropic inventor specializing in energy in general and lightning in particular: Benjamin Franklin.

Which leads us back to the Livermores. The Founding Father (1706-1790), Ambassador to France, and inventor of both the lightning rod and the Franklin stove, appears in the minutes of more than 50 of the séances held in the banker's various homes. This is how Charles Livermore described the ghostly guest on December 12, 1861, in front of Robert Dale Owen and the four other witnesses who signed the minutes of séance No 179:

> We could see Dr. Franklin's shape sitting in my big armchair before the window, which was hidden by a black curtain. Once the light from the lantern stayed on his face for 10 full minutes, affording us the opportunity to examine it at our leisure, as well as the rest of his body. To begin with, the face seemed to be composed of true living flesh, the hair seemed real, and the details of his shining eyes were so clear that we could see the

whites. But I soon noticed that the apparition, including the eyes, melted away in natural light, losing the appearance of vitality that it conserved as long as it was lit by the spirit lamp.[6]

He is referring to a globe lamp with which the presumptive Benjamin Franklin often appeared for the late Estelle's amorous appearances, particularly when she arrived on the Enlightenment diplomat's arm to "respond to her inconsolable spouse's ardor."

I am not making this stuff up. The situation's muddled surrealism is equaled only by the austere seriousness with which the reports of ectoplasmic *Kama Sutra* rituals were written up by the banker, the congressman, and the doctor.

So the amiable Ben Franklin lit the way, while also reporting like a sports commentator on the Civil War battles that raged during the couple's virtual reunions. For that matter, the revenant had no trouble announcing the skirmishes' outcomes even before they had begun. This was the case with the Confederates' surrender of Fort Donelson to the Federal Army on February 16, 1862, which he had announced the night before during the wife-from-beyond-the-grave's sensual dance.

To hear the participants from the hereafter tell it, the occultism à la Groucho Marx was in no way gratuitous. "With these proofs, can the world still doubt our existence?" Franklin's image declared, wielding his little globe of light. "If we work so hard, it is to convince them. It is all to benefit humanity."[7]

Obviously, things are far less flashy with Geneviève Delpech: no observers, no minutes taken, no spirit-petting. Tesla or Einstein's hologram appears at the foot of her bed to begin the "guidance," as she puts it. Then, as audiovisual mode probably uses up too much of their energy, they gradually fade their images out. The sound always comes to her through her left ear, and she takes notes.

It's not some kind of automatic writing—she applies herself carefully while taking dictation. The entity's voice makes no bones about correcting his spokeswoman's transcription mistakes, particularly when it comes to equations, proper noun, and references to articles or patent numbers, let alone the diagrams and drawings that take shape under her hand. During the "guidance," the speaker's image reconstitutes as necessary (when she slips up, or if her attention lapses briefly). So much for the style; now for the substance.

"Consciousness is a non-localized phenomenon," our Tesla declares. "It is as old as the physical universe. When a human being is alive, their consciousness is located inside the structure of microtubules in their brain, which provide a bridge between the brain and the soul."

When I receive the text message into which the medium has copied that information, the word microtubule really leaps out at me. I first stumbled across that discovery, on the cusp between biology and quantum physics, a year ago. Microtubules, which can be seen through a microscope, are tube-shaped fibers providing a cytoskeleton for our eukaryotic nerve cells. They are composed of proto-filaments and a protein called tubulin.

Here is what I wrote about them in *The New Dictionary of the Impossible*:[8] "The physicist Roger Penrose declared that electrons present inside those microtubules are delocalized in a quantum sense (i.e. they can interact coherently despite significant distances)." For Penrose, the tubes are neither more nor less than a support for consciousness, which he describes as "a quantum computer program contained inside the brain, which persists in the universe after the person's death."

That is the same thing Mme. Delpech's informer has just summarized, only somewhat more prosaically. What conclusion should I come to? That he was quoting me? That he was drawing on the very same dense writings by Penrose that I had tried to simplify and popularize?[9] My questions lead me to a more overarching query.

I know that the medium had not yet read my *Dictionaries* on December 21, the day she received the message, as I didn't give them to her until the following week. Allow me to repeat myself: this strictly literary woman has absolutely no science background, nor does she have the slightest curiosity about the subject. Since Penrose talks about thought transmission at the cellular level, might she have picked up the definition of human consciousness from my memory and "played it back" in the shape of a message from Nikola Tesla?

Like the incredulous people before me who have tested her psychic abilities, I have repeatedly seen for myself that she receives confoundingly precise, verifiable information that comes from elsewhere. Fine, but from where? Is the re-composed image of Nikola Tesla, the thwarted genius who was forced into the shadows and whom I had promised myself to write about someday, just a prop that facilitates our communication by personalizing it?

Here is the concerned party's reply: "Upon death, the microtubules lose their physical state, but the quantum information they held is not destroyed. It is distributed and dissipated into the whole of the universe."

That is almost word for word what it says on page 495 of my *New Dictionary of the Impossible*, which was printed seven months ago. I'm not sure if I should see the communication as plagiarism or validation. Tesla concludes his message by addressing an apostrophe to his medium, "That's what you felt during your experience of Everything."

Now he's quoting her: "Experience of Everything" is the title of a chapter in her book, *The Gift of Elsewhere*. The chapter is about an experience that changed her life. One day, she was sipping coffee on a terrace in the Luberon region of Provence, admiring the landscape, when she suddenly felt herself "leaving" at stunning speed:

> I was no longer in my bodily envelope, I couldn't feel it anymore, although I was still myself. Suddenly I had passed into another dimension: I realized that I was inside the bark of one of the magnolia trees on my left, and then inside the trunk. I could hear the sap circulating inside the tree, making a noise like veins pulsing. But the really striking thing was that the tree was alive, with a sort of consciousness. I could tell that it was capable of feeling love and pain. Next I knew I was inside a leaf... then in the ant pacing across the leaf. It all happened at astonishing speed.[10]

When Geneviève came back to herself, literally, she felt—as Eben Alexander had during his temporary-death experience[11]—as though she had acquired universal knowledge, but then had forgotten it instantly. All that was left was a sort of absolute empathy, an unconditional love for all forms of life. For years afterward, she was unable to eat meat, swat at mosquitos, or mow a lawn.

That is what her nocturnal correspondent was referring to on December 21. Skeptics will conclude that the medium was actually talking to herself vicariously through a pseudo-phantom. Others will see the fruit of a certain evolution. In fact, it seems to me that the mental dialogue established for the first time between an emitter and his receiver implies that, by that point, she was more than just Tesla's transmission channel.

He had made an assessment, if I may put it that way. Although he was still speaking through this woman, he was now also speaking to her, about herself. Other references to their shared experiences on Earth would follow over the course of the coming weeks. For the time being, the hologram keeps at it, belaboring his lesson about eternity without worrying about repeating himself. My apologies to my readers, but it seems wrong to edit the talking dead. And so:

> Quantum information is your consciousness. It can subsist independently of any organism, and can even reside in bodies that reside in parallel universes. Consciousness is more like music than calculus. It is connected

to a more profound order in space-time geometry. It's the least—
The message ends abruptly, mid-sentence. Was there some kind of space-time bug? No, it was actually an earthly emergency, as Geneviève would explain the next day when I managed to reach her. A call from the hospital had forced her to abandon the deceased in order to dash to her dying husband's bedside.

1. Arthur Conan Doyle, *History of Spiritualism*, 1926. Re-published by Cambridge Scholars Publishing, 2009.
2. Benjamin Coleman, *Spiritualism in America*, F. Pittman, 1861.
3. Robert Dale Owen, "The Debatable Land between this World and the Next," in *Quarterly Journal of Science*, 1872.
4. www.metapsychique.org
5. *Idem.*
6. Gabriel Delanne, *Les Apparitions matérialisées des vivants et des morts*, Volume 2, Leymarie, 1911; www.spirite.free.fr
7. *Spiritual Magazine*, 1862.
8. Plon, 2015; J'ai Lu, 2016.
9. Roger Penrose, *The Emperor's New Mind: Concerning Computers, Minds and the Laws of Physics*, Oxford University Press, 1989
10. Geneviève Delpech, *Le Don d'ailleurs, op. cit.*
11. Eben Alexander, Raymond Moody, *Conversations Beyond Proof of Heaven*, DVD.

9
Wavelength

Michel Delpech is at death's door. His wife hardly leaves the hospice-care facility that he's been transferred to. She no longer has the heart to keep her ears cocked for early-morning visitors, but Michel is actually encouraging her to keep at it. He wants to share one last adventure with her. The year they met, when—unbeknownst to him—he was in mortal danger, his future wife's psychic capacities saved his life, as he is fond of saying. Now, they are helping him face death, help him listen to it. On New Year's Day, she reads him the "coming-out" statement Tesla dictated to her the night before:

> I used to take a lot of potassium bromide. When the images appeared, they were accompanied by flashes of blinding light. I traveled in my thoughts until I was 17 years old. After that, I decided to focus on research. I never married because I was a scientist, and I wasn't attracted to women. It's sad, because I was often lonely, but the possibilities that determination and self-control offered made a strong impression on my lively imagination. At the age of eight, I began imposing tremendous discipline on myself. If I had a sweet or a piece of fruit, I would give it to another child. I was tormented. I imposed veritable torture upon myself. But I was pleased with myself when I achieved what I had set out to do. Tell Didier. Day after day, from morning till night, I forced my will and my desires to become one and the same.

Torn between the suffering of her dying spouse and the insistence of a loquacious spirit who's drowning her in post-scriptum meant for me, Geneviève is doing her best to cope with everything at once: Michel's relatives, the doctors, the dictation in her left ear, the tear-stained notes she's been taking, and the trouble she's having re-reading those notes as she copies them into text messages for me. She now reads those messages out loud as she writes them, so that Michel, who insists he wants to hear them, can be the first to know what they say. He has always been at Geneviève's side in her encounters with the invisible, and he's not about to abandon her now.

Indifferent to the context—unless he's trying to fill the singer in before he sets off on his farewell tour, Tesla's hologram forges ahead in a much less abstract fashion.

> To understand free radiant energy, you first need to understand the many force fields in the universe, such as the huge magnetic halos that surround the galaxies and stretch out over twice their distance. They are charged electrified-particle halos. In the same way that a stone thrown into a pond creates concentric ripples on the surface of the water, the universe is strewn with gravitational waves caused by the turbulent death of stars.

I should specify that the messages containing this information arrived on my phone on January 1, 2016. Einstein had predicted the discovery of gravitational waves 100 years before, but the scientific community as a whole had always resisted the notion. To the best of my knowledge, the first confidential leaks on the web from astrophysicists excited about the probable detection of these very same gravitational waves didn't start until January 11 of that year, and they were not published in the French press until two days later.[1]

As a reminder, the gravitational waves I'm talking about, which deform space-time "like a stone thrown into a pond," are caused by the collision-merger of two black holes whose very existence is still being denied by some physicists, making it a two-in-one proof! Astronomers wouldn't officially announce the stunning discovery until February 11.[2] Therefore, 40 days before their press conference—as the text messages Mrs. Delpech sent me prove—her Nikola Tesla continued his exclusive pre-announcement about gravitational waves in the following terms:

> They will become visible to you soon, overturning your understanding of space-time and of the unlimited free energy that you can draw from it for practical use. My friend Einstein was right, but, once here, he was surprised to realize that, as a whole, space-time is dynamic.

That one furrows my brow. In this case, "*Here*," means in the afterlife, I suppose, but I thought Einstein had understood the space-time dynamic while he was still alive. And what does he mean by, "as a whole"? I keep reading: "I too was right, when I spoke of many extraterrestrial life forms. You will soon find the macro-molecules at the origin of life. Protein. Then the existence of wormholes... Then you'll understand that your Big Bang is a fake. Instead, it's a huge white fountain created by the Big Bounce."

It took me hours to decipher that one. Googling the key words contained in the message kept bringing me back to the same theme: how share prices have bounced back for the electric-car manufacturer, Tesla, a company founded in 2003 using the engineer's last name, —and who knows how many of his inventions—for free.

Digging deeper, I stumble across the news that the Serb's first name has also been copyrighted—by a competing firm specializing in premium electric trucks: Nikola Motor Company. Let's think of the free use of his names as a kind of tribute; after all, it's better than fading into oblivion, right? In any case, that's how Elon Musk sees it.

Musk, the co-founder and CEO of Tesla, Inc. (a.k.a. Tesla Motors) has also announced his intention to build a plane with vertical take-off and landing, as well as a project to colonize Mars. Two more "borrowings" from the man whose name he has put back into the limelight, along with his suicidal generosity. Hasn't the gentleman-millionaire, as the French press has nicknamed Musk, followed in the Serbian's footsteps by going open-source and releasing all of Tesla, Inc.'s patents to "stimulate the competition"?

Unlike Nikola, however, Musk is a shrewd businessman. His extravagant gesture was fabulous publicity for his brand's image. When the press describes him as crazy, they mean it as a compliment. And his net worth is believed to be about $20 billion, according to *Forbes* magazine.

An astrophysics book eventually informs me that "white fountains" was the original name for what are now called white holes. For some specialists, white holes are like an exit door for the black ones, a sort of emergency exit that a celestial body, wave, particle, or even a UFO might pop out of after having passed through one of the space-time shortcuts known as "wormholes."[3]

As for the "Big Bounce," it's a controversial theory about the "endless return of time before time," i.e., the hypothetical existence of an infinite number of Big Bangs preceding the one from which our universe is thought to have emerged.

The day after that long message and the headaches it led to, the nearly daily message from my receptionist for the afterlife contained just three words: "Michel is gone."

*

As you would expect, after that, the medium had just one hope, one thing to look forward to: entering into contact with her own dearly departed. It would happen eventually, but not right away and not in the "usual"—at least, for her—way. For the moment, the Tesla correspondent, whose technical communications hardly suit the new widow's mood, has made himself scarce, though without entirely abandoning his antenna. His transmissions won't pick up steam again until a week later, the day after the funeral in Paris's Saint Sulpice Church.

During the ceremony, as the organ plays an arrangement of Michel's cult single, "Chez Laurette," a trio of pigeons offers an ethereal, aerobatic performance to our astonished gaze, soaring over the casket and between the stained-glass windows in a ballet of light and color. Has Tesla sent his favorite birds to execute an elegant welcome for Michel, to the tune of one of his immortal songs, no less? Even if one is loath to believe that, the aerial tribute is a magical, moving moment.

*

The audiovisual messages in Mme. Delpech's bedroom soon get back to speed with even greater technical precision than before. In retrospect, Geneviève has told me that her role as a spokesperson for an obsessive but very "present" stranger helped her cope with the suffering and loneliness of that bleak time, when the constant, close embrace of friends and relatives loosened after they'd gone back to their lives and concerns, as they had to do.

"Tesla is as tenacious as ever," she writes, just two days after the pigeons' dance in Saint Sulpice.

> He stopped in very briefly, just long enough to tell me that it was a scientist called Shangess or Changess or Shang Esse (I'm not really sure) who discovered the huge radio and energy halos around the galaxies a few days ago. Maybe it's Chang Ess? I think there's a space between the Chang and the Ess. My computer's still not working, but I'm sure you'll look into it right away.

She's right on that score. But since I follow a red herring, I have to explore dozens of web pages before I stumble across an article including the elements I'm searching for. She made just one small error. Chang Es isn't the name of any single scientist—it's a consortium: *Continuum Halos in Nearby Galaxies—an EVLA Survey.*

The program's mission is to study emissions from 35 galaxies based on observations from the Karl G. Jansky Very Large Array radio telescope at the National Radio Astronomy Observatory, a few hours south of

Albuquerque, New Mexico. Then I find out that, to their surprise, an international team of astrophysicists has recently discovered that gigantic halos are present in all spiral galaxies. What's more, the scientists learned that the halos emitted electromagnetic rays spilling over into the galaxies' "outskirts," offering priceless data about their formation, composition, and evolution—perhaps even the possibility of the presence of life forms.[4]

It's almost as though solving the riddles I've been receiving by text has allowed me to move up a level, like in a video game, increasing both the pace of the information I'm accumulating and the capacity for action it provides. Because from here on in, events start speeding up, both in terms of prediction and actual occurrence.

A message dated January 13 reads as follows:

This morning at dawn, old man Einstein snuck in, with a case of the giggles, announcing excitedly that, "They're going to find it... they're going to find it... It's in the gravitational waves... the curving waves... the space-time deformation waves. It's all there. Detection is imminent! Simultaneity is not universal. Time dilates, space contracts. Time is not universal." And then, miming writing on a blackboard, he told me, "ik, lm, *so ist* Gim = Ekl g (ik,lm). Gim = – k (Tim – 1sur2 Gim T)." There you have it, Didier... I've transmitted the equations and symbols as best I can, but I can't swear I got everything down correctly.

She's pretty close. At least, that's what the physicist Jean-Pierre Garnier Malet says when I forward the text to him. We met through mutual friends, but the day I first ask him to enlighten me, I had no idea how perfectly suited to the role he will turn out to be. Garnier Malet is a specialist in fluid mechanics who came up with a revolutionary theory about the doubling of time,[5] and co-authored an accessible book about the theory's practical applications.[6] Less than a month after our conversation, he will be thrilled to pieces over the official announcement of the detection of gravitational waves.

Garnier Malet is one of the only scientists in the world who has been defending Einstein's predictions tooth and nail for the past 30 years. Here are some excerpts from his reply (I have removed the driest, most technical parts), explaining why and how physicists have now "simplified" the formula I transmitted to him.

It remains to be seen how this equation can respect dimensional physics, but what is clear is that we should be able to connect universal gravitational constant, G, to Gim, gravitation of the doubled mass. Getting rid of the idea of a single space-time is actually the fundamental idea in my doubling theory… Your equation might be an interesting complementary path to explore.

I'll take his word for it. The fact that "the formula from the ether" has been validated by a scientist specialized in the field adds a new element. Until now, all the information that has come via the medium—Marco Metrovic's defense of Tesla's ashes, the Chang Es study, the detection of gravitational waves—was either already available online or was just about to be.

This equation, however, seems both to be original and not to be available anywhere else. Which means one of three things: Einstein—if we're willing to accept that it actually is him—either brought a previously unpublished formula to the afterlife or developed it posthumously, or, if a living brain came up with it, then the medium has somehow been able to tap into the thought processes of a contemporary scientist working on the same space-time plane as Garnier Malet. That wouldn't resolve the mystery, but it would add certain ramifications to it. In that case, there would be no reason not to think that the scientist in question might have been inspired by Einstein's post-mortem activities, the way Garnier Malet may have been via my intervention.

Knowing how open-minded Garnier Malet, an exceptional physicist, is, I decide to let him know where I came up with "my" equation. The confession doesn't seem to bother him very much. In fact, he seems quite pleased for me. He even mentions something Nikola Tesla once said (when he was still alive, in this case): "My brain is just a receiver: there is a sort of nucleus in the universe from which we draw knowledge, strength and inspiration. I haven't penetrated the secrets of that nucleus, but I know that it exists."[7]

Physicist prodigy Christophe Galfard, host of a science program on France Inter radio[8] and an eminent disciple of Stephen Hawking, his dissertation adviser at Cambridge, seems less convinced when I show him the equation. He is willing to admit that it contains elements from Einstein's general theory of relativity—the G that corresponds to space-time geometry, and a T related to the energy contained in that space-time. "But," he points out at the outdoor café where he gives me up an intensive brush-up class in theoretical physics, "everything depends on the i-m indexes."

This might be quantum, in which case it could be interesting, but we can't know for sure. There are things missing from your notation. If the indexes go from 0 to 3 (or 1 to 4), it's regular gravitation. It's only if they go from 0 to 4 (or 1 to 5) that we could try to recuperate electromagnetism through an additional dimension. Now that would be exciting. So where did you find this equation?

Taking a moment to compose myself, I pour water that has gone cold over a teabag whose very existence I had forgotten. Since I don't know him, I confess that I am loath to be entirely aboveboard with him... and then, throwing caution to the winds, I dive in, telling him the whole story: from the compass and the ashes to the ghosts and the messages.

A long silence follows. He's staring at me as though I've just stepped out of a UFO, and he's one of the Men in Black. He's very alert, attentive and still behind his dark glasses. Then, a weary, half-smile lights up his brilliant, Cambridge-educated face as he quips, "If you get an equation with an h, or an h-bar—i.e. Planck's constant—you'll have to give me your medium's number, okay? I am definitely interested in a quantum-gravitation theory. It's what we're all looking for."

I take my leave, feeling a bit swamped by the theoretical-physics lesson, which wasn't exactly what I had been hoping for. I have tremendous admiration for this young physicist's skill at making the subject accessible, but I feel a bit like an equation salesman who has failed to unload some made-in-the-afterlife calculations on a reticent customer. Fatigue, loneliness, and the question, "Why bother?" are running through my brain, replacing the enthusiasm his original glimmer of interest had inspired.

What if the apparitions and messages have all been just smoke and mirrors, something fabricated by our unconscious, a chain reaction set off by our need for a sense of amazement and a desire to believe in a hidden intelligence in response to the barbaric stupidity that saturates the visible world? Are we dealing with a practical joke on the part of some overlooked spirits? Is this just a step above the table-knockers and glass-lifters pretending to be Napoleon or Michael Jackson in those old-fashioned spiritualist séances the Web has popularized once again? Are there lost souls out there who are that desperate for us to believe in them? Are the anonymously departed—the "homeless" ones evicted from our living memory—forced to resort to imposture to keep themselves from dissolving into oblivion?

I've been trying to reach Geneviève Delpech. I hadn't invited her to the assessments of the equations she'd received. As she has said herself, it's all Greek to her. For me, too, but I have been trying to concentrate on the subtitles. Her voicemail is full. I go home with six pages of notes so abstruse that I should have at least numbered them. Six more pages of equations the young physics Ph.D. has so generously shared with me. I'll have to ask Einstein to explain them to me.

Speaking of the devil, he's back the next morning at dawn, him or his doppelganger, the emanation of a "thought form" that has escaped from that "nucleus of knowledge" to which his travel companion had referred.

"The universe's expanding acceleration is a phenomenon that is irremediably tied to both the infinitely large and the infinitely small," he dictates to poor Geneviève, who had been hoping to sleep in. Instead, here she is, obliged to look for her notebook at 5 a.m. to write down a codicil to his cosmic will and testament. "General relativity announced that from the beginning. I regret having backed down about that; I shouldn't have. I had laid the foundations for quantum theory."

Later she tells me that the "fugitive from the nucleus" hammered away at the concepts with compulsive fervor, not even leaving her time to make herself breakfast.

> From now on, both space itself and time are fated to vanish like shadows, and only a sort of union between the two will conserve an independent reality. My theory is not the ultimate one, but it is the theory. Gravitation and electromagnetism have to be brought together, but the string theory that flows from there will run up against this identity: container (space-time)/contents (matter and energy). You will see that space-time is only an illusion. Whoever replaces me will find the theory that will prove there is neither space nor time.

Geneviève scrupulously asks him to repeat the last few phrases so as not to accidentally obfuscate his already hermetic ideas, but the message is actually fairly clear for me. Christophe Galfard explained string theory to me, very superficially. The universe isn't composed of only particles and/or waves but also of strings that vibrate. Sometimes they're open, other times closed, but the universe is—or rather, all universes are—produced by their vibrations. Quantum theory sees their existence as a certitude, but they can't be located in our world, which is limited to four dimensions (the three spatial ones, plus time). They need six more.

Thanks to another flesh-and-blood physicist, Thibault Damour, I will learn the very next day that our pen-pal from beyond the grave's comments echoed one of Einstein's least-known lectures. One he delivered in 1954, at the very last seminar he attended on Earth. His dream of unifying gravitation and electromagnetism reverberates through it.

"There are many reasons to be attracted to a theory that contains neither space nor time," he said in a lecture hall at Princeton a few months before his death, "but no one knows how to construct such a theory." A theory like that would lead to an impossible equation: container equals content. Apparently, he's still searching for it, or he has decided to let the living find it all by themselves.

The rest of "his" communication of January 14, 2016 reads as follows:

Getting back to the Big Bang: it wasn't the beginning of the universe, and certainly not its creation. Electro-magnetic rays, gravitational waves... that's what you should be looking into. Different physical laws exist in very distant regions of your universe. So although my theory is perfect, it isn't the ultimate one."

On that note, the "thought form" evaporates. Mme. Delpech puts her notebook down and tries to go back to sleep when... whoosh! Tesla shows up. She barely has time to turn her bedside lamp back on when, without so much as a by-your-leave, the ectoplasm starts haranguing her. "You're confusing precognition and clairvoyance! You have a gift for precognition: you see the effect before the cause. That's precisely where the principle of causality is hard to apply, but physics sees the appearance of retrograde causality."

The message startles me. I happen to know what retrograde causality is. I was in attendance when Dr. René Peoc'h performed a fascinating experiment that shed very straightforward light on a concept that requires some effort to get your head around. This is how Peoc'h, whose doctoral thesis demonstrated that thought could affect matter,[9] describes the astounding protocol he designed in 2002: "The experiment does not consist in modifying the past, but in sending a mental message through time to the moment when the event took place, a few months earlier."

Concretely, you place a tychoscope (a random-event generator that looks like a tin can on wheels) in the middle of a 1 × 1.6-meter rectangle. The self-propelling little vehicle uses radio waves to communicate its movements to a computer, which records them in an Excel file. Six months after a series of 1,720 random, 20-minute movements, volunteers (who don't know what the experiment's goal is) are asked to open a file at random after having spent five seconds concentrating on trying to get more movement to the right (or the left, or backwards, or circular, or whatever they want, as long as their mental projection, which they have first put in writing, is clear and firm).

One key detail: the experiment performed six months prior to the volunteers' contribution had no human witnesses. The robot-movement data recorded was also printed on paper, but no one has seen it. Therefore, the first person to observe the measurements is the volunteer trying to mentally modify them a half a year later. Will the volunteer's thoughts be more potent than the laws of chance?

The answer is yes. Irrefutably so. In statistical terms, for each experiment involving 860 files opened at random, there is less than one chance in 10,000 that the path will match the volunteer's thoughts. So Peoc'h has proven that mental action aimed at the past can independently influence a result that's "sleeping" in a machine.[10]

On the other hand, it is absolutely impossible to modify measurements that have already been recorded by a human consciousness. But in all other cases, the path the volunteers discovered (or created) when they opened the file reflected their wishes. The volunteers get what they want (such as more movement to the right) in statistically significant proportions, even though the "abnormal" path was printed paper in real time, six months before the volunteers put their "two cents' worth" into the experiment. In our ordinary, linear conception of time, it appears flagrant that effect has preceded cause.

I'll let Peoc'h explain the meaning of that amazing experiment, reported with great fanfare by Princeton University's PEAR lab,

> Our experiments demonstrate that thought may be able to travel through time to participate in events that normally take place at random. You can't say that the past has been modified, but rather that an action that is taking place in the present (observation of the path) is also contemporary to events in the past (influence on the random generator). No matter how you describe it, the results prove that a random event that has not been observed by a living being remains partially influenceable.[11]

*

Let's get back to January 14, 2016. Nikola Tesla's speaking image (arriving from the past, the future, a string universe, a parallel world, or all of the above?) adds this to his message mentioning retrograde causality:

"The scientific progress being made in regards to wormholes, quantum mechanics, and its extra-temporal paradoxes show that the arrow of time is neither linear nor unequivocal. In closing, meditate upon my friend's equation: $N = R^* \times f_p \times n_e \times f_l \times f_i \times f_c \times L$."

What friend? Einstein?

I call the medium to ask if she wrote everything down carefully.

"I think so."

"There weren't any h's?"

"H's? No, why?"

It's like playing quantum Scrabble—no h's? Oh well. Looks like the quantum-gravitation equation is going to have to wait.

Still, let's check this one out.

As soon as I copy the complex assemblage of letters, symbols, indices, and subscript indications into Google's search field, I find out who the friend Tesla referred to is. The formula is known as the Drake Equation. In 1961, Cornell University astrophysicist and astronomer Frank Drake achieved international renown when he published a statistical formula used to establish the number (N) of extraterrestrial civilizations we could come into contact with (in other words, the odds of finding intelligent life in the universe): R^* being the rate of formation of stars per year in our galaxy; f_p, the fraction of those stars possessing planets; n, the average number of planets potentially suitable for life; f_p, the fraction of those planets on which life actually appears; f_p, the fraction of those on which intelligent life appears; fc, the fraction with the capacity and desire to instigate interplanetary dialogue; and L, the average life span of a civilization.

The values used by Drake and his colleagues established the number of civilizations in the Milky Way with the ability to communicate at 10. We're still waiting to hear from them, but if the message Drake's teams launched into space from the Arecibo Observatory in 1974 hasn't gotten a reply yet, it might be because our means of reception are inadequate, or because the reply isn't coming from where we've been expecting.

But why did the presumptive Tesla invite us to "meditate" upon that probability study? Bear in mind that he stated in his Colorado Springs notes that he had rediscovered the secrets of mastering energy that had been revealed to ancient Egyptians by technical advisers from another planet. Was it just a reflexive reminder, a bit of publicity for the extraterrestrial intelligence the Serbian engineer had promoted so frequently during his lifetime, or was the cosmos finally about to send us a reply? Or else humanity has forgotten it for millennia, and we're about to rediscover it.

The next day, January 15, I receive a text message from Mme. Delpech at 7:36 A.M.: "Sorry, I know it's early. I saw Einstein. He didn't say anything, but he was waving a copy of *L'Express* magazine, and a piece of paper that said, 'lexpress.com,' too. It just happened, and he seemed really insistent, so I'm passing it on to you. Now I'm going to try to go back to sleep."

What is the point of these one-ghost shows that our reconstituted geniuses keep staging? Are they improvising an ectoplasmic stand-up routine in response to news here on Earth, or are they inviting us to the dress rehearsal of events that have been planned for a long time?

And if so, why?

I'm holding my breath as I turn on my laptop. Mme. Delpech's Einstein has made a mistake, just like the original often used to. Oh, not a big one, the kind of trivial thing that happened frequently when he was alive. Having arrived at the solution before he finished his calculations, he would already be focusing on something else by the time he got around to retroactively finishing the calculations for the sake of a public demonstration, and they'd be strewn with careless mistakes. Typically, today's mistake doesn't affect my overall understanding: *L'Express's* URL ends in *.fr*, not *.com*.

Nevertheless, his tribute to the staff of the magazine's website is well-founded. They are indeed the first to publish the rumor swirling around the small society of astronomers about the "possible detection of gravitational waves." Although the event is "still awaiting confirmation, it is already being described as the 'discovery of the century.'"

*

Let's not be blasé: I'm practically in shock.

An irresistible desire to step outside has convinced me to abandon the morning's work. I'm strolling through the streets of Paris, where an icy wind is swirling exhaust fumes through the weak January sunlight, and I feel both lighthearted and incredibly weighty at the same time. I know a secret, even if it's one the general public will learn about soon. Two weeks ago, I received the first key to a door that astronomers are about to open, one that practically no one in the world has even been willing to acknowledge might exist until this very morning. I want to take the whole world as my witness, to shout at the passers-by who couldn't care less: "I knew it! Einstein told me!" And who do I bump into just then? Laurent Seksik, the author of an excellent biography of Einstein.

I'm not even surprised. Seeing him pop up at this precise moment may be statistically improbable, but by now it practically makes sense. Although we are always pleased to see each other in Nice, where we both sit on the annual Baie des Anges Prize jury, we never seem to have time to get together in Paris. Still, it's the second time I've run into him there "by chance"—and the quotation marks are intentional.

The first time was three years ago, at the entrance to a parking lot. I was running late, but he looked distraught, so I cut the engine and asked if he was all right. He didn't even bother to try to put up a brave front. He knew how much I'd enjoyed his biography of Einstein, which had increased my appreciation for the eccentric genius tenfold. He confessed that, although he was in utter despair over it, he was about to abandon his projected novel focusing on Einstein's debatable attitude toward his schizophrenic son, Eduard. "I just don't feel like I have the right to tarnish the great man's reputation," my fellow writer sighed.

I immediately found myself protesting, arguing with him with such intensity that anyone watching would have thought my own reputation was at stake. That same night, he called me to tell me he had gotten back to work, that the project "felt right" to him once again. A few months later, when his *Case of Eduard Einstein*,[12] came out, the book's quality and success filled me with a pride that was unearned, but absolutely sincere. I deserved no credit for it, I told myself, I just happened to be in the right place at the right time. It was as though Einstein's essence had used me to lift his biographer's spirits, to let him know how much he was looking forward to a book that, by also giving his point of view, would re-establish the somewhat mangled truth of his painful ties to his younger son.

And now we've met again, at the precise moment when one of us—although this time it's me—needs someone to talk about "our" pet subject. Except this time, the situation is reversed: rather than shedding light on a shadowy element of the physicist's past, I am hoping to put his amazing intuition about gravitational waves back into the spotlight! The whole world will finally do justice to the clairvoyance of the aging Einstein, who inspired little more than ridicule, hatred, and talk-show voyeurism.

I tell Laurent about the scoop I got on my iPhone and show him the dateline of the text messages. All he can do is say, "Amazing" over and over.

He's never shown any interest in mediums, but like me, he believes his eyes. When you get right down to it, the specific channel the information uses to reach me counts less than the object itself. The transmission process has become secondary to the outcome. We are both just thrilled that technological progress had proven our friend Einstein right once again.

Moments of plain humanity like that one are what I like best about my connection to the invisible: when the prefix in the word *supernatural* became an intensifier—rather than a disrupter—of "normality." Those supremely natural moments when the magical is seen and shared in broad daylight, in an otherwise ordinary, everyday setting, becoming a matter of course, like when we were children.

1. www.lexpress.fr, January 13 2016.
2. www.2.cnrs.fr, 11 February 2016.
3. Trinh Xuan Thuan, *Dictionnaire amoureux du ciel et des étoiles (A Sky- and Star-Lover's Dictionary)* , Plon-Fayard, 2009.
4. *The Astronomical Journal*, vol. 150 ; www.queensu.ca/changes/.
5. http://www.garnier-malet.com/fr-scien/articles.php?pg=90
6. Lucile and Jean-Pierre Garnier Malet, *Changez votre futur par les ouvertures temporelles (Change Your Future through Temporal Openings)*, Le Temps Présent, 2006.
7. Nikola Tesla, *My Inventions*, op. cit.
8. Christophe Galfard, *L'Univers à portée de main (The Universe Within Reach)*, Flammarion, 2015; as well as a radio program of the same name on France Inter.
9. See Chapter 1.
10. *Journal of the Society for Scientific Exploration.*
11. René Peoc'h, *"Expériences de psychokinèse,"* in *Paranormal: Entre Mythes et Réalité"* (Minutes from a conference in Paris), Dervy, 2002.
12. Op. cit.

10
Playing hooky with death

Twenty-six days later, on February 11, the official announcement of the detection of gravitational waves attracts considerable media coverage. As soon as the executive director of LIGO (the Laser Interferometer Gravitational-Wave Observatory) pronounces the magic words, "We did it!" the shockwave goes around the planet, lighting up social media.

"Einstein was right!" Barack Obama proclaims, congratulating the observatory's sponsors. Putin is thrilled, François Hollande is, too, although somewhat less so. For him, the timing isn't very good: the news comes out on the very day that he had been hoping to get some mileage out of announcing a new Cabinet.

"This is one of the biggest discoveries of modern science!" Mark Zuckerberg, the head of Facebook, crows.

"We haven't seen anything like it since Galileo!" Christophe Galfard gushes on France Inter radio.

"It is a result that is at least as important as the discovery of the Higgs Boson," his friend and teacher, Stephen Hawking, adds—while trying to bask in some of Einstein's glory. "These experimental observations are consistent with my theoretical work on black holes in the 1970s… It is thrilling to see predictions I made over 40 years ago… being observed within my lifetime."

At the observatory on the Côte d'Azur—where many of the French astronomers who had first suggested using an interferometer to detect gravitational waves (way back in the 1980s, under the leadership of Alain Brillet) currently work, happiness outweighs the bitterness of "We told you so."

"At the time, everyone said we were nuts, that what we were trying to do was tantamount to using a device on Earth to measure the width of a hair placed on the Sun!" exclaims Catherine Nary Man, research director at the National Science Research Centre's Artemis Laboratory.[1]

Physicist Thibault Damour has a very modest reaction. The magazine *Sciences et Avenir* quotes him as simply emphasizing "how quickly this discovery was made," without bothering to remind them that he had been one of the few scientists who had long believed it possible. Just a year earlier, he had defined the waves in this somewhat unexpected way: "Space-time is like veal in aspic: if you shake it, the gelled aspic ripples, shuddering from vibrations that are space-deformation waves called 'gravitational waves.'"

With the same instinct as the man who had predicted them a century before, Damour, a theoretical physicist from the Institute of Higher Scientific Studies not only *saw* the reality before it was observable, but he found a concrete analogy to describe it. Continuing his French cookery image with scientific rigor and an iconoclastic sense of humor not unlike Einstein's own, he added, "Moreover, the possible presence of the meat, which modifies the density of the aspic locally, supplies an analogy for how matter warps the geometry of space. In general-relativity theory, matter is in fact represented by lines that are analogous to meat's fibers."[2]

In a nutshell, the whole world has been digging into Einstein's meaty theory for months until—as my publisher points out just as I'm correcting page proofs for this manuscript—a "vegetarian" (you might say) tries to spoil everyone's fun. The French newsweekly *Marianne* has run an article in a summer series called "Improbable Scientific Theories" in which the journalist criticizes "the greatest physicist of all time's blind spots." The article includes this surprising statement, which sweeps away five months of unanimous rehabilitation with the stroke of a pen: "Einstein made another mistake in 1936, in an article in which he denied the major consequences of his own theory of relativity: the existence of gravitational waves."[3]

What the journalist sees as a "mistake" is an about-face that should, as we have seen, really be blamed on pressure from the university administration and the scientific press. You could conceivably describe it as a character flaw; Einstein himself later admitted as much, in reference both to that and to the concept of a cosmological constant, which he had been forced to recant in a similar way. But it seems a bit much to insult the visionary who, in 1916, became the first person in the world to predict—in print—both the existence and the eventual detection of those waves, just because he didn't have the wherewithal to defend his ideas tooth and nail.[4] Marianne doesn't even bother to mention the earlier text. Sadly, in posterity's opinion of some trailblazers, precedence is sometimes confused with outdatedness.

Fortunately, the original texts are still available for consultation by anyone who is aware of them and willing to give the authors credit. The real problem arises, of course, when the proof has disappeared. The Yugoslav science journal, *Review*, for instance, asserts that Tesla's concept for a plane with vertical lift-off and landing, which the American Patent Office didn't register until 1928, actually dates to considerably earlier than that. The idea even predates motorized aircraft, but "the earliest sketches of those planes, as well as drawings of rocket engines, were destroyed in a lab fire in 1895,"[5] as were his notes about the remote transmission of images in nearly live conditions. Nothing is left of that collection except one letter from 1919, preserved in the American Library of Congress.

In it, the engineer describes in loving detail to a baseball-fan friend of his how baseball games could be watched, almost live, on a device placed in one's living room:

> In the present state of the art, the best suggestion I can make to this end is to employ nine flying machines (wing- and propeller-less) of my invention capable of a speed of 500 miles per hour or more, to take the film of an inning, develop the films in transit and then reel them off as fast as they arrive…The above is offered merely on the principle that something is better than nothing. The simultaneous transmission [sic] is a hard nut to crack. It calls for an invention to which I have devoted 20 years of careful study and which I hope I will ultimately realize, that is, *television*, making [it] possible to see at [a] distance through a wire.[6]

Tesla never made claims to the process involved in the development of television. They had already stolen the invention of radio from him, and that was enough to nurture a bitterness profoundly unsuited to his profession as an inventor. Einstein has been blamed for over-protecting his theories by imagining hidden variations. Tesla, on the other hand, imprudently had too many ideas and not enough funds. He applied for "only" 112 patents out of the more than 700 inventions found in his files.

"Other people did Tesla in, Einstein did himself in," pianist Marguerite Merington, who was madly in love with the former and may have been a mistress of the latter, quipped somewhat succinctly, but with a kernel of truth.[7] The comment brings us back to the other major "mistake" wrongfully attributed to the theorist of relativity: his refusal to acknowledge the principles of quantum mechanics, when he is, in fact, their one true and uncontested sire!

"He didn't have anything against the probabilities, which he mastered," Thibault Damour reminds us. "He just wanted them to be deduced from a more complete theory." It was a theory Einstein sought throughout his life, refusing to accept the probabilities solely on the basis of the so-called Copenhagen interpretation (the existence of a classic world separated from the quantum one), which he compared to "a soft pillow…that the true believer has a hard time leaving."[8]

What bothered Einstein the most about the consequences of his discoveries involving light (which can be both wave and particle, depending on who is measuring it, and why—which happens to be the starting point for quantum physics) was the observer's decisive role in the phenomenon being observed. That role falls outside any theoretical framework, since the observer's consciousness alone creates the reality observed, leaving a lot of room for randomness and subjectivity. Could the physicist now be enjoying the advantages of the very situation he used to deplore?

Allow me to explain. In the famous quantum-inspired thought experiment devised by Erwin Schrödinger, a cat locked in a room without a window and with a vial of poison that might or might not break is considered to be *both* dead *and* alive until the observer can verify the cat's condition by opening the door. Could the same thing apply to the apparitions I've been relating here?

If, for the sake of argument, we assume that they do, in fact, emanate from actual dead people, are they meant to fuel *our* reflections or to nurture their own "post-life" energy? If I observe that some type of their individuality persists and my readers believe it—or rather, *think* it (i.e., by being willing to envisage the possibility and its range of possible interpretations with me), could that help Einstein and Tesla's remnant consciousnesses become more active? Since quantum mechanics posits that reality is created by our observations, could our observations also offer a new dimension of existence to those among the departed who wish to remain in touch with the living?

But let me get my feet back on the ground; a shadow has somewhat veiled the enthusiasm that has been buoying me up ever since "my" gravitational waves made headlines around the world. Was the scoop of which I was so proud just an illusion?

After the fact, Christophe Galfard informed me of a tweet posted by Lawrence Krauss, an American science writer, on September 25, 2015.

Krauss tweeted the rumor that LIGO might have detected the waves. The tweet launched a flurry of debate amongst cosmologists. Michael Merrifield, an astronomer at the University of Nottingham, mirrored the community's outraged reactions, remonstrating "If true, you are trying to steal their glory; if false, you are damaging scientific credibility." LIGO's spokesperson, Argentine physicist Gabriela Gonzales, published an official denial in *Nature* magazine, saying, "We'll certainly let you know when we have news to share; I'm worried that the public and the media's hopes will be dashed." The media was convinced the rumor was just that: a rumor, and nothing more.

The general public wasn't aware of the tempest in a cosmic teapot, but for a small core of astrophysicists, the likelihood of detection "was in the air," Galfard says. Could the "thought forms" with the appearance of Tesla and Einstein have drawn the information from "the air" and then served it up to me? Was the prediction I thought was an exclusive, the spirit scoop that had thrilled me so, nothing more than the echo of a rumor in the Tweetosphere, the egregore of the stubborn hope of a handful of researchers?

*

In any case, while the supposed phantoms of Einstein and Tesla are taking turns soliloquizing Geneviève Delpech in her bedroom, her late husband remains despairingly silent. It weighs on her sometimes to be conducting such an intense relationship with two strangers from the hereafter while waiting, in vain, for a sign from her man. She would so love to catch his posthumous image and voice, but the two imperturbable geniuses overstay their welcome at the foot of her bed, monopolizing her channel with equations, discoveries, and theories that leave her cold. She takes their dictation, "feeds me information" at their request, and is generous enough to be happy for me when I'm thrilled with the precision of the data she transmits. In the midst of the yawning void of mourning, it cheers her up a little to think she's "making herself useful," but it really isn't fair—Michel's silence is wearing her down.

That's when Marie-France Cazeaux steps back into the picture. You might remember that toward the end of their collaboration, "her" Einstein was getting more and more annoyed with her. He grumbled that she never had a pen when he wanted her to write something down. If by chance she found one, she'd lose the scrap of paper on which she had jotted the words and figures he'd dictated, which, in any case, were both meaningless and indecipherable to her.

Not having heard from him in weeks, she often calls to ask me about the reasons for his extended absence. After a while, I confess as gently as I can that her fickle phantom has been frolicking with another woman's neurons. "Some people never change," she says, sighing stoically. "May I ask who she is?" Alas, her clairvoyance is of no avail in this case, obliging me to be the tattletale. Trying but failing to sound indifferent, she asks in a jealous tone of voice what he talks to Mme. Delpech about. I keep things vague, saying only that it's very technical.

Changing the subject, the retired nurse points out, somewhat sniffily, that she, "wasn't a big fan of her husband, Michel. I didn't *dislike* him, per se, I just didn't really know his work. But he keeps insisting, 'You never liked my music.'"

Suddenly I'm fully alert. I make sure I've understood correctly: has she really been feeling his presence? "Oh, yes," she confirms off-handedly. "He's here; he's fine. He showed me that Albert took him to explore the stars. He's happy. He says he's playing hooky with death." She rattles off names, describes items of clothing, the color of bed linens, romantic details, and more. I interrupt her and insist on giving her his widow's number—I don't want to be the go-between in such an intimate context.

An hour later, Geneviève calls me, sounding shaken. For someone who could very well have a high opinion of her skills, she tells me, instead, how amazed she is by Marie-France. She's so overcome with emotion that for the first time in all these months, she addresses me with the familiar *tu*, as opposed to her usual, more formal *vous*.

"She saw him in his old V-necked sweater—you know, the fuzzy one. She said, 'He was wearing the gray cashmere you got him at Old England!' It's true! He wore it all the time at the hospital. Didier, nobody knows that except the people who visited him there. He even showed her his slippers—she mentioned some bleach stains on the left one! You couldn't make that up!"

I nod. To each their own. While Marie-France might not be the type to transcribe equations, she's unbeatable for domestic details, the little nothings that seem to occupy so much of the memories of the departed. One thing I know for sure is that she didn't get the info from me. The one and only time I ever met Michel Delpech, it was on December 26, 2015, at his request. He was lying in his hospital bed, barefoot and wearing a blue sweat suit.

"And get this: she told me about the baby we didn't have!" Of all the secrets that no one outside of their couple knew, and that Marie-France had captured as a sort of calling card, I'll mention only that one—with Geneviève's permission. For a few seconds, as she had told me herself an hour before, the retired nurse had seen the singer with a little boy. The kid told Michel that his name was both Gabriel *and* Samuel, and then impatiently commented that it was time for his parents to make up their minds.

"I lost a baby when I was four months pregnant," Geneviève informs me. "He had serious birth defects and wouldn't have been viable. Michel and I hadn't had time to choose a name for him. We had left it at, 'If it's a boy, we'll call him either Gabriel or Samuel.'"

There is a long silence. I swallow, and then find the courage to ask, "And which one are you leaning toward now?" Without a moment's hesitation, she replies, "Samuel."

Then she says that she feels better all of a sudden. As though the never-even-born baby had somehow survived and was able to vicariously celebrate continuing his posthumous growth with a single, official name, chosen by his mother. Even the dead, it would seem, need an identity.

I share in the emotion washing over her, while at the same time trying to explain the situation she's being subjected to with prudent hypotheses. If the singer can't manifest himself "live" to his newly-widowed wife a month after their physical separation, it must be to avoid compromising his phase of detaching from life on Earth and learning to accept his new, disincarnated status. So he whispers the sweet nothings, the proof of love he's as yet unable to transmit directly, to a retired hospice-care nurse from the Riviera instead.

Geneviève says she understands. It saddens her, but she accepts it.

*

Marie-France's stunning comeback makes my day. I could tell how upset she was that Einstein's spirit had left her for a younger woman. Now, not only has the neglected woman been entrusted with her rival's husband, but she's doing her best to pass him back to her. From that point on, the two mediums' competitiveness turns into friendship. Consequently—at least, that's how I see it—Einstein reconnects with Marie-France's channel without abandoning Geneviève's.

An interesting compensation phenomenon occurs in terms of ubiquity. At the same time as the genius's hologram is triumphantly waving a copy of *L'Express* at Geneviève's pillow, he's also crying on Marie-France's shoulder.

"I was a terrible father," he says with a sigh, clearly upset with himself. "I couldn't cope with having children who weren't 'normal.' I abandoned my poor Eduard to that lunatic asylum. He wasn't crazy, just depressed. They tortured him, erased him, destroyed him."

One morning, Marie-France asks me the name of the daughter Einstein lost when he was still single. She thought she'd heard "Lieserl." I'm not sure, so I check my copy of Laurent Seksik's book. Lieserl is, indeed, the mystery child's name, although it's unclear whether that was her actual name or if it is was a nickname for Elizabeth. Historians only learned of her existence in 1986 through letters between Einstein and his first wife, Mileva. She had given birth to the girl in secret in 1902, a year before she and Einstein were married. The child, who probably had Down's syndrome, was kept hidden and died of scarlet fever when she was about a year old.

I am accustomed to the instinctive way that Marie-France—whose house, family and mediumship for the bereaved keep her so busy that the afterlife is her only real source of information—manages to capture the family secrets of everyone from ordinary people to the offspring of great dynasties. I have seen for myself how, thanks to her, Napoleon's descendants were able to find objects and information whose very existence they had been previously unaware of, but this is more than just her usual service as a seer. She is deeply affected by the distress emanating from the spirit, whose presence is very strong. She says she hears him endlessly begging, "Help me. Pray that my children will forgive me. I won't be in peace until they allow me to be with them."

So she prays in her way; and I in mine. While she lights candles to Saint Rita, I focus on Einstein and his children as though they were characters in one of my novels. I mentally storyboard the scene of the prodigal father's return. I picture Einstein in his favorite setting, in his element: on the *Tinef,* the scrappy little sailboat he steered awkwardly and happily while playing the violin and elaborating his most important theories at the same time. I watch him navigating the lake for a while, and then I have him aim towards a boathouse where I've prepared a little surprise for him. I've gathered all of his offspring there: Lieserl, the mentally handicapped little girl who had been erased from his biography; Eduard, the depressed son who was committed; and Hans-Albert, the unexceptional physicist who would have so liked to have been recognized by his peers as a worthy successor to his famous father.

The boat draws up to the dock, the doors to the boathouse open. Einstein is welcomed by his children. Their dialogue has the solemn familiarity appropriate to the occasion of a virtual family reunion.

"We've been hoping you would come, Father. It was your pride plus your awareness of your own mistakes that convinced you we didn't want to have anything to do with you. We had no way to overcome the soundproof barrier you erected between us. You had to break through it yourself in order to be able to hear us."

Cut.

The next day, I get a call from Marie-France, who I didn't say anything about my virtual scriptwriting to. Along with the myriad details of her daily life, she casually comments, "Oh, I saw Albert this morning. He said to thank you for the boathouse."

Once again, I'm tempted to impute the "proof of receipt" of my mental activity to telepathy, but the outcome matters more than the media. If it's that easy to help deceased people trapped in their misunderstandings, then it would be cruel not to, right? In any case, whether or not it was of any use in the other world, the "thought experiment," to use Einstein's phrase, was exhilarating for me. I sensed tremendous gratitude, which, even if it was an illusion, gave me back the energy I'd devoted to a distress that, at first glance, didn't seem to have anything to do with me.

Could our daydreams constitute a kind of reality for the deceased? Inversely, does not believing in the hereafter lead to its desertification? And what about those who project fanatical violence and artificial paradises populated with virgins offered as rewards for kamikazes? Might that turn it into a horrific hell? For my money, real questions have always been more enlightening than dazzlingly definitive answers.

But let's leave the generalities to the theorists. The question preoccupying me the most about the situation I seem to have at least partially brought upon my two informers is this: what might explain the "split personality" of the itinerant spirit appearing in the guise of Einstein, complete with his features, character, memories, and aspirations? Why does he appear in triumphant high spirits to Geneviève, and as a shamefaced, penitential father before Marie-France? Is he in the grip of some kind of reverse empathy? Is he sparing the already-suffering recent widow his lamentations, while confiding in a generous and fulfilled mother and grandmother, knowing it won't do her any harm?

Their roles seem clearly defined in terms of what the entity wants from each of them: one is the psychic secretary; the other the custodian of unfinished personal business and unresolved chagrin. His mood follows suit: a joyful soul who cheers up lonely Geneviève; a tormented one who confides a rewarding mission of consolation to Marie-France.

At the end of the day, it works out pretty well, whether you believe in survival of the consciousness or not. A renowned neuro-psychiatrist to whom I described the situation (and who, like many former militant rationalists, has asked to remain anonymous; a sign of the times, alas) resolves the case of my two mediums in a single phrase: "Your subconscious is projecting those mental constructions on them."

Fine, I can buy that… even though I don't see how my subconscious could project names and information I know nothing about via incorporeal apparitions. My eminent clinician and disciple of Henri Bergson—who wrote, in *Matter and Memory* (1896), "Consciousness overflows the brain on all sides," was thinking of the famous Philip experiment.

Here is a quick summary of that extraordinary demonstration, which the "serious" media tried to ignore for years…almost understandably. In 1972, a group of eight researchers led by the mathematician George Owen, emeritus professor at Cambridge University, composed a fictitious ghost called Philip. Like the creative team on a TV series, they started by inventing an entire life for their revenant: identity, address, family, career, love life, and personal dramas that led to his committing suicide.

Once they were done, they decided to try to communicate with their fictional Philip via séances with a table the ghost could rap, shake, or cause to levitate. It was a stunning success. Even in their absence, the table rapped out the biography and moods of this invented person who became a fabricated phantom. As can be seen on *Dailymotion*, the pseudo-spirit's "spokes-table" participated in a live program on CityTV, a Toronto channel. The table even climbed the stairs to the podium all by itself in order to answer the journalists' questions.[9]

What's even more amazing about it all is that many of the answers supplied by the haunted table, particularly ones relating to historical events, had been previously unknown to the synthetic specter's "programmers." Even when the group believed the ghost had been mistaken, it always turned out to have been right. It's almost as though a real Philip had infiltrated their imagination at the beginning of the experiment. Perhaps the combined power of the group's mental energy allowed a previously anonymous ghost to acquire a kind of social existence, enabling it to transmit information.

The mindboggling phenomenon went on for ten years, and no paranormal investigator or illusionist was ever able to discover the slightest hint of cheating, nor was anyone ever able to debunk it in any way. Professor Chauvin studied the experiment and gave a lecture at the Sorbonne about it. His verdict came in the shape of a question: "Would it be overstating the evidence to conclude that human thought has creative possibilities that are able to invent 'thought forms' that are at least partially capable of disenfranchising themselves from their creators?"[10]

The neuro-psychiatrist insisted on reassuring me. Even if we assume the ghosts of Einstein and Tesla are products of my subconscious hopes and expectations, considering the release they represent for me and the hope that my readership is likely to draw from them, they should be seen as a public service as much as a personal necessity.

By the time I left his office, I have to admit that I was pretty close to subscribing to his analysis, but as usual, getting answers only leads me to ask new questions. Besides, Bergson's aphorism may pose an interesting problem, but it doesn't resolve it. If our consciousness overflows our brains, might that not be because it is being fed by other consciousnesses, whether attracted via empathy or called on for moral support?

I ponder the case of Jean Jaurès.[11] Although they are not often mentioned, the Socialist leader's ideas about the invisible world were as enlightening and enlightened as the ones he had about society. In 1891, he defended his philosophy thesis, entitled, "On the Reality of the World of Substance." It describes a possible future for human beings in which their spiritual evolution has taught them to overcome the limitations of egotism and fatality here on Earth as elsewhere. "An ego alone could cause other bodies besides its own to move through direct will; it would no longer be the soul of a single organism exclusively, but indeed the soul of all things, as far as its action could spread. If it could apply to the whole universe, it would become the soul of the world."[12]

*

A few days after the boathouse episode, Marie-France is bedridden with terrible pain in her knees. When I call to see how she's doing, she says, "Eduard had a wheelbarrow when he came to see me last night. He was dressed like a gardener. Isn't that strange?"

When I reply that tending the garden was Einstein's son's appointed task in the asylum, a hopeful note creeps into the nurse's voice.

"Then he must know a lot about vegetables, right? You'll never guess what he told me to put on my knees to ease the pain: green cabbages."

When she inquires about the long silence on my end of the line, I explain my reaction by providing a possible caption for Eduard's comment: the French translation of my name, which dogged me during my grade-school years, and how my father had appeared to Geneviève, whom I didn't know then, in a kind of otherworldly bait-and-switch operation. Now it's her turn to be momentarily speechless. When she takes her leave, she seems pensive.

The next day, she informs me that even though she followed the ghostly gardener's advice scrupulously, draping one open volume of my *Dictionary of the Impossible* like a cataplasm over each knee, she's not really feeling any better.

Which just goes to show that books don't always work wonders.

1. *Sciences et Avenir*, March 2016.
2. *Le Monde*, Special issue "La Révolution Einstein," July 2015.
3. *Marianne*, 21 July 2016.
4. Albert Einstein, *Näherungsweise Integration der Feldgleichungen der Gravitation*
5. *The Yugoslav Monthly Magazine*, July 1964.
6. Letter from Nikola Tesla to Robert U. Johnson, 29 November 1919, Library of Congress.
7. Margaret Cheney, *Tesla, Man Out of Time, op. cit.*
8. *Once Upon Einstein*, Thibault Damour CRC Press, Taylor & Francis Group 2006
9. www.dailymotion.com/video/xgbfxm_philippe-le-fantôme- imaginaire_news
10. Rémy Chauvin, *L'Autre science, in A l'écoute de l'au-delà, op. cit.*
11. Translator's note: Jean Jaurès (1859-1914), an anti-militarist, was assassinated in 1914, and remains an iconic figure of the French left to this day.
12. Jean Jaurès, *De la réalité du monde sensible*, Alcuin, 1994.

11
The magpie, the black hole and the white fountain

The two mediums are staying in closer and closer touch, but despite the reassuring news she's been getting from Marie-France, Geneviève is still waiting for a *direct* sign from her husband. One evening, as she's flipping through the book that her fellow medium on the other side of France is applying to her left knee as a cataplasm, she falls asleep reading the story of the fledgling that fell from its nest and was adopted by composer and pianist Michel Legrand in 1970.

Saved from an untimely death, the little ball of feathers eventually grew into a lovely magpie. The bird was fiercely attached to the composer, who taught her both to feed and to fly. Accustomed to hearing him at work on the piano, the magpie never reacted to it very much, unless Legrand played anything by Bach. Every time he did, she came zooming in through the window that had been left open for her and threw herself at the sheet music in a rage, shredding it with her beak.

Legrand told me that he still didn't understand how the bird was able to make the connection between destroying paper and stopping the music, or in musical terms, what she had against Bach in particular. Unless it was the passion that Legrand poured into playing Bach… Could it be that the magpie was jealous?

The next morning, Geneviève is startled awake by something knocking on her window. Uncharacteristically, she slept with the shutters open, because the motor that runs them had suddenly stopped working the night before. So without even having to get out of bed, she is able to see a magpie tapping at the window as though it had flown straight from the pages of my book. With a lump in her throat, she gets up, walks cautiously toward the window and gently lays her forehead against the pane. The magpie stays on the ledge, gazing at her for quite some time. Almost in spite of herself, Geneviève whispers "Michel?"

Now I know full well that when people are in mourning, they grasp at straws and seek meaning in coincidence or unusual events that seem to resonate with what they're going through. Since time immemorial, birds have been seen as psychic pumps, conduits or loaner vehicles for disincarnated souls, but until that morning, Geneviève had never noticed a magpie near her building in Neuilly, on the outskirts of Paris.

Had her morning visitor been "drawn" there by the magpie mentioned in my book, "called to her" by the image of the temperamental bird she had fallen asleep reading about, or had her late husband sent it to her? Had he *finally* found a way to mark his territory, to display a kind of jealousy toward his rivals, those pesky ghosts who had established their winter quarters in his recently bereaved wife's bedroom? Geneviève, in any case, is moved enough at the wonder of it all that she feels no need for an answer. She is too happy with the hope it has inspired to want to turn doubt into certitude and risk exposing herself to disillusionment.

The magpie comes back two mornings in a row. At the same time, for the same length of time, and performing the same observation ritual both days. Then, as though the point of the visits has been to help the widow come to these conclusions, it stops showing up. By chance or by design, the motorized shutters suddenly start to work again.

*

Text message received on January 22:

No magpie at my window this morning. On the other hand, Nikola Tesla dropped in at 5:30. Here is what he dictated: "To understand electricity's atomic nature, the field equations have to lead to the following proposition only: a portion of three-dimensional space, at the edge of which current density disappears everywhere, always holds a total electric charge represented by a whole number. People are right to say that the theory of relativity provided a kind of conclusion to the grandiose architecture of Maxwell and Lorentz's ideas. The concept of an electromagnetic field revised the foundations of the new physics."

He paused for a few seconds, and then he added, "$do^2 = c^2dt^2$."

Another pause and then, "$ds^2 = dx^1\,2 + dx^2\,2 + dx^3\,2 + dx^4\,2 = 0$."

After yet another pause, "$s^2 = Eguvdx\ u\ dx\ v,\ uv$."

That's it.

I toss the unfathomable formulas into Google's search bar right away. There are no results except for the first one, which sends me to Maxwell's Equation and the Lorentz force law, the foundations of electromagnetism (1865). They contributed to Einstein's intuition about gravitational waves. Although the other equations borrow elements from the Pythagorean Theorem and the theory of relativity, they are unknown on the web. My pulse starts to race. Still no "h" or "h-bar" in view, so nothing quantum. But could this be the formula for the famous "gravitation/electromagnetism" union that Einstein's hologram had been pleading for a week ago, the one that would radically change our conception of space-time? The weekend has just begun; I decide to contact an expert on Monday morning.

*

After that message, whose style and substance both went way over my head, Tesla maintains radio silence and stays away for a week. As for Einstein, he has only left the boathouse once, to thank Marie-France for the family reunion. Deprived of her bedside geniuses, with neither ghost nor bird to keep her company, Geneviève starts to feel lonely, when the Sky Engineer shows up again at his usual time. Soft-spoken and lugubrious, he delivers a statement that is totally unlike the requests and scientific communications he has made until then:

Peace, which you have never given so much lip service to, has never been further from reigning over the world. What the prophet Jeremiah said about the people of his day applies even more fully to those of yours. "You declare, 'peace, peace,' and there is no peace." You counsel remedies to each other that will grant peace of mind, yet you are still devoured by anxiety. You come up with plans for disarmament, for harmony between the nations, but all they do is change the type and methods of aggression. The rich can buy everything but happiness, and the poor are sacrificed to the unhappiness of the rich. How will you find peace, true peace, if you forget that you are not machines for earning and spending money, but spiritual beings?

The question would be followed by ten days of absence. It should be said that Geneviève is moving. Caught up between packing and the painful emotions and memories that it stirs up, her mind isn't very accessible, even if she does miss her early morning tête-à-têtes with the voyeur magpie and the stubborn ghosts.

As for the equations that were unknown on the web, and that I had had such high hopes for, the physicists I submitted them to tell me their defining characteristic is notation errors. A "plus" instead of a "minus" in front of dx42, a do2 that should be dxo2, etc. On the bright side, "ds2 = 0" is a geodesic: the equation for the shortest path light can take through the void. Live and learn. For the rest, I'm told to check my sources. But there's nothing revolutionary on the cosmic scale.

So much for electromagnetic gravitation. Maybe next time.

*

The Dead Team makes a comeback on February 12. In radiantly good spirits, the physicist stands silently behind the inventor, allowing him to give a speech in an exceptionally eager tone that will set the timetable for the next few years:

> Now you're going to discover a whole new way of studying and understanding the driving force behind your universe, as well as what makes up the very texture of your space and time. After that will come proof of the existence of micro black holes, with the size of a proton and the mass of the Himalayas. They emit phenomenal quantities of electromagnetic rays. Discovering them will lead to a new theory of gravitation that combines general relativity and quantum mechanics. Then white fountains connected to the black holes via wormholes will appear, and so on and so forth until the discovery of cascading worlds.

Once again, Tesla's avatar shows himself to be a pretty good search engine. With a few terms, he sends me packing in record time, heading for the information he wants me to look into and the encounters he's hoping I'll make. This time, it's with astrophysicist Jean-Pierre Luminet, an internationally renowned specialist in black holes. He educates me about the predictions I have just received. According to Luminet:

> Some scientific—not science-fictional—scenarios consider the possibility of multiple universes, some of which could be connected by those mysterious wormholes. We can also conceive of structures that would be like reverse black holes: "white fountains." The matter

swallowed up by black holes would gush out of those white fountains. If that were the case, then the Big Bang might have been a huge white fountain connected—who knows? —to a colossal black hole in another universe that poured some of its matter into ours. And we, in turn, may be fuelling other Big Bangs via our black holes. From black holes to white fountains via wormholes, it would add up to cascading universes. And if the last one were connected to the first one, then we would have come full circle. Where does matter come from? Perhaps it's simply looping around and around.[1]

It is hard not to see that gorgeous text as the extension, or perhaps the source, of the concepts sketched out by my incorporeal informers. Once again, it's a chicken-and-egg situation: has the defunct Tesla inspired the alive-and-well Luminet, or is the voice from beyond the grave being fuelled by the thought processes of the research director at the National Scientific Research Center? Could death itself be a sort of black hole connected via a wormhole (perhaps that tunnel of light described by patients who have been resuscitated after being declared clinically dead) to the thought processes of those among the living who are somehow "compatible"?

As for those "micro black holes," a persistent rumor has been going around since 2015 that the LHC[2] in Geneva–the world's most powerful particle accelerator and the largest machine ever built—is already producing them. From what I see on his blog, Luminet doesn't think so: "The LHC will deliver 14,000 giga-electron volts of power... It would take a million billion times more energy than what is accessible to the LHC for a particle to be both massive and compact enough to create a black hole!"[3]

The astrophysicist does, however, add a sort of disclaimer to his reticence: his calculations are only correct within the framework of classic general relativity. String theory postulates that gravitation might be propagated in extra dimensions of space-time, which could supply the energy for micro-black holes. If that were true, then the Geneva LHC would be capable of producing a hole a second.

Luminet concludes:

Those micro black holes would have such a small diameter (10^{-18}m) that, based on Hawking's process of quantum evaporation (…) they would only survive for a 10^{-27} of a second. As soon as they were created, those lab-made black holes would disintegrate, leaving a spectacular signature behind. It would be an immense discovery that would provide proof of the existence of the hidden dimensions in the universe that are postulated by string theory.

I'll leave it to the specialists and the dreamers to contemplate these infinite perspectives… and ignore the doomsday prophets who insist the end of the world is nigh because of what is going on on the banks of Lake Geneva, since our entire planet could be sucked into a man-made black hole.

"Big Bang Machine Could Destroy Earth," screamed a *Sunday Times* headline back in 1999. No, most scientists, including Luminet, replied. On the contrary, he hypothesizes the Earth might be able to provoke an infinite number of new Big Bangs, each of them nurturing future extra-terrestrial civilizations. In other words, the LHC might be seeding life *elsewhere*. It's a very cosmic view of bio-generosity, one that seems to reflect Tesla's own… unless something is trying to make me think so.

I spend a lot of time dwelling on my own doubts. Is a presumptive ghost the emanation of a single earthly mind—its own—or is it nurtured by the mental activity, dreams, research, and conversations of the living, as well as their yearning to believe in personal contact? Are the brains of the living a source of energy for the dead? Does our empathy fuel them? If "something" is making me write these lines, am I serving as a reservoir to be replenished or to be drawn on? In other words, who's in charge here: are Einstein and Tesla the subjects of my book, or am I a character in their plot?

Einstein obviously doesn't need my help to stay in the public eye, but his energy might have come looking for me to help get Tesla's work, ideas, and humanitarian ideals, which have been largely forgotten, back into the spotlight. "His" energy, or perhaps energy from a sort of databank nurturing our brains, the "nucleus of knowledge" at the heart of the cosmos whose existence Tesla postulated in 1919. Of everything he wrote while he was still alive, it was the text that he poured his most deeply held beliefs into.[4]

If it turns out that I am being manipulated, that I am just a cog in a wheel, I'd at least like to be able to believe the cause is worth the trouble.

1. Jean-Pierre Luminet and Elisa Brune, *Bonnes Nouvelles des étoiles ("Good News from the Stars")* Odile Jacob, 2009.
2. Large Hadron Collider
3. blogs.futura-sciences.com/luminet, 7 April 2015.
4. Nikola Tesla, *My Inventions, op. cit.*

12
Big bang and pyramids

O n March 15, the avatar of the forgotten inventor goes back to the subject of the origins of the world.

I repeat: what you think is the beginning, the famous Big Bang, is just a bottleneck between the current universe—the one you know—and another one, which is contracting and which preceded yours. And it will always be thus. Above and beyond all this, what encompasses everything, the true face of God: knowledge, information, the pure Mathematical Object. In addition, please tell your friend to read between the lines of the story of the Prophet Elijah and the Priest Ezekiel. He should also look into the French historian Bleuette Diot.

This time, what I'm supposed to do next is spelled right out: my "research director" doesn't want me to waste any more time dawdling in soccer clubrooms. The pretty, old-fashioned name I had never heard before comes up with a single click. From the home page of her site, I learn that Bleuette Diot is indeed a historian, a graduate of the Sorbonne, specializing in lost civilizations. Among other books, she has written a cycle of historical novels[1] for which a friend of mine who is knowledgeable about that sort of thing, Mireille Calmel, wrote the preface. I leave a message for Mireille right away.

While I wait for her to get back to me, I look into Elijah and Ezekiel, "Occupation: prophet," their (French) Wikipedia pages announce from the get-go. Elijah, born in 927 B.C., predicted the coming of the Messiah, then successfully ordered the rain not to fall for three years in order to prove the Spirit's power over outside elements. After that, he departed this mortal coil in a "celestial chariot."

As for Ezekiel, in the 6th century B.C., he thundered that our ills didn't come from "original sin" and that we shouldn't accuse others of the trials we bring upon ourselves. We can thank him for what UFOlogists believe are the earliest descriptions of aliens and UFOs in the Bible: "Spread over the heads of the living creatures there was the likeness of an expanse, shining like awe-inspiring crystal."[2] Scholars of the "Martian arts" also point out that when Ezekiel says, "The Spirit lifted me up between the Earth and Heaven, and brought me...to Jerusalem,"[3] "Spirit" ought to be interpreted as "flying saucer."

I refine my search, but reading between the lines in Elijah and Ezekiel's stories doesn't get me anywhere except to unlikely extrapolations harped on by esoteric sites, not to mention the e-commerce guru on YouTube who goes all out, calling himself "the apostle Elijah-Ezekiel." On the strength of that fusion-acquisition identity, he offers visitors to his website recipes for protecting themselves from the evil eye.

I'm outta here: black holes—fine; two-bit obscurantism—no thanks. Tossing Bleuette out with the murky bathwater, I move on to other things.

Two days later, Tesla's hologram calls me back to order. He appears before Geneviève Delpech around 6 a.m. "with a cheerful grin, for the first time ever," she points out. All he has to say is, "Bleuette Diot got it right about ancient lost civilizations that were visited by aliens. Look into what she has written."

Intrigued by his insistence, I go back to the web to learn more about the historian. A summary of her most-commented-upon essay reads as follows:

> For two million years, mankind lived a nomadic, hunter-gatherer existence. Then, all of a sudden, for no reason that we are aware of, major changes took place, an unprecedented upheaval that paleontologists call the "Neolithic revolution." Mankind suddenly became aware of its ability to modify its environment and adapt it to its own needs. No other creature has ever experienced so spectacular a change over the course of its evolution... what was the catalyst for that change? Could Göbekli Tepe, humankind's first temple, be the key to this fascinating mystery? What influence did that sacred place in the Middle East have over Sumer, a brilliant civilization that seems to have arisen out of nowhere?[4]

I try to buy the essay online, but it's out of print. Just then, Mireille Calmel gets back to me. I summarize the situation for her as briefly as I can. She doesn't bat an eyelash. To begin with, she points out that she shares the fan-from-beyond-the-grave's opinion of the historian whose work she has prefaced. Besides, in her work as a novelist, she periodically feels connected to people from the Middle Ages, like the bewitching Eleanor of Aquitaine, who inspire the characters in her sagas.[5] She's thrilled to learn that I'm "working with" the greatest inventor known to mankind, although she does impishly add that I should try not to get too smug about it. Personally, I'd trade my asexual genius for her sensual Eleanor of Aquitaine any day, but no one asks our opinion.

Mireille gives me Bleuette Diot's number and wishes me luck. Her mischievous tone of voice only adds to my discomfort. How, exactly, should I broach the subject with the historian? "Good morning, ma'am. I'm calling at the suggestion of Nikola Tesla, who has read your books and recommends them highly"? Instead, I settle for a prudently bland message, saying I would appreciate it if she could get back to me about her work on ancient civilizations.

But the Serbian spirit, who has followed Geneviève Delpech to her new home in the suburbs, doesn't leave the historian time to reply. He's already leading me down a new path into another field of research, as though he were running out of time. Perhaps his green card for our planet is about to expire. Perhaps it's time for him to complete my roadmap, filling me in as best he can before I have to sail off on my own toward the ports of call he has indicated.

You will discover that after molecules, which are made up of atoms, then protons, neutrons, and quarks, there's something smaller still, all linked. There is always something to form things because there's something besides matter that allows objects to cohere. It's a Spirit, an Infinite Knowledge, a conception you're not aware of. We are a link in an enormous mechanism that you don't know about yet.

As I used to say, energy will become freely available to everyone someday, but because of the selfishness of a few people who don't want the situation to change, mankind can't access that energy yet, can't use it to make the world a better place. For political, military, and economic reasons, my discoveries were hushed up. The irony is that new weapons were created based on those same discoveries. Their purpose: global domination of the planet and its population.

But thanks to the energy of the quantum void, harnessing antimatter and electromagnetic propulsion will become possible for mankind, as will travel at the speed of light. Imagine a world with unlimited free, clean energy for all. Inequality between peoples would disappear; there would be no more war, famine, or poverty; pollution would be eradicated and nature preserved… "What a shame!"

In 2239, mankind will make its first journey into space-time, but before that, humanity will have acquired a global comprehension of the brain and of thought; it will discover the existence of a quantum brain, a magnetic brain that acts as a two-way radio connected to both the universe and other beings. At that point, the mystery of telepathy, foreknowledge of events, mystical ecstasies, synchronicity, and more will be explained.

Two days later, his tone is more pressing: "Please transmit my knowledge for a better world. I beg of you."

Fine, but *what* knowledge? What has the so-called Tesla revealed up until now that we couldn't have learned from reading his patents, press releases, and autobiography, or the rare research papers devoted to him? As though my annoyance were perceptible, he suddenly shows up at Marie-France Cazeaux's place, vehemently insisting that humanity needs to enjoy free, unlimited energy. She calls me to complain about the newcomer, a "tall, sinister-looking scoundrel," who has crammed her head full of calls for an electrical revolution. I defend him as best I can, but I don't have a lot of arguments in his favor. After all, what kind of revolution can he hope to foment with the intermediaries he has chosen: a painter, a retired nurse, and a novelist?

"Seriously, how could we possibly be considered competent, credible, or even connected to all this?" the first of the three exclaims somewhat indignantly. She's getting fed up with being awakened at dawn by an energy-obsessed troublemaker instead of her loving crooner, whose voice has remained stubbornly silent.

The answer she receives the next day startles me as much as it does her: "I'm pleased to inform you, Geneviève, that the important gravitational-wave discovery was made on your birthday, September 14, 2015."

For real?

I decide to check.

Although the official announcement wasn't released until February 11, 2016, it was indeed on September 14, 2015, at 4:51 a.m. (EST) that the American research project LIGO, in conjunction with the Franco-Italian VIRGO, detected significant vibrations at the same moment on both of its "arms"—two enormous, four-kilometer-long laser interferometers located thousands of miles apart.

Refuting rumors, leaks, and tweets, the crews of the observatories chose not to communicate their fabulous discovery for the five months it took to confirm that the vibrations hadn't come from some sort of background noise but had in fact been caused by the collision of two enormous black holes, thirty times the mass of the Sun each! The famous "waves" in space-time that Einstein had predicted a century before had finally been perceived and measured for the first time.

That double absolute proof—both of the actual existence of black holes *and* of the dynamic nature of space-time— that astrophysicists had hardly dared to even dream of, turned out to be a "birthday present" from the universe to Geneviève Delpech.

"Nice," she says, sounding distinctly underwhelmed.

I have to wonder: is it just a coincidence, which our informer from the hereafter has elevated to the status of a sign in order to make her feel more personally involved, to motivate her anew by granting her a more flattering role than "go-between?" Or is it really proof of synchronicity, one more element in the celestial scenario, a link, a cog in the "enormous mechanism," as he puts it, connecting the people and facts serving the "Infinite Knowledge" to which he referred last time?

Instead of weighing in on that path of research, on March 7 he inflicts yet another detour on me. This time, it's practically a 180°-degree turn.

> Dr. Blanke. Ask Didier to look into his hypotheses, which are close, but not exactly right, as well as Dr. de Ridder's, from the teaching hospital in Antwerp. They got the main thing right: it all comes from the temporal lobe. But only in gifted subjects who are healthy in mind and body. Which you are. But they haven't really lifted the veil from the mystery of OBEs.

No, he's not talking about Orders of the British Empire. In plain English, he means Out of Body Experiences. Taking place when you're asleep or in a state of modified consciousness, those who experience them are able to mentally travel through the reality around them or even through parallel universes, which seems to be what happens from time to time to Geneviève, a "gifted, healthy subject," let it be duly noted.

Why is he deliberately sending me running after red herrings, if I understand our informer correctly? What's the point of looking into the work of researchers who are barking up the wrong tree? It's not like I don't have anything better to do with my time. Still, at the end of the day, curiosity wins out. The least I can do is to check that the doctors in question actually exist.

Since Antwerp happens to be the city in Belgium that my family is from, I start with Dr. de Ridder. Google sends me straight to these surprising lines from the *Gazette Médicale Belge*: "Dr. de Ridder hanged himself this week after political journals erroneously announced he was a member of the Academy."

Seriously? Is the Flemish physician who caused his own permanent OBE about to join the Dead Team that's already overwhelming me with missions? I soon realize that the answer to that question is no. The news brief I just read dates back to 1845.

Launching a new search, I find a present-day Dr. Dirk de Ridder, neurosurgeon and director of the Brain Clinic at University Hospital in Antwerp. He is also the author of a 2007 study about a malfunction in a specific area of the brain that makes subjects perceive themselves as being outside of their bodies. The study follows up on those published in 2002 and 2005 by Dr. Olaf Blanke from Geneva University Hospital.

So, once again, the information is accurate. The Tesla source likes to stay decidedly up-to-date on scientific research here on Earth. When it comes to lost civilizations, though, I can't help noticing that it takes a lot longer to get an answer. I've been waiting for Bleuette Diot to call me back for three weeks now.

I decide to leave a third message on her cell. This time, a man picks up, a car mechanic in the town of Loches. He sounds very busy and pretty gruff. Could he be her husband?

When I introduce myself, he grumbles, "Not again!"

That's when I realize that I had written the historian's number down wrong, so there wasn't much chance she would to get back to me. Could the precise but disparate bits of information Mme. Diot's posthumous fan had transmitted to me in the meantime have been meant to keep the pressure on, a way of keeping me from getting distracted while I waited for a reply that was never going to come?

I reiterate my request, only on the right voicemail system this time. And to pass some time (quite a bit of it, actually), while I await a reply, I watch the very long conference/interview the historian gave in 2015 on a Web TV channel.[6] Based on the discovery in Turkey of "the world's oldest temple," Göbekli Tepe, which has been dated to 12,000 years ago, Mme. Diot overturns the accepted chronology of the Neolithic period. Which means that five thousand years before the Sumerian civilization—hitherto believed to have been the oldest in the world—there was a human society able to raise five-ton pillars in a T-shape and to sculpt artwork of "a complexity worthy of Michelangelo's *David*." But had it primarily been a place of worship or a teaching center?

Based on her readings of the Vedic and Sumerian texts, Mme. Diot has revived a theory that Tesla endorsed during his lifetime. The texts relate that an essentially benevolent alien civilization brought its genetic material and know-how to the Earthling hunter-gatherers, in exchange, they said, for the gold powder the aliens needed to purify the atmosphere on their own planet.

What exactly should we understand by the term, "genetic material"? In a nutshell, Homo erectus's interbreeding with aliens is what led to Homo sapiens. Although that's not quite right either, because Bleuette Diot disagrees with Tesla on one point: she doesn't think the inter-mingling with cosmic immigrants involved Homo erectus. Based on a series of comparisons between Sapiens and its contemporary, Neanderthal, she sets the gene-blending a little later, toward the -35,000-year mark. Neanderthals, she says, were devoid of language[7] precisely because, unlike Sapiens, they never interbred, and only the latter experienced the "Big Brain Bang," as she puts it.

Exactly what knowledge did those extra-terrestrial colonizers—those "giants," or "gods"—transmit before fading into the collective imagination of human mythology? First of all, agriculture, to feed humanity as they went from nomadic to sedentary societies. Next, jewelry-making, to add skill and refinement. An obsidian bracelet found at A ikli Höyük (Turkey) in 1995, engraved with a micron-level precision that could not be achieved today without resorting to laser tools, has been dated to the Neolithic (10,000 years ago).[8]

Then came anti-gravity techniques, enabling the transportation, shaping, and raising of enormous blocks of stone "alongside" the tools of the time, which were supposedly used to build the pyramids. Bear in mind that ropes and stone rollers are the only tools recognized by "official" Egyptologists. Finally, harnessing free energy and scalar waves. So the pyramids served, not as tombs, but as electrical-power stations, wirelessly transmitting information and electrical current to every point on the planet where other "terminals" based on similar technology stood.

As Jacques Grimault—the "serious" Egyptologists' real-life nightmare —has pointed out, from Giza to Angkor via Peru, China, Japan, Mexico, and Easter Island, all located 30 degrees from the equinoctial line, an axis connects the various production sites [sic] around the Earth. A documentary about the subject has gone viral online.[9] In line with those wacky, for some, appealing for others, hypotheses, the other megaliths (obelisks, standing stones, dolmens, tumuli, etc.) acted as stone relay stations.

As for harnessing anti-gravity, Jean Cocteau referred to it in on January 1, 1962 in an extraordinary television appearance. The ghost he would be by then offers New Year's greetings to the youth of the year 2000.[10] Among the mysteries Cocteau says he hopes they will be able to solve are the inscriptions found on several South American pyramids, in which the Mayans "thank the visitors from space who taught them the secret of anti-gravity."

If we accept that it was used by the Earth's earliest civilizations, it seems reasonable to wonder how such important knowledge could have been lost. Why was the "teaching temple" at Göbekli Tepe, like so many others, deliberately buried under a manmade hill some 8,000 years ago? Can barbarian invasions, the evolution of human stupidity, or hypothetical conflicts between alien races explain this unbelievable loss on their own?

I would like to ask Mme. Diot if she came up with her theories on her own, based on her research as a historian and archeologist, or if she, too, has received visits from the "air-traffic controller" who has led me to her work. We mustn't forget that one of the reasons for the tower Tesla built at Wardenclyffe was to recreate the "pyramid effect:" a condenser, or capacitor, able to accumulate a considerable electrical charge, allowing for an "abundant discharge of energetic ions" to be generated at the top.[11]

As I await her reply, an unforeseen development will disturb things, turning me, yet again, away from a road whose path and purpose were unknown to me. It is a development that will upset me to the point of calling the continuation of the journey into question.

1. Bleuette Diot, *Sumerian Codex*, Dorval, 2013.
2. Ezekiel, I, 22.
3. Ibid., VIII 3.
4. Bleuette Diot, *Histoires secrètes des civilisations anciennes*, N° 1: *De Göbekli Tepe à Sumer*, Dorval, 2014.
5. Mireille Calmel, *Le Lit d'Aliénor ("Eleanor's Bed")*, XO Editions, 2001 ; *La Rivière des âmes ("The River of Souls")*, XO Editions, 2007.
6. Bleuette Diot and Jean-Raymond Binet, *Les Origines de la civilisation*, Meta TV, February 17, 2015, YouTube.
7. A controversial opinion since the Neanderthal genome has been analyzed, www. sciencesetavenir.fr, October 25, 2007.
8. Communiqué from the CNRS (National Scientific Research Center), December 6, 2011: "The (very smooth, mirror-like) finish on the bracelet's surface required the use of complex polishing techniques

enabling the achievement of polish to the scale of a nanometer, worthy of those used on modern telescope lenses." www.francetvinfo.fr

9. Patrice Pooyard, *La Révélation des pyramides*, documentary film based on the work of Jacques Grimault, 2009 (over 5 million unauthorized views in a single year on YouTube).

10. Jean Cocteau, *Vœux pour l'an 2000 (Year 2000 New Year's Greetings)*, pre-recorded in Saint Jean Cap Ferrat, www.ina.fr

11. Nikola Tesla, *Colorado Springs Notes*, op.cit.

13
New revelations, proof and doubts

The message that was such a game-changer was delivered on the night of March 23-24th. Here is the full text:

I didn't manage to accomplish the great things I had hoped to achieve. I was defeated. I had hoped to light up the entire planet... I had said: Matter was created by the eternal energy you call light. It illuminated, and the stars and planets appeared, and mankind and everything that is on Earth and in the Cosmos.

There are four laws of creation.

The first is that the source of this entire dark, stunning scheme—which is too great for the mind to grasp—is mathematical measurement. The universe is contained within that scheme.

The second law is the propagation of darkness, which is the veritable nature of light, from the inexplicable until it is transformed into matter. The third law is the absolute necessity for light to turn into matter composed of light.

And the fourth law is no beginning and no end. The three preceding laws are in perpetual activity, and creation is eternal.

Become parts of that light. It is music. Light will fulfill your six senses of perception. See it, breathe it, feel it, touch it, and think it. Light particles are notes of music. With a hundred bolts of lightning you can have an entire sonata; with a thousand bolts of lightning, you will obtain a concert. Numbers and equations are signs that mark the music of the spheres. If Einstein had heard those sounds, he wouldn't have invented the theory of relativity. Those sounds are messages from the spirit proving that life has meaning, that the universe exists in perfect harmony—its beauty is the cause and the effects of creation. You are living on the planet Earth which, along with its atmosphere, forms a system of resonance, a vast condenser that is a reservoir that could be drawn on. Humanity wasn't ready for goodness; it still isn't. Oh, if you could see, feel and hear what I saw, felt and heard from the time I was a small child...

Listen to Bach and Mozart; read the great poets: you will know mental energy... The energy of joy, peace, and love. I spent my entire life doing everything I could to help that energy influence human beings. I wanted to destroy the power of the evil and suffering to which people lose their lives. They spread like an epidemic throughout the universe. You must fight against disease, deprivation, and societies that injure people through stupidity. Fight against incomprehension, persecution. There are many fallen angels on Earth.

Tell your friend this: Nikola Tesla was happy. Nikola Tesla enjoyed himself. Nikola Tesla followed the paths of Indri, Peron, Buddha, and Jesus. Feel the rhythm of life. Knowledge will come from space. Your body must tune into the rhythm of the universe: your hearing, your sight, your breath. Talk to the earth, the plants, the stones, the lightning. Talk to the universe. Lightning is an entity, talk to it; it is brilliant.

Jesus knew the secret of returning to earlier energy: it's a very straight kind of light. Tell Didier that. The universe is spiritual. Our souls are connected by energies that are like unbreakable threads; a sudden wave of sadness could mean that somewhere on the other side of the planet, a good person has died. The entire universe falls ill at times. The remedy is in your hearts.

Look into my friends Shiuji Inomata, Bruce De Palma, and so many others who were laughed at, harassed, and financially ruined, as I was. Some were tortured and jailed.

Death doesn't exist in the reality of the universe. Only life exists. It is everywhere present, including in what seems dead to your five physical senses. All life is nothing but energy. Free energy comes directly from the heart of the universe and is subject to the laws of Universal Harmony; but to feel it, understand it and use it, mankind must live according to the vibration of the righteous conscious, without aggressiveness, with the lucidity and clarity of supra-mental levels. Mankind must stop behaving like animals in order to open itself to the

Intelligence of the Heart. Read the Vedic texts.
Tell your friend this: No, the Nazis didn't get my files. Some of them reached Hitler's hands, nonetheless. Practically all of my research has simply been kept by the FBI in Washington. The Americans retrieved files from the Nazis. It's the Black Program. The Paperclip Project. I invented the Great Eye. Archives of the Tokyo *Asahi Evening News*, 22 June, 1982. *Marine Observer*, Volume 47, 1977, page 66.
I like your contemporary, Searl. And Moray, too.
The reference number for the Tesla file the FBI kept is 100-2239. Department of Justice. Mr. J. Edgar Hoover. Washington, DC.

*

Investigating the names and references dotting this message would provide plenty of surprises, as we will soon see, but when it was first received, I was more than a bit puzzled by the strange blend of fuzzy, New Age-style spirituality and poetical allegories, larded with verifiable, high-level, technical references. Once again, I have to wonder: was that Tesla's spirit talking to us? If so, is *all of it* from him? I should point out that the last part of the message—whose purely factual tone contrasts so sharply with what precedes—is actually a reply to one of my questions. I had asked Geneviève Delpech to ask Tesla which of his inventions had been stolen by the Nazis the next time she had him "on the line."

The last thing I'd expected was a negative response leading to my being pointed in yet another new direction.

I type the keywords he'd provided into the search field—22 June 1982/Asahi Evening News—and am sent directly to a site devoted to the USSR's use of scalar-electromagnetic weapons invented by Tesla![1]

Incidents involving Soviet tests of weapons including the "Tesla globe" and the "Tesla shield" are frequently observed by airline pilots who fly over the North Pacific heading to or from Japan. Here is a typical instance: two regularly scheduled Japan Air Lines flights—403 and 421—observed and notified air-traffic control about a glowing globe hovering just over the horizon and spreading over it. The plane was at a point about 42 degrees latitude and 153 degrees longitude at the time. So the observation was some 700 miles east of Kushiro. The pilots guessed that the ball was about 10 to 18 miles wide. Depending on how far away it was, it might even have been considerably larger. The incident was reported in Tokyo's English-language newspaper, the *Asahi Evening News* on June 22, 1982.

No sooner had I checked the Japanese source, pursuing my navigation of the site decrying military use of scalar waves, I came across a similar phenomenon observed from 9:13 p.m. to 9:40 p.m. by the crew of a vessel in the North Atlantic. That incident was also on June 22, but in 1976. This is what the ship's logbook says:

> We observed an orange glow behind some distant clouds. A few minutes later, a bright white sphere was observed to the left of the orange glow, just above the clouds. The white sphere gradually grew larger, eventually becoming the larger of the two, but weakening in intensity as it grew in size. At its peak, the top of the white sphere reached an angle of elevation of about 24 degrees, relative to the observer, which lasted for about 30 minutes. It took about 10 minutes to reach full size. By 9:40 p.m., the sphere had faded away. It was sheer enough that the stars could be seen through it at all times. This incident conforms, yet again, to the Soviet scalar EM interferometer "giant Tesla globe" mode. The meaning and purpose of the orange glow are unknown at this point in time.

The article goes on to say that the incident in question "was reported in the *Marine Observer*, vol. 47, 1977, p. 66." Which is, word-for-word and figure-for-figure the reference the medium had received—her handwritten notes, which she had sent me a photo of from her phone, attest to that.

Once again, materialists, who don't believe in the existence of this kind of psychic communication, are reduced to parrying the inconceivable with the irrational, suspecting Michel Delpech's widow of duping me by scouring the Internet for old military secrets and serving them up in the guise of fresh communications from her spectral informer. Oh, and by the way, her computer hasn't been working since we've met, and I can confirm that. Between her husband's final illness and funeral and her having to deal with the estate, getting her laptop fixed has not been very high on her to-do list. Her friends lament the fact that she doesn't even know how to go online or check her e-mail on her cell phone.

So, excluding the psychologically and realistically absurd hypothesis of a long-term hoax, then it's important not to let myself be deceived about the source, nature, and purpose of the information she's been transmitting without understanding it. Discounting the small talk and poetical commentary in which it is wrapped, is Tesla's consciousness in the hereafter really trying to get me to alert the world to the potential dangers of what Red Army scientists and their successors have been doing with his discoveries?

Because that is what this is really all about.

To simplify to the extreme the highly-sophisticated information on the website he referred to—one where invisible-war buffs can deepen and intensify both their anxiety and their fantasies—allow me to explain that scalar waves, which were identified and harnessed by Tesla, radiate neutrinos arriving from the cosmos. The latter are received and retransmitted by moving water, rocks, plants, and human beings. Unlike "normal" electromagnetic waves, whose intensity weakens as they radiate outward, scalar waves feed off the fields of energy they traverse, delivering more power when they arrive than when they started out.

Tesla invented devices to "trap" those waves and point them at targets as therapeutic tools, unstoppable weapons, or protective shields. The phenomena related in the *Asahi Evening News* and the *Marine Observer* would fall into the latter two categories. I should mention here what Tesla's actual and surprising goal, which I learned while flipping through the very few biographies that have been written about him, was. I only just found out today, well after I analyzed the message from March 24.

As unlikely as it sounds, the Sky Engineer had decided to develop the ultimate weapon *in order to prevent war*. Indeed, the principle of using cosmic waves enabled the production of *both* the most precise long-range weapons *and* infallible protection from them in the shape of the scalar shield. Every bit as utopian as Einstein with his dreams of "global governance," Tesla decided to break the descriptions and sketches of his technological arsenal into several segments, cheerfully giving different pieces to the American, Canadian, British, and Soviet governments, so that they would be "obliged to work together instead of going to war against each other."

I know, it's hard to keep a straight face.

The kind-hearted, absent-minded genius whose excellent intuition applied only to his inventions, had forgotten just one small but key detail: industrial espionage. It would seem the Soviets were the first to steal the information they needed to build scalar cannons and shields from their WWII allies.

Washington later managed to get its hands on some secret Nazi technology (particularly through the White House's "purchase" of aerospace engineer Wernher von Braun, the father of Nazi Germany's V-2 rockets, American ballistic missiles, and the American Saturn V launch vehicle, which propelled the Apollo space program), which helped them catch up somewhat.

Nevertheless, based on hundreds of military documents declassified after the collapse of the Soviet Union, it seems likely the Kremlin was still a step or two ahead. Conspiracy theorists believe the USSR got a secret thrill from testing America's reaction to the "accidental" destruction (via Tesla's technology) of its warships and space shuttles. Rumor, as well some expert accounts, accuse Moscow of having pulverized both the atomic submarine *USS Thresher* in 1963 and the *Challenger* in 1986,[2] among other targets. So how credible are seemingly off-the-wall allegations like these?

We'll examine the evidence in the next chapter.

For now, let's get back to my reaction to the message of March 24 and the dramatic events to which it led. Among the names mentioned, the first ones to catch my eye were "Indri" and "Peron." Since I hardly think Nikola Tesla would credit his spiritual evolution to a lemur from Madagascar or an Argentine dictator, I google the names, looking for possible homonyms. What I find literally knocks me off my seat. Pairing the two words sends me to an infinite number of sites reproducing, in a range of different translations, a "secret 1899 Nikola Tesla interview."[3]

I stare, dumbstruck, as *entire passages* of the message Geneviève Delpech received the night before appear verbatim on the screen. Despite the fact that they seemed to be highly personalized revelations, the intimate details shared by her visitor from beyond the grave—including those relating to his failure as a savior, the origins of matter, the promulgation of the four laws of creation, and more—turn out to have been cut-and-pasted straight from an interview Tesla reportedly gave in 1899 in his Colorado Springs laboratory to one John Smith, stringer for a magazine called *The Bulletin of Immortality*.

What really gets my goat is not just the style (i.e., how precisely some of what he said in that interview matched what was dictated to the medium, all the way down to details like certain turns of phrases that would seem to be due to translation errors). The substance itself poses real problems, as well.

How could Tesla have expressed reservations about Albert Einstein's first theory of relativity back in 1899? Limited relativity, as we have already discussed, ignored energy from the void, which Tesla termed "ether" and whose existence he defended ardently. The offense to his precious ether could justify the gibe at the physicist's expense ("If Einstein had heard those sounds, he wouldn't have invented the theory of relativity"), except that Einstein's theory *wasn't published until 1905*.

Even more edifying: a full version of this apocryphal 1899 interview, including polite greetings and other small talk, refers to Emily Dickinson, described as the magazine's editorial director of sorts.[4] When the journalist mentions her name, Tesla politely replies that she is "a wonderful poetess whom I admire greatly." But Emily Dickinson had died 13 years before the article was published, and in pathological isolation, much like Tesla's own, later in life. The only reliable reference to the *Bulletin of Immortality* I can find is that it happens to be the title of a play based on Emily Dickinson's poetry staged at the Theatre Centaur in Quebec in 2015.[5]

What kind of game is our electrician from beyond the grave playing—if it is indeed him?

"Tell your friend Didier, 'Nikola Tesla enjoyed himself,'"… and he is still doing so, apparently.

In some versions of the pseudo-interview, when he evokes those whose "path he followed," Zeus's name is mentioned along with Indri's and Peron's, which makes me wonder if there might have been a spelling problem for the latter two. The medium might have misheard, or the specter pronounced them poorly. Geneviève has already mentioned that the Tesla who appears in her bedroom speaks French with a slight accent. Although he spoke 10 languages when he was alive, death does not seem to have freed him of his accent.

As it happens, *Indra* and *Perun* are counterparts to Zeus (i.e., the god of lightning in the Hindu and Slavic mythologies respectively, as Zeus is in the Greek tradition). Is the Sky Engineer, who managed to produce artificial lightning in his laboratory, simply admitting that he, too, had been playing God?

The references to Buddha and Jesus might have been a nod to their philosophy or—which would be more in keeping with the text—a way of evoking the ways in which those spiritual masters used light to free themselves from matter.

Assuming the message actually was an authentic communication with the spirit of the lightning master of Colorado Springs, the question becomes: why is he serving up a rehash of a fake from the Web? Is he making fun of us, testing us or trying to trap us? Could he be trying to validate the substance of the apocryphal interview? Or should I suspect the communicating entity— which is usually scrupulously precise—of having been interfered with by something in the sub-astral atmosphere that night? Must we conclude that the dearly departed absorb *anything* attributed to them, blending it with their memories, thoughts, and predictions, and that their "thought forms" will spit everything back uncritically?

Unless, not wanting to put all of his eggs in one basket, our talkative ghost-in-the-guise-of-Tesla has been pouring his obsessions into the ears of an infinite number of mediums. If one of them were Internet-savvy, he or she might have thought it funny—or more effective in terms of proselytism—to turn Tesla's posthumous communications into a "historical" interview online. An interview, which, by the way, the Nikola Tesla Museum in Belgrade says is not indexed anywhere in their archives. Officially, therefore, it's a hoax, presumably perpetrated by a New Age-influenced Tesla fan.

At the end of the day, it's enough to make you wonder if the entity communicating with us could be the result of a more-or-less haphazard assemblage, a sort of remnant wave unspooling a message, intertwining hackneyed reflections and vague cut-and-pasted ideas with precise technical information and announcements of imminent scientific discoveries. But even if that were the case, who is running the assemblage's show?

A series of precedents—which Father François Brune[6] and Professor Rémy Chauvin, two of the most eminent specialists in paranormal-contact phenomena, have studied and written about—do exist.[7] As extravagant as it might seem, interplanetary cultural exchanges have been occurring for over 40 years in a laboratory known as the CETL, the Luxembourg Centre for Trans-Communication Studies.

The CETL was founded by Jules Harsch-Fischbach, Chief of staff of Luxembourg's Ministry of Communication, and an electronics buff fascinated with the hereafter. During his free time, and working in close collaboration with Professor Ernst Senkowski of the Physics Institute of the University of Mainz (Germany), Harsch-Fischbach broadened the scope of his duties to include developing audiovisual liaison systems with other worlds. I won't go into detail here about the amazing results they obtained, but they can be found in Chauvin and Brune's books, as well as on a number of websites.[8]

Let's just say the CETL's small crew seems to be working in tandem with a counterpart communication center located in another dimension, on a planet called Marduk, to be more precise. Among those volunteering their time to the alter-dimensional research unit are Thomas Edison (1847-1931) and the Latvian psychologist and author Konstant ns Raudive (1909-1974), both of whom, along with Friedrich Jürgenson, pioneered recording techniques for voices believed to be coming from beyond the grave.

The problem is that one of the "Tesla" messages Geneviève received—one of the only ones she didn't text me about, in fact (all I have is an undated, handwritten page), originated from that otherworldly communication center. It is a word-for-word copy of an allocution emerging from the static in a transistor at the CETL lab on June 22, 1987. Since the wording rang a vague bell for me, I searched for and found passages I had underscored 15 years earlier in Brune and Chauvin's book, which led me to the original radio text. In their own words, the two authors relate the indubitable phenomenon they had both been eye-, or rather, ear-witnesses to. This is Brune's version:

> A deep voice with a pleasant timber emerged slowly from the background noise. It was Konstantíns Raudive, speaking French in my honor: "Dear Friends, What proof can we give you that we are not trying to mislead you? None, except the intimate, absolute conviction of a connection, an exchange, of souls touching...

The only variant in the version transmitted in December 2015 to Geneviève Delpech by Tesla's holographic image: "Dear Friend," in the singular (and feminine, in French), rather than the previous (masculine) plural. The rest of the message referred to the place Tesla was staying, that same planet Marduk, renowned for both its communication center and its huge waterway, known as the River of Eternity.

And that's not all. As François Brune points out, the first two sentences pronounced by the presumptive Raudive and later echoed by the supposed Tesla were in fact borrowed word-for-word from a beautiful letter. One of several that the soldier Pierre Monnier (1891-1915) had composed and sent to his mother through automatic writing after getting killed in combat.[9]

And even that's not all! The name of the planet and the river, as well as other, subsidiary details supplied by our 2015 Tesla ("There are several deceased entities like myself, along with other entities who were never incarnated on Earth. We schedule contacts between different planes,") is another blatant rip-off. Re-reading Chauvin, I realize they derive in *extenso* from another message received by the CETL's computer in 1988—it had even turned on all by itself for the occasion. The (audiovisual) message had been dictated by a deceased woman who introduced herself as Swejen Salter, a scientist in charge of an inter-world communication program. Chauvin adds that even this message had clearly been inspired by a science-fiction saga written by novelist Philip José Farmer (1918-2009), who also invented planet Marduk and the River of Eternity.[10]

So what conclusion should I draw? That "our" Tesla and "our" Einstein are no more than composite apparitions, conveying reader-friendly gobbledygook dreamt up by "communicators" with vivid imaginations?

My gut instinct refuses to believe that interpretation, which would reduce our ghosts' personalities to nothing more than shells in which you hear the sea when you cup them to your ears. Despite the series of plagiaries, I know there was something intense and intimate—which felt real and from the heart—going on when the Light-Beam Rider shared news of the imminent detection of his gravitational waves, and when the Sky Engineer set me on the dual path of both his censors and his followers. It had the same urgent, altruistic sincerity as when our communications had first begun, when he had pleaded with me to find and thank the man who had opposed the hijacking of his ashes for politico-religious purposes.

Is this necessarily an either/or situation?

No matter how you look at it, there is a form of intelligence at work behind all of this. It is an "out of this world" intelligence whose intentions focus on knowledge, love, and the greater good, even if that means resorting to borrowed identities in role play so true to the original models that possible trickery becomes excusable. If that's true, then what is the ultimate goal of the tactics? The discernment I have been asked to show, and all the tests pertaining to it, may well be the only key able to open the door I might find at the end of the path on which I'm being guided.

We shall see, but I've gone too far to give up now.

For the moment, I can't resist the temptation to share the delightful, though hardly flattering for us Earthlings, "justification" of the posthumous counterfeiting the late Swejen Salter, head of planet Marduk's communication program, offered in response to the demystification performed by Rémy Chauvin in 1988:

> Only things that exist in your real universe can be shown to you, because otherwise you would neither recognize nor understand the elements we would wish to indicate to you. Therefore, we choose a particularly important fragment of text and offer it to you repeatedly, rather as you would show an infant a ball, and repeat the word, "ball," over and over until the infant learns to associate the word to the object.

*

A few days later, it's Marie-France Cazeaux's turn to have the ball tossed to her.

Tesla's hologram has chosen her to criticize the hijacking of his inventions, this time not by the Soviets but by the Nazis. She is the one he rails vehemently to about the Americans' highhandedness. When the Third Reich collapsed, they recovered prototypes built from sketches that had been stolen from him, while at the same time clandestinely bringing the scientists in charge of developing them to the USA. The operation went by the code names "Black Program" and "Operation Paperclip."

Why had one of the mediums been pointed toward the KGB and the other toward Hitler's headquarters? When queried about the bicephalous transmission system he had set up involving both the painter and the nurse, he replied, "I'm dividing up the work load." My task is to collect everyone's homework, sort out the information, go through it with a fine-tooth comb, and arrange it into something coherent... But for the sake of what cause?

During the months of spring 2016, I alternate between phases of feverish excitement and dubitative exhaustion. Sometimes, I'm as puffed up as the Frog in Aesop's fable, convinced I have been entrusted with knowledge that could be decisive for the future of mankind. At others, I feel like a pinball that an invisible player is flipping from target to target to accumulate points, but toward what goal?

As anyone can imagine, I wasted no time in googling the information closing the March 27 message, the number of the FBI's secret Nikola Tesla file. *Your search—"Tesla FBI 100-2239"—did not match any documents*, the server replies.

I contact some journalists I know. Thanks to the Freedom of Information Act (FOIA), over 30,000 files from American intelligence agencies were declassified in the 1980s. The journalists explain how to consult whatever the FBI had been obliged to reveal about Tesla, which is how I come across 290 pages of Nikola Tesla's file on an official FBI site.[11] The first page of the file bears the number 100-2237—my incorporeal informer got a single digit wrong, having said 9 instead of 7.

This minor disappointment doesn't last long: the file, which, as one might expect, has been copiously redacted, starts by describing the technical characteristics and properties of *teleforce*, an umbrella term Tesla used for inventions relating to "death rays" and the "scalar shield." Right there on my screen, on FBI letterhead, I can read a description from October 1940, predating the observation recorded in the *Marine Observer* in 1977.

The first conclusion: the lies are leaping off the screen. Until the disclosure law (I checked), the FBI had strenuously denied being in possession of plans for secret weapons invented by Tesla. The unmovable J. Edgar Hoover, head of the FBI from 1935 to 1972, had even sworn that "the old man died without leaving any archives or the slightest trace of work in progress," as though he were some senile old man who tossed everything to the pigeons.

Out of curiosity, you can consult the other 289 mostly-redacted pages. Aside from a few curious gaps in censorship concerning the FBI's attitude after Tesla's death, they offer no dramatic revelations about his secret plans or the "appropriations" to which he was subjected.

More on the FBI later.

What the other file, the famous 100-2239, might contain remains to be seen. Bearing in mind that the subject of the file had specifically said that the FBI had "kept it for itself." Does that mean they "forgot" to disclose it, in hopes that researchers would swoop down on 100-2237 and settle for gnawing on that skimpy bone? That would seem to be the case.

Despite longstanding reports and rumors, the FBI was not involved in searching Tesla's effects, and it never had possession of his papers or any microfilm that may have been made of those papers… which were thought to include plans for a particle-beam weapon, dubbed a 'death ray' by the press.

According to the agency's site, that "rumor" is still number ten on the list of "Top Ten Myths in FBI History." A myth? That would imply that the FBI agents, if they are in good faith, haven't read the agency's own files.

I have neither the relations nor the skills required to dig further into whatever still-classified documents might lay dormant in a safe somewhere in Washington, D.C. Hopefully, skilled investigative journalists will follow that lead soon. Instead, I rummage through the documents that have been made public, focusing, at our posthumous correspondent's suggestion, on "spin-off" uses for his inventions, those ultimate weapons the Soviets, the Third Reich, and the U.S. Army are said to have developed.

1.   www.cyberspaceorbit.com/teshield.text. version française : www. scientox.net/Tesla-Armes-Electromagnetiques.html
2.   www.scientox.net/Tesla-Armes-Electromagnetiques.html
3.   https://www.linkedin.com/pulse/nikola-tesla-everything-light-1899-interview-prasannakumar-j-n/ - www.rustyjames.canalblog.com etc.
4.   www.nikola-tesla.it/intervista
5.   www.ledevoir.com, May 7 2015.
6.   François Brune, *Les morts nous parlent, op.cit.*
7.   Rémy Chauvin, *A l'écoute de l'au-delà, op. cit.*

8. www.lepaysdapres.eklablog.fr, www.worlditc.org, www.spirit-faces.com...
9. *Lettres de Pierre*, introduction de Jean Prieur, Fernand Lanore, t. I, 1980, 7 tomes.
10. Philip José Farmer, *Les Dieux du Fleuve*, robert Laffont, 1984.
11. https://vault.fbi.gov/nikola-tesla

14
Tesla's legacy?

Let's get back to deciphering the message of March 24. Just before the publication dates for the articles in the *Asahi Evening News* and *Marine Observer* that describe instances of the use of his "teleforce," the sender stated, "I invented the Big Eye." In slightly more scientific terms, the "eye" is an endothermic scalar interferometer, a system combining the capacities of a radar device and a scanner. It enables surveillance anywhere, including inside buildings, deep belowground, and even on the ocean floor. And observation isn't the only thing it's good for!

Using a pair of rays separated in exothermic mode, powerful scalar pulsations can be sent toward a submarine, intertwining to create a violent EMP (Electro-Magnetic Pulse) effect that spreads throughout the submersible craft and its weaponry. In this way, the submarine and all its missiles are instantly destroyed.[1]

Is that what happened to the *USS Thresher* on April 10, 1963, when it sunk off the coast of Boston with all hands on board? Did Nikita Khrushchev do that to avenge his humiliation at Kennedy's hands a few months earlier during the Cuban Missile Crisis? The very next day, on April 11, 1963, a huge underwater explosion, whose cause remains unknown, occurred 100 miles north of Cuba, in the Puerto Rico Trench.

Years later, conspiracy-theory physicists retroactively attributed the loss of several American F-111 fighter planes during the Vietnam War to the Soviets having developed Tesla's arsenal. The culmination of their argument: the presumed attack on the space shuttle *Challenger* on January 28, 1986 used a combination of techniques, including reducing the metal's resistance with scalar waves, and climate control, another "borrowing" from Tesla's work. The idea was to manipulate the jet stream in such a way as to send unusually cold air down from Canada to the launch site in Florida in order to weaken the shuttle's booster joint.

The only thing we know for sure is that a leak in the joint was pinpointed by the Rogers Commission's investigation as the main cause of the explosion. But conspiracy theorists point out that for the USSR, it was only a test. Moscow had been trying to find out if Washington would be able to detect Tesla's weapons at that stage of their development.[2]

That's the theory, anyway. Of all the technical arguments put forth by those who have denounced that sub-zero Cold War (Washington, it seems, never suspected a thing), I will retain only the least abstruse: birds. The presence of such powerful waves is extremely painful for small brains such as theirs. According to bird-watching groups that try to assess the damage NASA programs cause to bird populations, January 28, 1986 was unlike any other launch day. In the hours preceding the launch of the *Challenger* on that fateful day, not a single bird was observed flying or singing within miles of the launch site. So, it would seem that birds are the only witnesses for the prosecution to support this serious, retroactive charge against the USSR. So does that make it a bird-brained theory?

That's as far as I've gotten in my fact-checking when the phone rings. Marie-France Cazeaux had pen and paper on her bedside table for once, and she reads me what Tesla dictated when he woke her up that morning; *her* Tesla, whose personality is quite different from the one who appears to her fellow medium. You might say it's the principle of communicating vessels: just as Einstein is boastful to one and tearful to the other, the gently melancholic Tesla of the Paris area turns into a fuming bundle of anger and hatred on the Riviera. It seems that Marie-France and Geneviève are fated to see different ghosts.

"You simply can't imagine how much he resents the Nazis! He's wound up as tight as a clock, especially over Speer. The worst of them all, he says. He was the only one who was really bright, and he pulled the wool over everyone's eyes."

I find the statement disconcerting. Albert Speer had been Hitler's architect, his one true aesthete and final Minister of Armaments. By pleading guilty to "unjustifiable blindness," he was the only member of Hitler's inner circle who managed to avoid the death penalty at the Nuremberg trials. After twenty years in Spandau Prison, the still-elegant Speer published his best-selling autobiography,[3] which procured him lasting fame until his death in 1981.

I had read it while researching the workings of the Third Reich for my book *The Woman of Our Lives*. The most interesting thing about the 800-page memoir was the scathing portrait of the idiots and bandits who composed the rest of the Fuhrer's "inner circle." The Fuhrer himself is described by his one-time right-hand man as being only moderately intelligent, but possessing irresistible charisma—a psychic ogre "whose approval it was impossible not to wish for." With his icy lucidity and uncompromising style, when he blames himself for his initial fascination with Adolf Hitler, the incisive chronicler and philosopher of Nazism could practically make you forget his war crimes.

"Fascination, my eye!" Marie-France exclaims, having caught her visitor's infectious anger. "Speer was pulling all the strings! Hitler was his puppet! It was Speer who planned everything! He was a snake, worming his way into people's minds. He held forth in literary programs and posed in gossip magazines, acting like the village idiot, pretending to be a naïve intellectual who hadn't been aware of the Holocaust. Lies—all lies!"

Trying to confirm all this, I quickly learn that, according to the *Daily Telegraph*,[4] documents extremely compromising to Speer had indeed been found in 2005. Speer had both signed and annotated paperwork allocating supplies for enlarging the camp at Auschwitz. The decision had been based on recommendations from two of his assistants who had just visited the "over-populated" camp—where over 800 Jews had been murdered that very day.

"And you know what else Tesla told me?" the retired nurse went on in the same indignant tone of voice. "Speer is the one who stole Tesla's secret inventions and had scholar weapons built—"

"*Scholar* or *scalar*?"

"I'm not sure—I can't read my notes very well."

I think back to Speer's taped declarations from 1944, announcing that his scientists had finalized "an absolute weapon the size of a matchbox, capable of destroying New York City in the blink of an eye." At the trials in Nuremberg, he swore he had just been bluffing.

"He mentioned other names, too," Marie-France went on. "Von Braun, the Nazis' rocket man who wound up working for NASA; and Hans Kammler, an SS officer who had been promoted by Himmler. My God, such horrors! Tesla showed me everything: Mauthausen, Dora... plus the atrocities taking place in the concentration camps. It was hellish underneath them!"

"*Underneath* them?"

"He showed me the huge underground galleries where scientists had been locked up and forced to build secret weapons. Anti-gravity, I think he said, right? He made me write it ten times. Underneath the camps, there were thousands of slaves building these sort of flying saucers, perfecting their anti-gravity inventions... And the Bell. The Nazis were getting the scientists to build some kind of bell. The bell seemed like the most important thing of all. Does that ring any bells, as it were?"

Only vaguely, but I check. The "Bell," or *Die Glocke* in German, was the name for the most unlikely of all Nazi research programs. It was, indeed, an anti-gravitational system, something like a flying saucer, according to its inventors.[5] But it was meant to be able to travel not just through space, but through space-time, too. In his final madness, Hitler, encouraged by various gurus, had still hoped to win the war by using the Bell to change the past.[6] Until the Russian and American archives had been declassified, most people believed the Bell to be no more than urban legend, but the Bell's ringing has grown louder lately, as has talk of the above-mentioned Hans Kammler.

The self-proclaimed inventor of the gas chambers, the *Gruppenführer SS*, who Speer portrayed in his book as "a cold and calculating brute, an unscrupulous fanatic," was promoted to head of rockets and secret weapons in July 1943, six months after Tesla's death. A document he signed, which has recently been discovered by the Polish military historian Igor Witkowski, confirms that *Die Glocke* was the most important of the "ultimate-weapon programs" the SS had underway.

Moreover, Albert Speer acknowledged their existence when he was interrogated at the Nuremberg trials. He also had the cheek to claim that although he had been Minister of Armaments, he had been "kept in the dark about that kind of research" by Kammler, who had assumed full responsibility for it.

Had *Die Glocke* been the implementation of a project stolen from Tesla? That's what he drummed into Marie-France's ears, with a kind of guilt-induced anger. In concrete terms, according to the transcriptions of the Allies' interrogations, the Nazi Bell, measuring approximately 12 feet high and 9 feet wide, used magnetic fields to generate extremely rapid rotation. It had been built and tested on several sites, including Góry Sowie in Polish Silesia. The first known description of the unidentified machine is in the words of the German General Jakob Sporrenberg, who was interrogated by the Polish Army in 1945.

While historians agree that the ultimate goal of the so-called Bell (i.e.

time travel through mastering anti-gravity) remains an inconsequential fantasy, several of its side effects—such as radioactivity, cell-structure disintegration, aggressive cancers, heart attacks, and more—were observed on many of the foreign scientists who were mobilized to build it, as well as on the anonymous deportees used as guinea pigs. This is clear in documents found in archives seized by the Soviets.

By the time the Allies entered the underground laboratories dedicated to the project, however, the Bell had disappeared. Hans Kammler committed suicide on May 9, 1945, by either shooting himself in the head or swallowing poison, depending on your source. It's hard to confirm because his body has never been found. In fact, a documentary broadcast in 2014 on ZDF (*Zweites Deutsches Fernsehen*—Germany's Channel 2) revealed that his death had been staged by the Americans.[7] Determined to get their hands on the technology before the Soviets could, the USA spirited the SS officer out of Europe with fake I.D.

"Kammler... brought a special treasure from the Third Reich to the United States. Modern weapons," Donald Richardson's sons told the *Daily Mail*. As a personal advisor to General Eisenhower, and Kammler's "handler," Richardson had debriefed the SS officer. According to Richardson's sons, the escaped Nazi collaborated with American research teams for two years[8] before he was found dead in his cell, having committed "suicide"... again. For good, this time?

In the end, Kammler was probably eliminated for the same reason he had initially been kept alive: military secrecy. But why then? Perhaps the international press got a little too curious after the famous Roswell crash that had taken place a few months earlier, in mid-1947.

Another German documentary, *UFOs and the Third Reich*, claims that the pieces found in Roswell came from an American prototype of the Bell (built thanks to information from the former SS officer), rather than an extra-terrestrial spaceship, as is often believed. The military's amateurish, shambolic response to the event ranged from grotesque improvisation to information expertly tailored to distract people's attention, such as the "official version" of it being a weather balloon; "stolen," faked images of an alien's autopsy, and more. According to the documentary, it was all just an extraterrestrial smokescreen concocted to cover up the US Air Force's use of Nazi technology in an attempt to travel through space-time.

What is one supposed to think about all this? Is it science fiction, reality, or deliberately orchestrated fakes? Winding my way through the para-mythological jumble of flying saucers and time machines, I stumble across a story that is, unfortunately, indisputably real. In December 2014, an Austrian TV crew investigating a spot with exceptionally high radioactivity discovered "the Third Reich's largest secret-weapons factory."

In the words of filmmaker Andreas Sulzer, it is a maze of underground tunnels sprawling across an area of almost 200 acres, beneath the concentration camp at Mauthausen.[9] The place was infamous for exterminating the intelligentsia of occupied countries through work. Thousands of deportees literally slaved away at building and testing the nuclear, anti-gravitational, and scalar weapons on which Hitler founded his last hopes… exactly as Tesla had "revealed" to Marie-France Cazeaux.

"We owe it to the victims to open this site and expose the truth," the instigator of the report declared. But due to how much excavation work that would involve (to keep the Allies from discovering the tunnels, the Nazis cemented up the entrances at the time of their defeat), Austrian authorities are requiring that they first obtain a proper research permit. The permit request was filed in 2014 and is still "under consideration." There has been no more news about excavations or digs since that administrative roadblock went up.

As for the camp at Dora, which Tesla also mentioned to Marie-France, I discovered that a similar type of "test cave" has been described by several eyewitnesses, including a French deportee who managed to escape that high-tech death trap alive.[10]

After steeping myself in Nazi atrocities, Soviet strategies, and American manipulation, I need to reconnect with some human decency. Distancing myself from the vengeful fury displayed by his darker side on the shores of the Mediterranean, I re-read the message dictated in the suburbs of Paris on March 24, 2016, in which he had once again asked me to look into people whose names meant nothing to me.

And so I decide to try to find out who Inomata, De Palma, Searl, and Moray might be. Scientists with careers not unlike his own, I suppose. Predecessors or perpetuators that he describes as having been "laughed at, harassed, and financially ruined"… or worse. The last two, he says, are our contemporaries.

I am tormented by the urge to *do* something, the hope that the information supplied through this disconcerting channel will serve some actual purpose, do something other than prove its own precision at stirring up or anticipating the near future. What else can I do with the information I receive besides transmitting it, as I had earlier passed formulae on to Jean-Pierre Garnier Malet and Christophe Galfard? But they are specialists in theoretical physics. Could the pending or still-evolving discoveries being presented by the Tesla source inform, complete, or lead to concrete progress improving humanity's fate? Via my ghostly advisor, could I help an inventor who has stalled or, like Tesla, is being persecuted? At the end of the day, maybe that is the point of the scavenger hunt he's been leading me on.

As soon as I sit down in front of my computer to see what I can find out about those presumed colleagues of Tesla's, I receive two unexpected e-mails in a row. Both of them resonate so profoundly with the situation I'm going through that they completely distract me from what I was about to do. It's as though the elements transmitted from the deceased scientist were almost magnetically attracting complementary information from the living

1. www.cyberspaceorbit.com/teshield.text.
2. Lt. Col. T.E. Bearden, *Fer de Lance: A briefing on Soviet Scalar Electromagnetic Weapons*, 2002; www.cheniere.org
3. Albert Speer, *Inside the Third Reich*, Macmillan, 1970.
4. www.telegraph.co.uk, 11 May 2005.
5. "Les armes secrètes des Nazis," *Le Point*, 8 May 2014.
6. Pierre Lunel, *Les Magiciens fous de Hitler*, First, 2015.
7. www.lemonde.fr, 11 June 2014.
8. www.dailymail.co.uk, 10 June 2014.
9. www.rtbf.be, 31 December 2014.
10. Claude Quétel, *Le Camp des armes secrètes: Dora-Mittelbau*, Editions Ouest France, 1992.

15
Light, healing and synchronicity

The first of the two e-mails is from Dr. Gaston Ciais. A renowned dentist and laser-therapy specialist from Nice, he has been pulling off miracles in oncology wards across the region. His treatments considerably reduce the pain and side effects of chemo- and radiation-therapy, particularly the terrible inflammation of the mucous membranes they often cause, which laser beams can protect against or even prevent. And that's not all!

In Tesla's message from March 24, I read that matter was created by light. Out of the blue (uninformed about my "contacts" over the past few months, why had he chosen to write to me just then, when we hadn't been in touch for over a year?), Gaston decided to write to me about the classes he's been teaching at the Universities of Rome, Parma, and Liège (European Master's degree in laser-therapy, 2013 Erasmus program Bronze Medal). In his e-mail, he explains how he achieves surgical reconstruction of flesh through "light surgery" with a laser beam. In other words, he is telling me how he creates matter with his beam of light.

Concretely, his photons, projected luminous particles, "solicit" the patients' electrons, which then reconstitute missing tissue from the "blueprint" contained in the patients' DNA. Dr. Ciais had one patient, a little girl who, having lost all feeling in her right side after a stroke, had gnawed at the inside of her cheek to the point where she'd carved out a two-inch hole at the corner of her lips. Not only did Ciais' laser beam stimulate tissue regeneration *without scarring*, but the skin was identical in terms of both color and texture. Even the regenerated part of her lips spontaneously took on the same color and shape as before.

Both modest and dazzled by "his" light's effect on the human body, Dr. Ciais has had more stunning successes of this kind than he can keep track of. He regrets that his laser technology is not in broader use, despite the fact that he has revealed both the protocol and the outcomes in medical journals. A worthy disciple of Tesla, he has neither "blocked" his system with a patent, nor sought to profit from it financially.[1]

So as it happens—and as the disembodied voice claiming to be the Serbian engineer pointed out that very morning—light *does* create matter. And as it turns out, it can recreate it, too! Actually, it can do even more than that.

Ciais reminds me that in 2014, scientists at Imperial College London who wanted to test a theory (Ciais himself had simply used trial and error to find the right laser frequency) had achieved a near miracle in their lab.[2] Their experience consisted in provoking a collision between light photons. It led to the formation of both an electron and its anti-particle, a positron, every time.[3]

Although Albert Einstein had theorized the idea that energy and matter are equivalent entities in his famous formula, $E = mc^2$, until that experiment, materializing the idea through the use of light energy had been little more than a pipe dream. Once again, scientists have proven Einstein right! Could the effect revealed by the scientists in London be the very one that allows our departed scientists' bodies to materialize? Could it allow them to use the mediums' mental energy to reproduce their images as holograms, sometimes even going so far as to "create the impression of actual matter?"

Marie-France Cazeaux has already witnessed something similar in a dire emergency: the consciousness of a deceased person sitting next to her on a park bench was willing to do whatever it took to prevent the imminent suicide of the young woman sitting on Marie-France's other side. That young woman—the wraith's daughter—is still alive, and she can confirm the particulars of the incident that saved her life.[4]

While light can both create and recreate matter, Dr. Ciais has shown that, in a very specific case, it can also "de-create" it. "Jesus knew the secret of returning to earlier energy. It's a kind of extremely straight light," my informer disclosed, also in the message of March 24. At the time, I hadn't understood his meaning or the point of his digression, but now it suddenly makes sense. Because guess who first discovered the true nature of the image of Christ that appears on the Shroud of Turin: Gaston Ciais!

Allow me to remind everyone that from 1988 to 2001, the Shroud, which bears an authenticated bloody imprint of a scourged, crucified man who had been tortured in ways described in the Gospel, was believed to be a forgery from the Middle Ages. That was before the carbon-dating test that had placed it between 1260 and 1390 was "scientifically and definitively abandoned," in the terms used in the press release published by the world's largest carbon-dating lab.[5]

It turns out that in 1988, the labs dated a patch that had been woven in during Medieval times to repair fire damage. Was this simply an unfortunate choice for a sample or deliberate sabotage? With similar negligence, other "specialists" have decreed the image of the crucified man, not counting the marks of his wounds, to be the work of a painter.

What it actually represents is a superficial (40 micrometers) browning of some of the linen fibers, caused by an orthogonally polarized CO_2-type laser beam with a power output of 1 watt. In other words: a *very straight* beam of light. I am well aware of this, because Ciais and I demonstrated it on France 2's evening news on December 23, 2005. We produced a laser mark on a piece of antique linen that was analogous to the one you can see on the Holy Shroud, at least in terms of depth and hue. Because on the relic preserved in Turin, the image was not formed by a single line but could be described as being more like pixels, "To reproduce it identically," Gaston Ciais has explained, "would require thousands of orthogonally polarized laser beams functioning at the exact same nanosecond."

The question remains as to how, nineteen centuries before the invention of the laser beam—whose theoretical bases, I can't resist pointing out, were discovered by Albert Einstein in 1917—a laser image could have spontaneously browned the fibers of a shroud in Palestine. Aside from the carbon 14, every other dating method used—historical, cultural, or botanical; i.e. based on analyzing the weaving method, the folds, the type of linen, or the traces of flowers and pollen identified by Avinoam Danin of the Hebrew University of Jerusalem[6]—has always arrived at the same conclusion: the area around Jerusalem, first century.

The answer is that the image must have been formed from the inside. Based on the research of German physicist Fritz-Albert Popp,[7] in the fall of 2014, Gaston Ciais worked out the genetic mechanism behind the radiant energy that created the image, which no one else had thought of until then.

The thing is, our bodies give off light through our DNA nuclei. "The light is very low intensity," Dr. Ciais explains, "but it's sufficient to differentiate certain oncology diagnoses, for instance, because the light emitted varies depending on if it's coming from healthy cells or pathological ones. And that light, unlike sunlight or electric light, is by nature coherent, monochromatic and unidirectional. The very definition of a laser beam."

According to Dr. Marco Bischof, the head of the International Institute of Biophysics in Neuss, Germany, that natural laser light is a sort of "means of communication" amongst our bodies' cells. It is also where the thousands of pixels forming the image of the scourged, crucified man must have come from—via an inexplicable surge in the intensity of light—at the exact instant he disintegrated, because the image was printed *flat*.

We know this because there is no trace, either of blood clots or of linen fibers tearing, which would have been inevitable if the Shroud had been removed from a bloody corpse after—as analysis has proven—having spent over 30 hours in contact with it. Scientists who have studied the phenomenon call it "contact-free print-removal."

Here's the thing, though: someone else has claimed credit for Ciais's extraordinary explanation of dematerialization through a burst of radiant energy, which I described in 2005 in *Cloning Christ*. Eight years later, Paolo Di Lazzaro, the head of the Italian research center ENEA (National Agency for New Technologies, Energy, and Sustainable Development), wowed the press by declaring he had managed to reproduce the image on the Shroud of Turin with a laser "for the first time ever."[8]

Ciais felt obliged to correct that untruth, but he did so with the same apparent detachment displayed by Tesla when Marconi, who had plundered his patents, was fêted around the world as the inventor of the radio. What mattered most to both Tesla and Ciais was the importance of the discoveries and the progress they could lead to in terms of the greater good, rather than the fame or fortune it might have brought them personally.

*

Getting back to the contents of the oral surgeon from Nice's e-mail that arrived so soon after Tesla's message, one has to wonder what made Gaston Ciais think to send me information about the creative power of light *just then*. The timing is such that the data inevitably seems to offer medical validation of the concepts I had just received by way of the medium. The answer is actually quite obvious, because it is contained in the e-mail's own subject line: "Synchronicities," those extremely meaningful "coincidences" that Jung defined.

Gaston explains that the night before, while flipping through my *Dictionary of the Impossible*, he happened to stumble across the entry about physicist Jean-Emile Charon (1920-1998). A book by that brilliant "poet of electrons" had radically transformed my view of the world when I was 19. I had borrowed it from the library without even knowing what it was about, simply because the title, *Death, Here Is Thy Defeat,*[9] seemed a clear nod to the terribly erotic Christian novel, *Death, Where Is Thy Victory?*[10] by the illustrious author Henri Daniel-Rops. Rops' rather iconoclastic widow had been my summer vacation playmate from the time I was six until I was fifteen.

The book was an immediate and powerful shock. Not only did the eminent physicist and perpetuator of Einstein's work write in a clear, elegant, and flowing style, but even with my utter lack of scientific knowledge, I was able to grasp the ins and outs of his theories. As Charon sees it, we are all composed of *eons*, a category of memory-carrying electrons that, having caused the chemical reactions necessary for life on Earth out of "a need to increase information capacity," are now endlessly looping between the wave kingdom and the mineral, vegetable, animal, and human ones. Hence he concluded that our personalities are comparable to an orchestra composed of musicians from different backgrounds who have come together by choice to perform the musical score of our lives.

Then out of the blue, Ciais felt compelled to describe in an e-mail how he had found the very same book by Charon in the street at the foot of a garbage can one day in 2012, when he had gone out to grab a sandwich between two appointments.

You can easily imagine how I "devoured" the book, which had almost literally come out of nowhere. Charon's view of electrons as micro black holes that have been recording and storing everything since the beginning of time and that structure the world in its continuity finally explained what I had been observing with my patients every day. I have seen evidence of it in my most difficult cases, in the work of the electron-photon pair, which "re-structures" tissues that have been burned by chemo- and radiation-therapy, slashed by surgery, etc. But even more importantly, his concept provided a theoretical basis for the preventive technique I had devised empirically, using the laser... It allowed me to understand what "my" light was doing: reestablishing the world's memory thanks to the universal knowledge contained in the eons in our bodies that Charon describes.

Obviously, in that chain reaction of synchronicities, what strikes me most is the allusion to "micro black holes," which Tesla had referred to in his communication of February 12. I can't just keep my mouth shut and leave Gaston in the dark. Taking advantage of a book-signing scheduled in Nice the following weekend (another "coincidence"?), I suggest we get together, explaining that I'd like to learn more about the course he teaches.

The following week, the 70-plus-year-old professor, as sleekly turned out as a race-car driver from the 30s, is using his laptop to display photos, results, and statistical charts about his treatments, as well as graphic representations of the waves he uses to complement the laser. One of his diagrams really catches my eye. The sinusoidal series of bowties with vertical arrows and oblique cross-hatching alternating on either side of a horizontal axis is *exactly* the same as the image Geneviève Delpech received through "automatic drawing" at the end of the March 24 communication. Neither Geneviève nor I had thought of the sketch as anything more than a purely aesthetic figure. Its meaning had escaped us entirely. On Ciais' screen, I read the caption: "Scalar Waves."

Do these coherent sets of "coincidences" keep targeting me in order to fill in the gaps in my scientific knowledge and counteract my flashes of skepticism?

Of course I can't resist showing Gaston the photo of the handwritten notes Geneviève had taken and texted to me, including the sketch. Right above the drawing are four lines of strange equations riddled with Greek letters. Ciais recognizes them immediately. He explains that they are a well-known, revolutionary series of equations by the Scottish mathematician James Clerk Maxwell. Ciais adds that in the mid-19th century, the Scotsman had theorized the existence of that same scalar energy that Nikola Tesla later captured and put to use. "But who sent you those equations?" Gaston asks, sounding curious.

And so I spill the beans, telling him what I have been experiencing, day-by-day, since last December. My references to Einstein and Tesla elicit some skeptical looks, but when I mention Michel Delpech's widow, he really sits up and takes notice. With a bemused grin, he shows me the text of his Shroud of Turin conference. It ends with the following lines of poetry: "*Voici mon âme, séchez vos larmes, mes frères/ Je m'en vais là où brille la Lumière*" ("Here is my soul, dry your tears, oh brothers of mine/Where I am going, the Light never fails to shine").

It is an excerpt from a song by Michel Delpech.

As for the financial interests that felt threatened by Tesla's wireless electricity,

Ciais has run into similar problems. The low-energy laser he uses to get rid of mucous-membrane inflammation costs less than €10,000 ($11,000-$12,000). That may sound like a lot, but not if you compare it to the three or four vials a week, at a cost of €1,000 per vial, that cancer patients take for the duration of their sometimes months-long treatments. Laser treatment would render those vials obsolete, so it's no surprise the pharmaceutical companies are about as excited by light surgery as the oil companies have been by free energy.

*

Voilà.

That many synchronicities would have been more than enough to fill this entire chapter, but as you may recall, I mentioned two e-mails earlier, so let's go back to the previous Saturday. As soon as I read Gaston Ciais' message, I start to respond to it, yet before I can even finish my reply, I receive another, equally synchronous e-mail.

The second one is from François Bernard, an osteopath in Lorgues who wrote his thesis about Nikola Tesla's work.[11] Having read my *Dictionary of the Impossible*, he thinks I will be interested in the minutes of a medical conference about the SWD, a therapeutic Scalar Wave Device to which I devoted a few pages of my dictionary. The conference took place recently in Überlingen (Germany).

Somewhat taken aback by this avalanche of concordant "complementary" information, I learn that a household-use free-energy generator based on Tesla's discoveries is currently in production in South Korea. By pure coincidence, it is scheduled to go on the market at exactly the same time as this book is scheduled for publication.[12] Designed to provide sufficient energy *in perpetua* for a house and a car, the generator's price will be around $3,000.

Is Tesla's dearest dream about to come true? "A dream for individuals, a nightmare for the oil and nuclear-energy lobbies," in the words of Dr. Hervé Janecek, one of the conference organizers, who has been promoting the therapeutic Scalar Wave Device developed by the German physicist Prof. Konstantin Meyl to the French medical profession for over three years now.[13]

I google the household generator right away, and everything suddenly comes full circle. The very first page I click on mentions the inventors Tesla wanted me to look into. With him, it can be hard to tell the difference between a reminder and a coming attraction!

How am I supposed to react? This stampede of confirming particulars coming hard on each others' heels doesn't surprise me anymore. After four months, I've become almost blasé about it. What does impress me, on the other hand, is the twisting, turning path, filled with both detours and short-cuts, that the information always seems to take to be transmitted, cross-referenced, confirmed, and understood. It's the incredible cohort of diverse intermediaries that show up unbidden to enlighten me about the science that goes right over my head. Almost without my realizing it, they both encourage me to keep going and make it possible for me to do so.

In this particular case, by briefly suspending the research my informer had demanded of me, the nearly simultaneous e-mails from two specialists in therapeutic waves wound up allowing me to better measure the full meaning and urgency of what I was doing.

*

On September 19, 2016, as I'm doing final corrections on the page proofs of this chapter, by association of ideas, the reference to Jean-Emile Charon's important book suddenly causes a wave of regret to wash over me. Novelist and essayist Martine Le Coz is one of the few French authors to have taken an interest in Tesla. Of the two books she has written about him, I have only been able to read one,[14] because the other is out of print, and I haven't been able to get my hands on a copy.[15] Why, at this late stage of the game, am I suddenly overwhelmed with regret about that gap in my research? I should have tried to get in touch with her months ago. As a fellow writer, it surely would have been possible through our respective publishing houses, but now it's too late: the deadline for the page proofs is just three days from now.

Sigh.

That very night, at the awards ceremony for the Prix du Patrimoine (Cultural Heritage Prize) which I'm on the jury for, a journalist from France Inter radio comes up to me. She introduces herself as Manault Deva and mentions that we should have met several years before, when a show I had been invited to appear in was cancelled because of a strike. Then she asks what I've been up to lately. Her face lights up the instant I pronounce Nikola Tesla's name: she's been working on a piece about him ever since she met Martine Le Coz. I grab my chance: does she happen to have Le Coz's number on her? And has she got a copy of her book *Wardenclyffe Tower*? The answer is yes on both counts. So she gives me one and agrees to lend me the other.

And so I learn what I could not possibly have guessed from reading *The Electric Man*: for the past 10 years, Martine Le Coz, who is also a medium, has been in regular communication with Nikola Tesla. Like me, she has contacted scientists—particularly the physicist and quantic-medicine theorist[16] Nouredine Yahya-Bey from the University of Tours—in order to transmit data. Although we have not been receiving precisely the same information, it all reflects the same humanitarian concerns, the same feverish sense of urgency, and the same need to *keep working*.

Surprising coincidence or "logical" synchronicity? I have often wondered why what is apparently Tesla's spirit would have chosen me. Lacking an answer to that question, here is another one: if our posthumous informer seems attracted to award-winning novelists,[17] is it because the author Mark Twain was his truest friend on Earth, the person who both admired him deeply and understood him better than anyone else? Tesla liked to remind journalists that during the nine months when he had been laid up with cholera in his teens, reading the great American humorist had more than once saved him from "fading to black."

Martine Le Coz, who has delved deeply into Hindu spirituality, which was very dear to Tesla, has arranged an exhibit of mandalas by the children of Mithila, a major center for that traditional spiritual art form. The exhibit is on in Paris the day Manault Deva and I discover our shared interest, which makes it easy for me to meet Martine. She tells me about Tesla's decisive encounter with Swami Vivekananda, who initiated him into the Vedic texts at the Chicago World's Fair in 1893, and later deepened the instruction during a series of interviews at the home of the actress Sarah Bernhardt. We talk about much more than just our shared subject's past and the information he seems to be transmitting in hopes of making the world a better place.

Martine invites me to her Legion of Honor ceremony. It is to be held in a rather unusual spot, one she has chosen herself: Beauval Zoo, in the presence of elephants. She is a passionate defender of those gentle animals who are endangered by the ivory trade. As it happens, Geneviève Delpech recently launched a project in Africa that she has been preparing for quite some time: a school-cum-sanctuary where orphaned children and wounded animals will be able to live together. It goes without saying that I will introduce the two widows who have so much in common. Not only do they both fight for the same ideals, but they are both connected—albeit each in her own way—to the same source. Although Nikola Tesla is first and foremost an obsessively active consciousness, he is also an excellent go-between.

1. Gaston Ciais, "Laserthérapie dans la prévention et le traitement des mucites liées à la chimiothérapie," in *Bulletin du Cancer*, February 1992.
2. *Nature*, 18 May 2014.

3. *Sciences et Avenir*, May 2014.
4. See the "Matérialisation" entry in my *Nouveau Dictionnaire de l'impossible, op. cit.*
5. Beta Analytic Radiocarbon Dating, ISO 9001 certification, January 20, 2001.
6. A. Danin, A. Whanger, U. Baruch, M. Whanger, *Flora of the Shroud of Turin*, Missouri Botanical Garden Press, 1999.
7. Fritz-Albert Popp, *Biologie de la lumière*, Marco Pietteur, Résurgences Collection, 1998.
8. www.bulletins-electroniques.com, May 2013.
9. Albin Michel, 1979.
10. Daniel-Rops, *Mort, où est ta victoire ?*, Plon, 1934.
11. *Philosophie ostéopathique – Energie libre et technologie*, master's thesis for the Institut supérieur d'ostéopathie, Aix-en-Provence, 2004.
12. Translator's Note: The author was referring to the original, French publication of the book. The generator in question has since been put on the market. For more information: http://infinitysav.com/magneticgenerator.
13. www.cytobiotech.com
14. Martine Le Coz, *L'Homme électrique, op. cit.*
15. Martine Le Coz, *La Tour de Wardenclyffe*, éd. Michalon, 2011.
16. Nouredine Yahya-Bey, *Le Code caché des miracles de Jésus*, éd. véga, 2012.
17. Translator's Note: Martine Le Coz won the 2001 Renaudot Prize for *Céleste* (Le Rocher). As was mentioned in Chapter 4, the author won the 1994 Goncourt Prize, for *One Way* (*Un aller simple*).

16
Dream energy

"I like your contemporary, Searl," the presumptive Sky Engineer said at the end of his message of March 24. In light of what I'm finding out about Searl online, I can see why he would. A precocious genius in the same vein as Tesla, John Searl devoted himself to inventing with near-suicidal abnegation. An Englishman whom I had never heard of before, Searl has been discredited, persecuted, and erased from the history books. Born in 1932, he clearly seems to be a sort of spiritual heir to Nikola Tesla.

A gifted child whose poverty-stricken family didn't know what to do with him, Searl was placed in a foster home at age two. Haunted throughout his childhood by dreams in which electrical schemas and components appeared to him clearly, at age 14 he built the Searl Effect Generator, a "generator of energy from thin air," as he described his rotary transformer composed of copper plates, rollers, and magnets. Yet barely had he turned it on before it lifted off and flew straight up to the ceiling! Believing he had "only" invented a wireless generator, the teenager learned he had just built a flying saucer. Tesla having died three years earlier, Searl seems to be his obvious successor.

Discreet and self-taught, Searl earned a living making electronic components on an assembly line in the Midlands. Over the years, he perfected a system allowing for unlimited energy production through a combination of electromagnetic power and perpetual motion. The only problem was that the minute he opened a window, his invention would head for the wild blue yonder. Searl lost quite a few prototypes that way, exacerbating his financial woes each time. The accelerating rotary movement generated a magnetic field that modified gravity around his machines.

Having finally worked that wrinkle out, at age 18, Searl developed a portable device with a one-meter wingspan that was able to generate more than a million volts. As a bonus, once the motor had got the device going, the generator never stopped running, drawing potentially unlimited energy from the surrounding air.

Every bit as generous—and as lacking in business acumen—as his predecessor, in 1970, John Searl decided to send a prototype of his invention to Queen Elizabeth II. The accompanying cover letter declared, "If Your Majesty deigns to accept the homage of this patent-free invention, I could show her how to build this device in order to generate an inexhaustible supply of energy and to build a new kind of air vessel." Buckingham Palace's mail service thanked him warmly, but informed him that the Queen had declined his gift—she didn't have time to receive all of the kingdom's generous donors.

Somewhat miffed, Searl decided to offer his generator to the United States instead. He demonstrated the airborne version at Edwards Air Force Base, the home of the Air Force Test Center. When top Air Force brass saw his remote-controlled, free-energy craft pulling off turns at 25 g, they declared it "too dangerous for their crews" and turned the donation down, claiming they weren't interested. That's the official story, anyway.

As for his dream of unlimited production of free electricity for consumers, it encountered the same fate as Tesla's comparable fantasy—pressure from lobbies, mockery in the media, a mysterious laboratory fire, and destruction of his sketches and prototypes—with an extra twist: although his generator naturally captured energy present in the atmosphere, in 1982, he was charged with "fraudulent use of electricity," as though he had plugged his device into an electric pole! While he was in jail, the army emptied his workshop.

But the imperturbable Searl was also every bit as ornery and resistant to pressure as Tesla. So in 1996, he had the results of his device officially observed and measured at a conference at Middlesex University, in London. That day, he proved to the world that it was indeed possible to draw electricity "from thin air." Later, in response to the various threats to which he was still being subjected, he vanished. Some sources say he is continuing his research under an assumed name in New Zealand or perhaps Thailand. A number of videos online provide useful, concrete descriptions of his inventions and the many possibilities they offer.[1]

Nikola Tesla's other "friends" mentioned in the March 24 message are of the same ilk. The one who seems to have been persecuted the least is Dr. Shiuji Inomata (1932-2001). Employed by the government for forty years at the Space Center in Tsukuba, Japan's "Science City," he was officially tasked with doing research into the possibility of building a free-energy machine. Toshiba Corporation even invested two million dollars into developing the program. Has this simply proved to be a gentler way to bury it in the mass grave of unrealized projects?

In America, on the other hand, the free-energy generator built by the physicist (and brother of filmmaker Brian) Bruce De Palma (1935-1997), was confiscated by the authorities, supposedly because he was using it to supply his home with free electricity. De Palma emigrated to Japan to escape administrative persecution. Inspired by Nikola Tesla, who had stated years before that "Magnetism is the ideal conductor for drawing free energy from space and putting it to work," he improved his invention by adding extra-powerful magnets. In 1980, tests proved that—like the electric engine on his precursor's Pierce-Arrow— De Palma's generator produced infinitely more energy than it needed to run the machinery it was hooked up to.

As for Thomas Henry Moray (1892-1974), the last of the perpetuators Tesla mentioned, he is probably the one who suffered the most from their scientific bond. Another gifted child, Moray came across Tesla's texts at the age of eight and decided then and there to take up the challenge of producing free energy by "stimulating and increasing existing oscillations in space." Later, having become an electrical engineer, he built a radiant-energy generator whose efficiency has been demonstrated repeatedly.

His device, which looked like nothing more than a box sitting on a table, converted energy from space into accessible electricity, powering the light bulbs and engines around it. As technical experts' reports confirm, the machine ran for days without showing the slightest sign of slowing down; yet the U.S. Patent Office refused all seven of Moray's attempts to protect his invention… because the machine didn't hew to any physical laws known at the time.

"But you can see that it works," Moray protested, sputtering.

"Yes," the patent officer replied, "but I don't understand how."

Was it pure incompetence, an isolated idiot's resentful power play, or was the refusal dictated from on high?

Sadly, Moray's patent problems were but the first skirmish in a long series of hostilities. Not only were his generators destroyed several times—supposedly by vandals—but he was even shot at, and someone tried to kill his wife and children. Considering the Cold War context, the FBI, led by the unshakeable J. Edgar Hoover, insisted that the series of attacks must have been a Communist plot. But anyone can see whose interests were actually being threatened by Moray's invention.

His sons, John and Richard, both physicists like their father, have done their best to find financing to mass-produce their father's generator. They are determined but cautious. "I don't want to put my family through what we were subjected to," Richard Moray has said with admirable restraint.[2]

Other inventors who don't appear on Tesla's short list of successors are on the verge of making Tesla's seemingly impossible, century-old dream come true. Some of them have even reached the mass-production stage. A list of them can be found in an article in the *Huffington Post*, which provides an overview of the prospects for various free-energy devices. The prospects are as encouraging for consumers as they are alarming for the oil, nuclear power, and shale gas lobbies.[3] The thing is, the *Huff Post* article dates back to 2010, and from the consumer's point of view, nothing has changed since.

So, what happened to the new, free-energy household generator whose imminent, late-2016 release was announced at the Uberlingen International Conference? Did that revolutionary promise wind up with all the others on the junk heap of history, in a multinational's incinerators, or a secret service's files?

Although sadly, free, unlimited energy's time has not yet come, there is one field in which Tesla's dream *has* come true: therapeutic uses of his discoveries, to which I have already briefly referred. Here is what Dr. Hervé Janecek, the official French importer of the Scalar Wave Device, or SWD, says on his website:[4]

> Konstantin Meyl (1952-) has studied all of Nikola Tesla's work in great detail. A professor of physics and applied electronics at the University of Furtwangen (Germany), he assumed that the radiant effect discovered by Tesla corresponds to the flow of neutrinos we are constantly receiving in great abundance (60 billion particles per cm^2 of skin per second), from the sun, supernovae and black holes. These are particles whose trajectory is not—or only barely—affected by matter.
>
> Thanks to modern electronics, and based on diagrams patented by Nikola Tesla, Professor Meyl was able to build a small generator of those longitudinal waves, and their properties match those described by Tesla. He showed that not only was transmission of wireless energy by that type of wave possible, but the yield of energy transfer in space was far superior to 1 (between 1.5 and 12!)!
>
> Professor Meyl has made an experimental kit available for sale. Fitting

into an ordinary briefcase, it makes it possible to demonstrate the existence and transmission of scalar waves using only 2 to 20 volts (as opposed to the 400,000 volts Nikola Tesla used to require). Over the past 15 years, Professor Meyl's initial experiment has been reproduced hundreds of time around the world, in public and private research centers run by both universities and independent researchers.

Nikola Tesla called his wave generator a "magnifying transmitter," because of its super-unitary yield: more energy does in fact arrive at the receptor antenna than is given off by the producing antenna. Professor Meyl explains that this is not "a miracle," but simply the effect of recuperating a set of harmonic scalar waves that are usually masked by background noise. They attach themselves by resonance to the first artificially created carrier wave. This phenomenon increases the amount of energy received relative to the amount given off: it is typical of longitudinal waves, which progress in a vortex.

But how do the waves affect our organisms? By the same sort of resonance, no doubt. It seems that cells "reboot" (to borrow computer terminology) when they come into contact with this cosmic energy. They can use it to compensate for gaps caused by disease, broken bones, post-operatory stress, pollution, etc.[5] In any case, it would seem that more and more people around the world are being treated with scalar waves, considering the number of animals that have been cured by them.

Veterinarians have indeed been the pioneers in this kind of therapy, probably because they don't have to worry about losing their licenses for practicing alternative medicine if they observe and refer to cases where cancer has disappeared in dogs, cats, or horses, thanks to a simple vibrational re-harmonization. Scalar-wave generators seem to reset diseased cells at a "corrective frequency"—their own normal, healthy frequency, in fact.

In other words, the waves seem to refresh the cells' memories, enabling them to reprogram themselves. Consequently, there is a cascading effect of metastases dying off. The effect has been demonstrated three times at university-run research centers in Heidelberg (2012), Madrid, and Brescia (2013). The outcome is comparable to successful chemo- and/or radiation-therapy treatment, but without the collateral damage to healthy cells.[6]

*

Oddly, Tesla's presumed spirit has made no reference to the medical applications of his work in any of the messages received, yet they are the only positive outcomes that posterity has granted to any of the countless discoveries he made that were ignored during his lifetime. So why has he kept quiet about it?

To save energy, perhaps. Maybe he figures there's no point in telling me about scalar therapy, because he knows I already know about it. Moreover, I've actually even tried it.

In fall 2015, two months before Tesla's work took over my life, an osteopath and a G.P. allowed me to experience the benefits of the waves' apparent power. The results were impressive in terms of healing speed and bone consolidation after a fracture in my foot; and the outcome was confirmed by both the radiologist and the orthopedic surgeon who had operated on me. You could say that my body has an intimate knowledge of the subject. So rather than informing me about what I already know from experience, Tesla prefers to bring me new data, fill in my gaps, and broaden my field of investigation. Well, that's my interpretation of the curious omission, anyway.

Other times, information skips the "medium channel" altogether and settles for word-of-mouth. Like the day at a book fair in Corsica, when one of my readers asked me what my next book would be about. I mentioned Tesla's name and—having become used to the fact that the man who had once been known as "the greatest inventor of all time" had fallen into near oblivion—was about to start explaining who he was. But she cut me off with a big grin. Not only did she already know who Tesla was, thank you very much, but he had saved her life!

At that, she pulled a purple credit-card-sized dog-tag from under her jacket with a flourish. She explained that it had cured her of several problems that had stumped conventional medicine. She called her purple card her "Tesla tag." I was somewhat taken aback to see the name of a now-forgotten, former envelope-pushing inventor associated with such a superstitious home-shopping-network type of lucky charm. Seeing the somewhat skeptical look on my face, my reader explained—practically without stopping for breath—that thanks to a modification of the aluminum's molecular structure, Tesla had obtained a micro-crystalline surface that entered into resonance with negative ions' vital energy.

Try to picture the scene, which was totally surreal: decked out in camouflage dress, the lady had brought me some sheep-milk cheese to thank me for signing her book. This down-to-earth, no-frills woman was probably a sheep herder who had come into town to stock up on books for the winter… and here she was, giving me a lesson in applied physics under a bookstore parasol! Having rounded up a whole flock of her friends—all of them flaunting their purple tags and singing its praises to the skies—she informed me that her "health-insurance card", which had been made in Switzerland,[7] was based on a patent filed by Tesla in 1901.

Despite her enthusiasm and my own affinities with the hermit of the Hotel New Yorker, I was not entirely convinced by the demonstration. So I let my fingers do the walking. Back at the hotel, I checked the accuracy of her claim against the U.S. Patent Office's digitalized records… and I found it! Patent 685-958, filed on November 5, 1901: Method of Utilizing Radiant Energy. In addition to the radiant-energy tag, the patent also included the famous free-electricity receptor the Sky Engineer had dreamt of offering for the betterment of humanity.[8]

When the living get that good at transmitting cascades of information, ghosts can go into sleep mode. Still, in my particular ghost's case, the pause will be brief…

1. http://www.collective-evolution.com/2013/01/07/free-energy-searl-effect-generator/
2. Jeane Manning, *Energie libre et technologies*, Louise Courteau, 1997.
3. Archives-lepost.huffingtonpost.fr/article/2010/02/07/1928835_ l-energie-libre-illimitee-et-non-polluante-disponible-pour-tous.html
4. www.cytobiotech.com
5. www.alternativesante.fr/ondes-scalaires/les-ondes-scalaires-medecine-de-demain
6. Hervé Janecek, « Les Scalar waves, la lumière qui nourrit et qui guérit », www.yvescassard.com
7. www.swisstesla.swiss
8. https://en.wikipedia.org/wiki/List_of_Nikola_Tesla_patents

17

"Fetch!"

I don't know if it's due to experience, my improved reactivity (before, when my 'source' gave me a lead, I used to wonder what it was about and why he wanted me to look into it; now I just do it), or a desire to speed up the flow of information through a channel that may be closing down soon, but for whatever reason, Tesla's messages are getting ever more succinct, pressing and precise.

Revelations, dates, names, equations, missions. Ceaselessly intertwining new information with requests for investigation, my correspondent, who has always been so courteous, now tends to sound like an editor-in-chief: briefing, motivation, assignment. Thus, on April 8, he dictates the following to his Paris-area amanuensis:

> I had the same experience as you did, of an immaculate white dove bursting magnificently into intense but not blinding light.
> I met Ettore Majorana.
> Didier must research the following: October 17, 1945. Conroy. N.Y Office. Trump Report. Kosanovic. October 19, 1945. Military Intelligence in Washington. September 5, 1945: Lloyd Shaulis of the OAP. Lieutenant Colonel Tom Bearden. Andrija Puharich. $0 = 1\backslash2 - d\,E/2dt$.
> Thank you.

Not much to go on. I start with the only clue that rings any bells: the dove. In her first autobiographical book, Geneviève Delpech describes how, one night in the house near Paris where she and Michel were living back then, she suddenly saw a white bird "burst into very bright, yet not blinding, light."[1]

When I call her to discuss the *message du jour*, what surprises her most is not that her dawn visitor knew about the dove incident—whether he had read her mind or her book—but that he addressed her with the formal vous, as opposed to his usual, more familiar tu. Then she realized the vous was a plural. Her friend Jean had witnessed the radiant dove with her.

Geneviève had been playing her husband's cover of a song by Georges van Parys, "*Un jour, tu verras*" ("One Day, You'll See"), for him. George's wife was very close to Michel, who had been on tour in the south of France that day. They next day, they found out she had died at the exact moment that the white bird was performing its radiant dance in the backyard. It had fluttered and swayed throughout the song, disintegrating into particles of light on the last note.

But what about the other immaculate dove that "burst into light"?

I found the answer a few days later, in a book by John O'Neill, Tesla's first biographer. One day when the two of them were with *The New York Times'* science journalist, William L. Lawrence, Tesla had described the incident to them:

> I have been feeding pigeons, thousands of them for years…
>
> But there was one pigeon, a beautiful bird, pure white with light grey tips on its wings; that one was different. It was a female. I would know that pigeon anywhere.
>
> No matter where I was, that pigeon would find me; when I wanted her I had only to wish and call her and she would come flying to me. She understood me, and I understood her. I loved that pigeon.
>
> Yes, I loved that pigeon. I loved her as a man loves a woman, and she loved me… That pigeon was the joy of my life. If she needed me, nothing else mattered. As long as I had her, there was a purpose to my life.[2]

Imagine how many betrayals he must have suffered and the degree of bitter lucidity he must have achieved for his disappointment with human beings to turn into unconditional love… for a pigeon. The luckless inventor, as we know, was phobic about microbes. He never wore the same gloves twice, and he cleaned his silverware with three different napkins before every restaurant meal. Anything anyone else had touched was dangerous in his eyes, yet pigeons' notorious filth and the many diseases they are known to carry didn't bother him in the least. Tesla did everything he could for the sake of humanity, yet he knew he would get nothing but pathogens in return.

Einstein was equally lucid on that score, at least when it came to the parasite they had in common, the one he nicknamed, "the dirtiest virus in America": the unsinkable J. Edgar Hoover. It wasn't until 1955 that the head of the FBI was forced by lack of evidence to close the file he had been amassing on

Einstein for 22 years: 800 pages of errors and calumny desperately trying to prove that the esteemed physicist was a KGB mole.[3] Peeved, Hoover then decided to go after his bugbear's secretary, the faithful Helen Dukas, whom he accused in turn of spying for Moscow. Einstein's anger eventually killed him, when his abdominal aneurysm burst.

In the words of his biographer, O'Neill, Tesla goes on:

Then, one night, as I was lying in my bed in the dark solving problems, as usual, she flew in through the open window and stood on my desk. I knew she wanted me: she wanted to tell me something important, so I got up and went to her.

As I looked at her, I knew what she wanted to tell me: she was dying. And then, as I got her message, there came a light from her eyes—powerful beams of light. Yes…a powerful, dazzling, blinding light, a light more intense than I had ever produced by the most powerful lamps in my laboratory.[4]

In an academic digression, O'Neill muses about the psychoanalytic meaning of the experience: "If Tesla had not suppressed the rich mystical inheritance of his ancestors, that would have brought enlightenment. He would have understood the symbolism of the Dove." Although I hate to disappoint his biographer, Lady Bird's lover—if it is, indeed he who had dictated the message of April 8—had stuck entirely to the facts.

Time to move on to the names and dates that have come hard on the heels of the reference to the luminous-bird experience he shares with Mrs. Delpech.

I have noticed a change in my behavior in the last few weeks. When he sets me on a hunt, I know I'm going to find what I'm looking for. A kind of reflex reaction has replaced the thrill of the chase, the initial excitement. Not that I've gotten bored or blasé, but I have grown accustomed to it. There's no longer anything magical about the process itself, nor about realizing my role in it. I'm not incredulous, spellbound, or amazed anymore. I just set to work like an automaton. Efficiency and the outcome, which I can always consider later, are all that counts. I wouldn't say it is conditioning exactly, but it has become a habit, almost a reflex. It's more like the awakening of my hunter's instinct than a sign of yielding to his will. Show me the scent, and I'm on its tracks: I hunt it down and fetch it back.

For that matter, flushing out my prey is getting easier and easier to do. They seem to come out of the woodwork right before my eyes. All I have to do is clamp on and dissect them methodically: figure out where to bite and grind up the facts, eyewitness accounts, and intentions. All of which leads me to wonder if the point of all this research might not simply be to provide me with *practical drills* rather than getting me to discover and transmit startling revelations. Could it be that my capacity for assimilation and discernment is being tested? Is my scientific and psychological understanding being refined in order to develop my aptitude for achieving the posthumous goals of a forgotten genius? Or at least those of the entity, the egregore of all the "Tesla data"—the true and the unlikely, the false imprecisions and truncated truths, the fruit of true plots and conspiratorial hyperbole...

In other words, I am torn between two extremes: hypertrophy of the ego and growing paranoia. I need to calm down, stay neutral, smile slightly, give a piercing look, alternately raise my eyebrows and furrow my brow.

Here we go—it's deciphering time.

I take a deep breath and type the first date mentioned in the message—October 17, 1945—into the search field, which sends me to various events: a ruling about the legal status of tenant farmers; Colonel Peron's release from a Buenos Aires jail; and FBI file number 100-2237, concerning Nikola Tesla. Annex 2, Document 13 is a memo from October 17, 1945. It has been copiously redacted with a heavy black pen before being declassified.

It focuses on three of Tesla's inventions: the controversial "death ray," a plan for a revolutionary torpedo, and a kind of anti-tank cannon. All were developed with the help of his assistant, Bloyce Fitzgerald, presented in the memo as being able to provide access to many of the late inventor's secrets. He is the one who "voluntarily" steered the FBI to the Hotel Governor Clinton, where Tesla had lived from 1930 to 1933, and where he had left a model "related to wireless transmission of electricity" in a safe.

Once again, all it took was a single date to expose J. Edgar Hoover's lies. Hoover had publicly stated that "the late, senile inventor left no documents relating to any hypothetical research whatsoever." I get goose-bumps just *thinking* about what the not-yet-declassified file 100-2239—the one the incorporeal mole informed me about on March 24—might contain, if its existence were ever confirmed.

But I mustn't let speculation distract me from facts, so let's stay on the trail of what's in his message of April 8. I add the second element provided ("Conroy") to the date I had initially searched for. In the same file released by the FBI, replete with the usual redacting, is an older report dating back to March 19, 1943, and signed E. E. Conroy. I check: he was an FBI agent assigned to the New York bureau, just like the message said.

Agent Conroy sent Director Hoover a note in which he expressed his suspicion that one Sava Kosanovic (the third name mentioned by my informer) probably removed the documents from the inventor's safe after the older man died. Kosanovic is none other than Tesla's nephew!

Now here is where things start to get really crazy: the declassified FBI file (Annex 2, Document 5) specifies that the N.Y. bureau had been "asked" by Washington's top brass to "discreetly contact the New York City D.A.'s office to discuss the possibility of arresting Kosanovic and charging him with theft, in order to recuperate various documents he is believed to have taken from Tesla's safe."[5]

To add insult to injury, the inventor's nephew was a high-ranking diplomat with the Yugoslavian embassy![6] The astonishing idea of charging a diplomat from a Nazi-occupied nation in the midst of the war—for the the actual "theft" of documents pertaining to America's defense that he was an heir to, let alone to cover up their disappearance in order to avoid embarrassing the U.S. Army, as several witnesses' accounts suggest—was soon dropped. Instead, a new strategy was adopted, leading us to yet another enigma: no one knows what pressure, leaks, calculations, or blunders led Hoover's FBI to relinquish "Tesla's estate" to the OAP—the Office of Alien Property.

Granted, the "aliens" in question are the overseas kind, not the extraterrestrial kind, but still, the FBI's decision is all the harder to understand when one considers that Tesla had been a U.S. citizen since 1891. His belongings, therefore, had no business winding up at the OAP. The Office accepted the "gift" nonetheless. Had the idea been to drown his memory in international waters?

Let's get back to the notes and documents Tesla left behind. Although the FBI continued to strenuously deny their existence, they also sent them to a technical consultant for the National Defense Research Commission for thorough examination. The consultant in question was an eminent electrical engineer by the name of Trump. Having carefully studied the photostat copies and microfilms the federal agency had provided him, he wrote the "Trump report," mentioned in the message of April 8. The report's conclusion is as follows: "There is nothing in these documents of significant interest to our country or that could be considered a risk if it were to fall into enemy hands.

Therefore, I see no technical or military reason for preserving these goods any longer."[7]

How might that last sentence be understood? Was he suggesting the documents be handed over to Tesla's Yugoslavian heirs, or that they be "officially" destroyed, not because of any potential danger they might represent, but, as he makes clear, due to their lack of "significant interest"? It should be recalled that some of the documents concerned revolutionary weapons, while others explained how to provide unlimited power to the planet for free. Granted, the latter project might have represented a danger for the power industry, but the U.S. Army believed—as can be seen in Document 77 of FBI file 100-2237—that Tesla's "death ray" was their "only defense against the atomic bomb."

As my research unfolded, I was able to confirm that the above-mentioned documents had definitely been studied and perhaps even used, "in experiments being made for national defense purposes by the U.S. Army Air Force Equipment Laboratory, Propulsion and Accessories subdivision," as the subdivision's director, Colonel Holliday, put it.

And now the fifth person named in the message, Lloyd B. Shaulis, enters the scene. On September 5, 1945 (the third date provided), Shaulis, an OAP staff-member, received a letter from Colonel Holliday requesting photostat copies of the documents from Tesla's estate that had been annotated by John Trump (who had described them as "without interest" and advised destruction). Shaulis conveyed them to the Equipment Laboratory with a formal cover letter stipulating,

> These data are made available to the Army Air Force by this office on the understanding that they are to be used by you in certain experiments that are being made for national defense purposes. When the documents have served your purpose, please return them to this office.[8]

Nice try. Nothing was ever returned. In fact, it was the last time the OAP—or any other federal agency, for that matter—ever explicitly admitted to having Tesla's plans and projects for secret weapons in their possession. The second date in the message, October 19, 1945, seems to be an indirect reference to the weapons. It corresponds to a report from the Senate's Military Affairs Committee about "Top Secret Military" patents confiscated by the U.S. Army in the offices and factories of the Third Reich and transferred to American companies.

The one clear conclusion we can draw after having examined all the documents is that lies and contradictions were indeed rampant, as our informer seemed to be implying. To sum things up: between the 1943 official communiqué and the 1980 declassification that proved they had been lying, the FBI denied ever having found any documents whatsoever in Tesla's safe. During that time, they relinquished them to the OAP, the department for "alien property."

Over the course of several different Senate and journalistic investigations, the OAP went from acknowledging having studied Tesla's secret notes to denying their very existence, via declaring they had sealed the contents of Tesla's safe without having opened it. They eventually admitted having "lost" the documents that they hadn't, to hear the tell it, had anything to do with in the first place.

So, by the end of this absurd imbroglio, does anyone actually know what happened to Tesla's last projects? Did his nephew the ambassador get his hands on them, or was it the FBI, the USSR, the Nazis, or the U.S. Army after fall of the Third Reich? The only thing we know for sure is that after a long, drawn-out lawsuit against the United States, Tesla's nieces and nephews managed to get the inventor's ashes, the scale models of his inventions, and all of his documents returned to Belgrade in 1950. The only items not returned were the ones from the safe in the Hotel New Yorker. So, we're back to square one: where have the papers disappeared to?

The last word belongs to the commander of the Aeronautics Systems Division. On July 30, 1980, in response to a Freedom of Information Act request, a spokesperson for Wright-Patterson Air Force Base stated:

> The organization [Equipment Laboratory] that performed the evaluation of Tesla's papers was deactivated several years ago. After conducting an extensive search of lists of records retired by that organization, in which we found no mention of Tesla's papers, we concluded the documents were destroyed at the time the laboratory was deactivated.[9]

*

That's it? Then why bother dragging me on that wild-goose chase? Did the late Tesla, assuming it really was him, guide me through that long, military-administrative snafu just so that I would realize that the documents from his safe—successively stolen, impounded, declared imaginary, without interest, lost, and inadvertently destroyed—have actually been the basis for every more-or-less secret weapon made since? From the death beam to the HAARP[10] program's hypothetical ability to control everything from the climate to people's thoughts, relegating the atomic bomb to the rank of an obsolete bugaboo—is it all him?

I will leave ownership of those allegations to the deceased. It is true, however, that the Military Intelligence services he mentions in his message do seem to corroborate that notion. In a note from 1947, for instance, Tesla's documents are described as "extremely important"—the very same documents they would claim shortly afterward to have accidentally destroyed.

Are all of these contradictory disinformation operations aimed at convincing people that the death ray—or the death beam Superman went up against in a 1941 cartoon—was no more than an urban legend, the brainchild of a doddering old man trying to attract people's attention?

No documents, no beam: case closed.

Yet on February 11, 2014, at the Singapore Airshow, there was an official presentation of the Death Beam, which had been rechristened "Iron Beam" for the occasion. Financed by the Israeli Army and able to destroy rockets and artillery in four seconds—thanks to a "directed high-energy laser beam" —this "economical and precise" weapon is in final development stages at Rafael Advanced Defense Systems Ltd.[11] When asked if it was based on Nikola Tesla's Death Beam, one of the firm's spokespersons replied that he had never heard of that person.

*

The April 8 communication ends on a consolatory note—another red herring?—with a reference to a certain Lieutenant Colonel Tom Bearden. Considering what a little research tells me about the officer, I'm actually surprised my correspondent hadn't mentioned him in the March 23 message about his perpetuators.

With degrees in both math and physics, Bearden, a retired army officer whose specialty was missile guidance, is a member of the Academy of Sciences of Alabama, his home state. A colorful figure, he leads both the Society of Nuclear Engineers and the Association of Distinguished American Scientists. But first and foremost, he is the head of CTEC, a company doing R&D on systems for extracting the unlimited free wireless electricity from the quantic void that Nikola Tesla dreamed of. In terms of free energy, scalar waves, extraterrestrial intelligence, and "aggressive" humanitarian discourse, Bearden is the most hard-hitting, media-savvy, and controversial of the lonely reviled old pigeon lover's acolytes.

Bearden has discovered and written about a "remote quantic device that multiplies the space-time it is connected to." For more details about his innovations and promises, check out either Bearden's own site,[12] or any of the many sites devoted to free-energy researchers or those who disparage them.[13] Some people see him as a savior, others as a hoaxer... and still others as a smokescreen deliberately crafted by conventional-energy monopolies.

Without getting entangled in the polemic around the old soldier who neither the industrial lobbies nor the rationalists have managed to silence, it seems reasonable to wonder where he came up with all of his discoveries, and ideas for machines and devices. Did he come up with them all on his own, did he somehow acquire access to the supposedly mislaid or destroyed "Tesla documents"... or was the information communicated to him posthumously by the grandfather of free energy? When the various possibilities are raised in videotaped interviews,[14] the Lieutenant Colonel's wordless smile seems not to exclude any of them, while carefully avoiding spilling military secrets, damaging his own credibility or upsetting his investors.

Before leaving this topic, let me add that the last person named in Tesla's message, Andrija Puharich (1919-1995), is an American parapsychologist known for his work on human knowledge and mastery of electricity at the time of the Pharaohs.[15] Once again, it's a mix of the hard-hitting and the lightweight, the credible and the wooly. He, too, inspires as much questionable fervor as suspicious bad-mouthing. Puharich has repeatedly discussed the Soviets' use of scalar weapons "inspired" by Tesla's work.[16] He has also stated that extraterrestrial muses sent the Serbian inventor mental images of his inventions. These allegations provide a singular resonance to this unusual confession in Tesla's autobiography:

> As time went on, I began to realize that my thoughts were being forged by impressions that were external to my own personal sphere. It gradually became flagrant to me that I was both a vessel and an automaton. Someone is showing me things so that I can create them.[17]

Is that why Puharich's name is mentioned?

As far as the equation that ends the message goes, the physicists I have shown it to say that it "gives an approach to zero that doesn't actually exist." Well that sure helps. Taking pity on me, one of the physicists suggests I look into the work of a mathematician called Majorana. The name rings a vague bell. Eagle-eyed readers may have noticed that I had forgotten one of the names from the April 8 list. The very first one, in fact. Is this a gentle reminder?

"I met Ettore Majorana," the specter dictated to Geneviève, spelling out the name in a respectful tone of voice. Wikipedia informs me that Majorana was an Italian math prodigy. Described by the Nobel laureate Enrico Fermi as "a genius comparable to Galileo and Newton," he may have died at the age of 32 on March 27, 1938.

I say "may have" because his body has never been found.

In a farewell letter, Majorana told his friend, the physicist Carrelli, "I will keep a fond memory of them all[18] at least until 11 o'clock tonight, possibly later too." The most commonly accepted theory about his disappearance is that, depressed about the advent of the atomic bomb, whose development and military use he had predicted, he drowned himself by jumping into the sea off the ship he was taking from Palermo to Naples. The only problem with the theory is photos of him were taken in Argentina 17 years later. Rumor has it that he seemed not to have aged in the least.

Articles from the time offer a range of explanations for the Argentine sighting: a doppelganger, a face-lift, or time travel. With nothing else to go on, the event was soon forgotten, and Majorana's memory has lived on mostly through the equation his peers named after him. Until March 2011, that is, when the D.A. for Rome reopened the investigation because of an unsettling statement. An eyewitness swore that in 1955, Majorana had presented some significant scientific discoveries at a conference in Buenos Aires. But when the witness began to query him about his sources, the mathematician suddenly disappeared, and no one has ever reported seen him again.

So the Italian police dug the photos taken in Argentina out of their files and had them analyzed. *The Reparto Investigazioni Scientifiche*, Italy's answer to C.S.I., found 10 points of perfect similarity between the face in the Argentine photos and Majorana's in 1938. So it really had been him 17 years later.

It was then pointed out that the year before he first disappeared, Majorana had announced the discovery of a "stable particle that is both matter and antimatter." Sci-fi buffs instantly leapt to the conclusion that the Italian mathematician had vanished into thin air during a space-time experiment. Having disappeared in 1938, he instantly reappeared in 1955, long enough to communicate the results of his research to scientists from the future. On February 4, 2015, the D.A. of Rome settled for publishing a statement voiding his office's initial declaration of death. And that is how Majorana was officially resurrected, for the period from 1938 to 1955, anyway.

*

In his following messages, the presumptive Tesla doesn't say anything else about his "encounter" with Majorana. So what was the point of mentioning it? Had it been just a friendly chat between contemporary scientists, or a hologram-type "visit" that had taken place after the mathematician's mysterious disappearance? It wasn't until June 28, right after I proofread this chapter, that I received the following answer to my question… even though I hadn't raised it with the medium: "At 3 a.m., Tesla came to tell me, 'I met Ettore Majorana in New York. He came to see me at home after my accident. He had just arrived from Los Roques, Venezuela. He was coming from Germany, too. It was on January 11, 1942. I was still very weak.'"

The word "accident" undoubtedly refers to the incident when Tesla—who was 85 by then—got hit by a cab one evening on his way to feed the pigeons in Bryant Park. He never truly recovered from it. So was the post scriptum intended to confirm the theory of space-time ubiquity, or was it meant to prove that Majorana had indeed faked his death in 1938 and gone on to travel the world incognito?

When I add "Los Roques" to a search on the forever-young mathematician's name, what turns up is that several eyewitnesses corroborate having spotted him—still looking like a youthful dandy—in Venezuela between 1955 and 1959. The information was convincing enough that the prosecutor in Rome decided to extend his certificate of survival for an extra four years before closing the case for good. Etienne Klein, a physicist and renowned Einstein specialist, has written a fascinating book about Majorana's work and the "living riddle" he still represents for some people.[19]

*

Getting back to the morning of April 8, 2016, Geneviève Delpech calls right after texting me what her correspondent's voice dictated at dawn. "I forgot to write down the end of the message," she says. "It was so strange, Didier. I don't know what to make of it."

"Why, what did he say?"

"He's never said anything like that before."

She swallows.

I wait for her to go on.

Silence.

I prompt her.

After hesitating for about five whole seconds, she spits it out, sounding terribly serious, almost alarmed even: "He told me when he'd be back!"

1. Geneviève Delpech, *Le Don d'ailleurs*, op. cit.
2. John O'Neill, *Prodigal Genius*, David McKay Co, 1944.
3. *Le Point*, 18 August, 2016.
4. John O'Neill, *Prodigal Genius*, op. cit.
5. The FBI's Nikola Tesla file, No. 100-2237, note from January 9, 1943.
6. Serbia and Croatia were incorporated into Yugoslavia at the end of World War I.
7. Margaret Cheney, *Tesla: Man Out of Time*, op. cit.
8. Margaret Cheney, *Tesla: Man Out of Time*, op. cit.
9. Margaret Cheney, *Tesla: Man Out of Time*, op. cit.
10. See Chapter 19.
11. Reuters dispatch, February 11, 2014.
12. www.cheniere.org/toc.html
13. www.rationalwiki.org
14. www.youtube.com/watch?v=wypYFe3JXdE
15. Andrija Puharich, *Le Champignon magique, secret des pharaons*, Tchou, 1977.
16. www.marcseifer.com
17. Nikola Tesla, *My Inventions*, op. cit.
18. Translator's note: "them all" refers to his friends and colleagues at the Naples Physics Institute.
19. Etienne Klein, *En cherchant Majorana, le physicien absolu (Looking for Majorana, the Absolute Physicist*, Flammarion, Equateurs, 2013.

18

"See you on Tuesday!"

The weekend is drawing to a close, and the medium has had neither an apparition nor the slightest peep in her left ear since the message on Friday morning. There's nothing surprising about that: after all, her visitor from the hereafter had said, "See you on Tuesday," right? Making an appointment like that, which is highly unusual, could be a display of his omnipotent free will, or it could just as easily indicate submission to his connection's imperatives (i.e., his need to adapt to outside conditions, Geneviève's psychic state or even her schedule).

I have an important appointment this Tuesday, April 12, too; one that is perfectly down-to-earth but related to this whole experience nonetheless. Today's meeting should be crucial to the future of my film about Chloé, the medium Albert Einstein's spirit occupies and then abandons. In the midst of an interview with the actress I'm hoping will take the role, Geneviève calls.

"Can I see you this evening?"

I take that to mean the ghost was as good as his word. I ask for details, but she doesn't want to say anything on the phone.

At 7 p.m., I take a seat at the back of the bar where we're meeting. She rushes in with five pages of notes, explaining that she didn't have time to copy everything that Tesla, who was "in great shape," had dictated to her at 4 o'clock that morning. "But that's not all," she adds, whipping out her phone.

My pulse speeds up. Last week, when she explained that her correspondent had told her exactly when he'd be back, I made a daring request: "Do you think you could try to take a picture of him?" It was more about gathering complementary information than about wanting proof.

My entreaty didn't surprise her, but that didn't make her any less uncomfortable with it. She replied in a tone of voice that betrayed her qualms, "You don't mean sneaking a pic without asking first, do you?"

Without stopping to think, I answered, "No, ask if he's okay with it. We'll see how it goes."

She blushed and said, "I can try, but I've never done that before, Didier. *I* see them, but I have no idea if they can impact film or be captured digitally."

I explained what I was thinking. Knowing her night visitor, if he thought reproducing his ectoplasmic image would fit into his communication strategy, I was sure he'd figure out a way to make it happen.

"Have a look," Geneviève sighs, four days later, as she opens the photo roll on her phone. "But I should warn you, Didier, they didn't come out very well. You're going to be disappointed. Well, here they are, anyway."

At first glance, I'm so taken aback, I nearly drop her phone.

She sighs, adding, "When he's there with me, he's absolutely radiant. His presence is so much stronger than this."

What can I say? I've already seen plenty of so-called "paranormal" photos. They generally lean toward more or less vague suggestions of shapes, outlines or faces; whereas this is an actual portrait in black and white with a touch of sepia. [See Figure 1]

It shows a man in his fifties or sixties, in a formal pose. He looks as alive as you or me. The resemblance is striking. The shot is not a close-up, but it is in focus. The gaze is intense—even the crow's feet and the bridge of his nose, which contrast with the smooth, cloud-colored forehead, are quite clear. The feeling the photo generates is neither morbid nor sensational. But my very first impression, what strikes me right away, is that this disincarnated consciousness *is hard at work*. I can't help but wonder how much energy it required (and where he might have drawn it from) to materialize to that extent the likeness of a body that no longer exists.

I ask Geneviève how she took it.

"I didn't even have to ask him if it was all right. He walked toward me and struck a pose like a model, as though he were agreeing to let himself be *taken*. That was the impression I got, anyway. So I grabbed my phone. He gave himself a bit more contrast. I was trembling like a leaf. I'm actually surprised the photo isn't blurry, my hands were shaking so. The other strange thing is that although he was standing about 10 feet away from me,

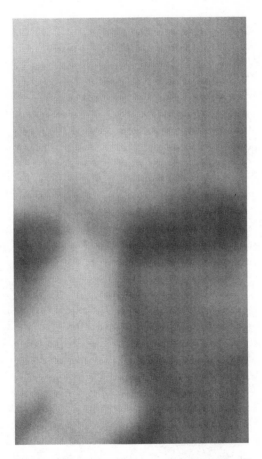

Figure 1. [April 12, 2016 - Tesla's "manifested" image]

I wound up with a close-up rather than a full-length portrait."

I try to suppress a smile. Thinking about which part of all this strikes her as implausible tickles my funny bone. She wound up taking six photos in short bursts, not counting the last one, which is completely black. There are three fuzzy, medium shots. I can't really make anything out in them, aside perhaps, from what my imagination suggests. I can't help thinking they're "typical" ectoplasmic photos, the kind you see in the archives of the International Metapsychical Institute.[1]

And then there are the three close-ups. They are so stunningly precise, so faithful in the expression, if not the skin or hair texture. It's as though the "subject" deliberately focused on making his attitude realistic in order to be recognizable. For what it's worth, in Google's portrait gallery of Tesla, which includes photos of him at different ages, I think I've found the portrait that seems to have inspired or *modeled* the materialization that Geneviève snapped.

I can practically hear the skeptics' sniggering at that hypothesis. As far as they're concerned, the medium took a photo of the old snapshot and photoshopped it in hologram mode.

What can I say? Do they really think Michel Delpech's widow and I are going to pull a stunt like that for the masochistic pleasure of making fools of ourselves? Granted, there were no witnesses to the photo session. All we can offer non-believers is our good faith, our good word, and the evidence, accompanied by a few expert opinions and comments.

Is it a photographable illusion, the capture of remanent waves, or the "pure and simple" projection of a disincarnated conscience deliberately reconstituting its own appearance the way a living person would get dressed before going out?

The photographic annals of parapsychology, including recent images from the Transcommunication Research Centre in Luxembourg, have established one thing conclusively: when the deceased attempt to make themselves visible to us, they always show themselves in a flattering light, at an age and with a bearing that respects both their physical and moral integrity. Geneviève, for instance, got a Tesla from the grand era, a spry gentleman in his 50s, thinly veiled behind an austere elegance. If you accept the Centre's logic, then of course he wouldn't have chosen to garb himself in the shell of the scrawny, zombie-like creature from his last years at the Hotel New Yorker. The same thing goes for my father, and Albert and Michel, too.

"Our conception of space is different from yours," the (even then) late Frederic Myers wrote via the pen of fellow medium Geraldine

Cummins. "I have but to concentrate my thought for what you might call a moment, and I can build up a likeness of myself, send that likeness speeding across our vast world to a friend, to one, that is, in tune with me."[2]

The only other possible explanation for this shot is a theory that is rational but could seem unreasonable to anyone who doesn't know about Ted Serios, a hotel employee who participated in experiments at the University of Denver in the 1970s. His case proved that the human mind could print an image on film through the power of thought alone. In strictly controlled tests in a university lab, Serios repeatedly managed to make mental images suggested to him—a moped, a steam locomotive, prehistoric people, etc.—appear on a Polaroid instead of his own face, which the researcher was photographing.[3]

Could it be that Geneviève managed to make the product of her own capacities as a clairvoyant appear on her phone? One way of answering those questions would reach me the very next day in the shape of three more photos. The first two would arrive through a different but equally mysterious channel, and the third would be "manufactured" right before my eyes.

"Look what I got when I woke up this morning," the medium writes at 10 a.m. on Wednesday. "I don't know where it came from. Is it your house?" [See Figures 2 and 3 below]

Two black-and-white photos are attached to her message. The first one is blurry, the second sharper. It is also framed somewhat differently, zooming in a bit on an old house with a thatched roof and a hill behind it. The house is surrounded by trees, and there is another building right next door. No, it isn't my house, though I have an inkling whose house it might be.

I've been reworking the beginning of the "Sky Engineer" chapter, the one about Nikola's youth on his family's farm near Smiljan. A quick Google search confirms my intuition: the images are of Tesla's Smiljan childhood home.

I'm only half-surprised by the search results. I actually come across the *selfsame* photo, give or take a few details—such as framing, leaves, and light. It probably dates back to the late 19th century, when Tesla's international fame was at its height, which would explain why a journalist would bother to take a photograph of an otherwise ordinary farm.

I also come across a photo of what the place looks like now. His

Figures 2 & 3 [April 13, 2016 - two photos of Tesla's Smiljan childhood
home mysteriously appear on Genevieve's phone]

birthplace has been entirely renovated, including the addition of a slate roof. Right next door, the church where Nikola's father used to celebrate Mass has also been restored. In front of it stands a huge statue of the Serbian national hero.

I ask Geneviève for the phone number from which she received the photos.

"My own," she replies.

How can we explain this strange phenomenon? The obvious, default explanation would only blow on the embers of suspicion and make the skeptics smirk: the medium had "obviously" used her phone to take pictures of photos on her computer screen, and then forwarded them to me.

Sure, why not?

Except that a) she doesn't have a computer, and b) why would she do such a thing? It wouldn't make any sense, although I'll grant that as absurd, complex, and pointless as it is, it isn't beyond the realm of imagination. It's not true, but it *is* humanly possible.

When it comes to the photo I wind up with shortly thereafter, however, I don't see how it can be explained away in normal, technical terms. It all started in a perfectly ordinary way: about two hours after Geneviève sent me the photo of the house in Smiljan, I get a call from my publisher. They want to know if I have an idea for the cover of the book I'm finishing up. Since Google is still open to my Tesla photo search, I pick four iconic portraits of him, make screen grabs of them, and send them to the publishing house.

When I check to see if they've been received, I realize something strange has happened. I'd sent my favorite one: the famous photo of the Serbian inventor posing with a light bulb in his hand—the one in which the light bulb is lit only by the current running through his body. The thing is, unbeknownst to me when I sent it, *I'm in the photo, too!* I'm a little above him, and behind him, too. My reflection is in the background. [See Figure 4 below]

By what sleight-of-hand could that have happened? The retina screen on my old MacBook isn't shiny enough to have enabled a result like that. Thanks to Laura Tenoudji, a Web specialist on France 2's "Télématin," I even manage to get an Apple technician to confirm that. For what it's worth, there isn't the slightest trace of my face in the other three screen

[Figure 4. April 13, 2016 photo - Unexplainable image of
Didier behind Tesla]

grabs I'd made only moments earlier, even though I was sitting in the exact same place, with the exact same light.

What's more, if you examine that one reflected portrait of me, it's actually quite strange: Tesla's portrait partially hides my face. My forehead is visible between his bangs, as though I were posing behind him. In addition, my face is cut off just below the nose, exactly the way his is in the picture the medium snapped of him from her bed.

Should I shrug it off as fortuitous or see it as a little dig? An image-editor I showed the photos to explained the long list of sophisticated special effects you would have to master to produce an image like that. Then, in that neutral tone of voice used by rational geeks for whom the virtual is in no way paranormal, he suggested a hypothesis, in the shape of a question. Might the mischievous ghost have chosen to react to my wish to immortalize his face posthumously by offering the symbolic counterpoint of our two *living* faces overlapping?

*

I cheated on my two mediums. With a third one. After a technical check-up, it is time for some ESP. I decided to pay a visit to the champion of dermo-optical perception, or "eyeless-sight," the woman whose perception of images inside sealed envelopes has been a standby of French magazines for three decades now: Yaguel Didier.

The *grande dame* of psychometric perception and loquacious tarot cards—whom heads of state and CEOs of major corporations have been known to consult with—shoehorns me into her busy schedule. She welcomes me with her signature cheerful simplicity: it has been known to disarm even the most hostile skeptics.

Once, a reporter made an appointment with Yaguel, passing herself off as an avid fan of fortune-telling in an attempt to trap her. Intending to throw up a mental block that would keep the psychic from capturing the slightest information, the journalist focused on a black screen. "What do you see, Madame Didier?" she asked in a falsely hopeful voice.

"A black screen."

Impressed, the journalist dropped the screen and was given a consultation she found to be entirely convincing.

Although we don't see each other often, I've known Yaguel for 30 years. Aside from the precision of her flashes of insight, it's her kindness that impresses me most. I'm thinking in particular of a day in 1986 when she realized that my grandmother, who showed no signs of ill health, was in fact at death's door. Yaguel later confessed that she felt she "had to" let me know, so I could be with her at the end. I will never be able to thank Yaguel enough for that combination of clairvoyance and thoughtfulness.

She fingers the thick envelope I hand her. It contains a printout of the spectral photo taken on April 12. I haven't said a word about the context or the messages I've been receiving. She closes her eyes, takes a deep breath, and starts talking. Her steady cadence refines her perceptions. I take notes, although I'm recording her as well. Here, in essence, is what she has to say:

"I can feel death. It's very present. There are three people involved, three living people, two women and a man. You feel as though you're being dragged along by your feet, don't you? You have to work fast. There's an action, a revelation, all very quick. You're being asked to fix something, to resolve it. You were chosen to do it. There are very luminous parts and very dark ones—military men, wars, trickery, and deceit. They want you to get involved. It's good, it's the right thing to do, but don't let yourself be defiled.

"The man in the photo is dead, isn't he? He always dressed in black. He was a great orator. A scientist, right? A researcher, in any case. Did he drink a lot? I see ecclesiastics around him early in life. He wants justice.

"What is this photo? An ectoplasm? Who was it?"

I pronounce Nikola Tesla's name. She doesn't recognize it. Aside from the possibility of a drinking problem that I hadn't been aware of, you could think she'd drawn everything else from the thoughts running through my brain.

I hand her a second envelope, which contains a photo of Einstein's face and a manuscript of his.

"This is exactly the opposite. I sense a living, lively, extrovert. A man... he's a writer, isn't he? He writes all the time... He's blond—

I interrupt her. "No, that's me. I'm in the photo, too, sorry. Look at the portrait that's above me in the photo."

It takes her a little while to decipher what I'm talking about. She concentrates, scanning her palm over the envelope again. Inside was a photo I'd taken as a souvenir of the day I was able to examine Einstein's handwritten notes with his calculations for the theory of special relativity at the Letters and Manuscripts museum. Einstein's portrait had been hanging over the display case.

"Oh, now this one is a horse of an entirely different color! This guy is brilliant! But he's dead. There's a lot of light around him. Cameras... he's very well known, right? Lots of honors. And hordes of women in his life. A real *bon vivant*. A sudden death, like an explosion. Someone's making a movie about him, or they're about to.

"He was Jewish, wasn't he? A very respected scientist. He lived in the United States for at least part of his life. The war was very painful for him, and there's a link between him and the man from before, a woman who connects them. It's as though the two men were from the same family. He reminds me of Einstein. Is he asking you for something, too?

"Sorry, I have to go. Someone's waiting for me."

I sum up the situation for her in a nutshell.

She nods, tells me not to worry, and ushers me out with this disconcerting piece of advice: "Don't go overboard, but do go for it."

*

It's becoming more apparent with every passing day: everyone who sees the photos of Tesla—both the close-up of his posthumous face and my reflection behind his living one—thinks they're incredible, amazing, mind-boggling… at first. Then, over time, *they get used it.* After a perfectly understandable outpouring of disbelief, of trying to figure out the optical illusion or to find a rational explanation that holds water, the authenticity emanating from the images gradually inspires a kind of serenity, of opening up to other possibilities. What if this weren't just an isolated paranormal event, but the first taste of a new normal? "Good fortune favors prepared minds," Louis Pasteur said. Signs, too. They mushroom if we accept them and try to decipher them without fear, obsession, or sacrificing our free will.

I am absolutely sure of one thing, though: the *climate* in which these phenomena take place, are shared and are commented upon definitely contributes, by resonance, to their replication. A capacity for wonder, a child's simplicity combined with an adult's serious reflection are the most efficient attributes for creating a snowball effect.

Here's a perfect example. Early in the summer, Geneviève Delpech was at the home of Dr. Jean-Jacques Charbonier, in southwest France. The two of them were giving a series of conferences under the aegis of the INREES (the Institute for Research into Extraordinary Experiences). The conferences had been meant to provide parents with ways of helping their children come to terms with the idea of death, which they have been confronted with quite a bit in the news of late.[4]

While they were driving, the medium was describing her latest exchanges with our honorable correspondents from the hereafter to the famous anesthesiologist (who has done so much to get temporary-death states officially recognized in France). When she told him about the photos, he wanted to see them, of course. Since she doesn't store anything on her phone, she called to ask me to forward them back to her. I complied.

Five minutes later, she called me back. "The most amazing thing just happened!" she exclaimed.

I'm always startled by how surprised she still is, even after decades of incredible experiences. But that enthusiasm, which never goes stale and which, by the way, she shares with Marie-France Cazeaux, surely contributes to the frequency and quality of the manifestations taking place in the two women's vicinity.

"Listen to this: I was just showing the close-up of Tesla to Jean-Jacques, who's driving, and his wife, who's in the back."

"It's fantastic!" the doctor cheerfully pipes up via the loudspeaker.

"But get this, Didier. I was telling them how I tried to take another picture of Tesla, but it didn't work. And precisely at that instant, the song on the car radio stopped—"

"It was Nino Ferrer singing 'Le Sud'" Charbonier interrupts in a clinically precise tone.

"And a woman's voice came out of the radio. It was perfectly clear, we all heard it. She said, 'Yes it did! The second photo worked, too!' And then the song came back."

The anesthesiologist and his wife confirmed the story. The three "ear-witnesses" disagreed about only one thing: at precisely what point the song had started up again. Opinions differed on whether it had picked up exactly where it had left off, or a measure further on.

Of course I immediately scanned through the photos on my phone for the last photo Geneviève had taken. I had forgotten all about it since it was so dark. It still is, except…

When I enlarge the non-image as much as possible, I find—and everyone I've shown it to without introduction describes the same thing—a night sky with constellations and unfamiliar shapes, some of which are in color. Black holes, wormholes, red dwarfs, UFOs, parallel universes? Who can say? It hadn't "worked," but that was then. In point of fact, it only hadn't worked *right away*.

"It's a star field," the astrophysicist Trinh Xuan Thuan confirms when I show him this potential slice of sky without revealing its origins.

As I enlarge the image on my iPhone, he identifies young blue stars, possibly interstellar clouds, and what might be a dwarf galaxy, although he specifies that everything would need to be confirmed.

"The reddish hue indicates both its venerable old age—about a billion years after the big bang—and the mark it leaves by the Doppler Effect as it draws away. That very bright mass over there might be in the Milky Way, near us, and the rest could be in the Andromeda galaxy, 2.5 million light-years away, but I can't say for sure. There are hundreds of billions of stars in Andromeda."

"So where did you get the photo?"

I explain to the eminent professor at the University of Virginia about the ectoplasmic photo shoot. He smiles, expressing polite surprise. Book after book, he has built ever-subtler bridges between the interplanetary void and the one defining Buddhism.[5] Yet even the fusion between science and spirituality running through his books still doesn't, he says, allow him to offer an authoritative opinion about the invisible.

I ask him, "What if it were something other than a starry sky? What if, instead of being stars, it was something infinitely small?"

"It would be less dense, wouldn't it?

The question mark is still echoing as we take our leave. Just as when I had consulted him for my *Dictionary of the Impossible*, this wise scientist never closes any doors. He hears me out, enlightens me, and allows me to make up my own mind.

*

As I write these lines, I get the feeling that the sky scene is "filling up," every time I look at it. Unfortunately, it hadn't crossed my mind at first to take successive screen shots of the picture. So I can't tell if the evolution I think I'm seeing is the fruit of my imagination or just the result of not having blown the photo up all the way at first.

Is this galaxy from nowhere a psychic projection or an illustration of earlier messages? Did it spring from that idea—suggested by the voice occupying Chérie FM—that there actually was something on that dark image after all? If so, it would bring us back to the decisive role of the observer in quantum physics, as well as the retrograde causality phenomenon that Dr. Peoc'h's experiments revealed and Tesla's message of January 14 referred to.

In the meantime, I had my own idea about whose voice had interrupted Nino Ferrer on the car radio to point us back to the photo. I had refrained from mentioning it to Marie-France Cazeaux when I told her the story on the phone, a few hours after the fact. Nevertheless, as soon as I mentioned the radio-crashing announcer, she exclaimed, "Hold on… that must have been Monique!"

Monique Simonet, retired school-teacher from Reims, France's pioneer in instrumental trans-communication, the old lady with twenty-thousand voices, had died just two weeks before. Marie-France had been in touch with her for years. On June 21, I was attending one of Charbonier and Delpech's conferences in Paris when she texted me the news of Monique's death.

And so, on this July day in 2016, "Team Tesla" was united by the subtle paths of chance and synchronicity, creating, unbeknownst to ourselves, a climate conducive to continuing the adventure… But that may prove to be pure speculation on my part. When I played a tape of Monique's voice for them, neither the Charboniers nor Geneviève were able to state unequivocally that it was the same voice they had heard on the radio.

The tape I played was from 2006. Monique is commenting on some messages she has received for me on her tape recorder. Apparently, they are from my father, who died the year before.

"I can dance!" he replies when she asks how he's feeling.

The comment doesn't surprise me, considering how much it had pained him to be an invalid for the last nine years of his life. Jean-Michel Mahieux, a sound engineer, used his software to compare the voice-without-vocal-cords to the one on my father's answering machine, which he recorded while he was still alive. Mahieux came to the conclusion there was a spectral similarity.

In a nutshell, I can't prove it was Monique's spirit that piggybacked on Nino Ferrer to join the conversation in the Charboniers' car. All I can say for sure is that, in this long series of extraordinary events, it would seem to be a logical step. Once again, there's that touch of humor I so need in order to believe in these phenomena one hundred percent. I know, there's nothing scientific about that. It's just how it is.

I'll never forget the fit of laughter we shared in Reims in 2009 in the small prefab house where Monique lived with her thousands of tapes. She'd just played the recording of the meal the family had shared after the funeral of her free-thinking spouse, who was totally hermetic to her theoretically posthumous messages. His cousins had been whining about their various ailments and the woes of old age, when everyone suddenly heard the voice of the recently deceased, as clear as a bell, mischievously commenting, "It sounds like I'm better off where I am then!"

Images and sounds materialized by a thought form, whether living or not; phenomena that seem to lead ineluctably to others: could Einstein's last prediction be starting to come true? Could we be bearing witness, with each of us contributing what we can, to the victory of his impossible Theory of Everything? Is this the end of the "soft pillow" he scorned, the end of the irrational (to his eyes) separation between the quantum world, where observers choose the reality they wish to create, and the conventional one, where they are simply subjected to it?

*

So the visual part of the message received on April 12—bursting with technical puzzles, winking allusions and unexpected extensions—wound up being quite exciting. Alas, that was not the case for the written part.

1. www.metapsychique.org (in French only)
2. Geraldine Cummins (& Frederic Myers), *The Road to Immortality*, op. cit.
3. *Journal of the American Society for Psychical Research*; Marie-Monique Robin and Mario Varvoglis, *Le Sixième Sens*, op. cit.
4. www.inrees.com
5. Trinh Xuan Thuan, *La Plénitude du vide* (*The Fullness of the Void*), Albin Michel, 2016.

19
Antenna issues

The information dictated on the morning of April 12 as a prelude to the ectoplasmic photo shoot concerns the array of thousands of towering antennae installed in Gakona, Alaska. It starts with a series of dates ranging from 1886—the year Tesla filed his first patents—to 2001. The only comment being "The HAARP system is fully operational."

For anyone who has managed to miss the hype, let me explain that HAARP stands for High-Frequency Active Auroral (as in Aurora Borealis) Research Program. A number of people—scientists, politicians, and ordinary citizens alike—believe it is probably a way to influence both the Earth's climate and its inhabitants' mental states.

I addressed this taboo subject in my *Dictionary of the Impossible*, under the letter H. It is one of my readers' favorite entries, but it also happened to be one of the most difficult and least agreeable to write. How can you ever be sure about anything to do with HAARP? Either it's one of the most destructive weapons ever developed or the biggest fake ever disseminated by conspiracy theorists. It would be tempting to prefer the second option, if it weren't for the fact that many of the rationalist critiques of the "Moby Dick of conspiracy theories" come from the program's own management. The "disinformation" branch of their PR service is every bit as impressive—in terms of stubbornness and contradictory assertions—as the unflappable J. Edgar Hoover's FBI was when they were handling the Einstein and Tesla files.

Even back in 2013, when I first started researching the topic, it strained my ability to distinguish fact from fiction. It wasn't easy to separate fake news from reality, to perceive what was a product of the omnipotent Machiavellianism of the sorcerer's apprentices and their unintentional foul-ups, or to choose between the American administration's claims of innocence and some retired employees' not-infrequent admissions of guilt.

Speaking of which, our informer had mentioned the name and address of one Dr. Patrick Flanagan. Born in the USA in 1944 and named 1997's Scientist of the Year, he lives, as indicated, in Sedona, Arizona. Another worthy heir to Tesla, he is undoubtedly one of the most gifted inventors on the planet. At age 14, he created the infamous Neurophone, still one of the most sophisticated devices in existence for controlling people's minds with electromagnetic waves. In Flanagan's expert opinion, HAARP is "not only the world's most powerful ionospheric heater, but also the most efficient device ever designed for influencing brain activity in huge swaths of the world's population."[1]

Outcome: scientists, investigators, fanatics, and retired army personnel periodically stir up the embers of this burning-hot topic, achieving little more than densifying the smokescreen. There is only one thing that we can be absolutely sure of: the measurements taken by the Demeter satellite. Every time HAARP's antennae light up to emit signals, the upper layers of the atmosphere become noticeably warmer. Physicist Jean-Jacques Berthelier, of the Centre for Terrestrial and Planetary Environment Studies, has this to say about it: "Emission coincides with a drop in atmospheric density by a factor of between two and three, and a noticeable increase in temperature, demonstrating that HAARP is able to modify the ionosphere fairly profoundly."[2]

It was on the basis of satellite measurements like those that a 1999 European Parliament investigatory committee concluded that "HAARP is a weapons system that disrupts the climate" and that "by virtue of its far-reaching impact on the environment, [it is] of global concern."[3] That sensational report had very little fallout... other than that two weeks later, the head of the investigatory committee, British Euro-MP Tom Spencer, was subjected to a customs check at a London airport and found to be in possession of gay porn and small amounts of both cannabis and cocaine. Which makes it somewhat easier to understand some British officials' embittered distrust of Brussels and Europe.

The main line of reasoning HAARP defenders harp on (as it were...) whenever they get the chance can be summarized in two points: the system was designed to *study* disturbances in the ionosphere, not to cause them. Besides, if the latter were true, they ask ingenuously, why would the

United States be the country most affected by climate change? The simplest answer to that is a biblical proverb: "He who sows the wind shall reap the whirlwind."

Other HAARP critics have pointed out that the Russians, the Chinese, and their allies have had plenty of time to develop their own HAARPs by now.[4] "Technology capable of seriously disturbing the mental health of whole populations," as a Russian parliamentary report criticizing the antennae in Alaska put it. That being said, according to some sources, the Russian equivalent of HAARP went into production some ten years prior to the American installation.[5]

What information does the presumptive Tesla have for us about a program that has been described by its supporters as perfectly inoffensive and its critics as potentially apocalyptic?

Nothing particularly ground-breaking at first glance. Nothing more than the usual explosive mix of fact and fantasy that my previous research led me to sum up in the following laundry list of issues:

> Seismic activation, global radar, particle-beam weapons, climate manipulation on a planetary scale, brain-wave manipulation, jeopardizing ecosystems, scrambling electronic-communication systems, and affecting human emotional states and mental processes.

The message, however, also mentions two issues of the *New York Times* (December 8, 1915, and December 22, 1940) in reference to a Dr. Bernard Eastlund (1938-2007). A quick investigation shows that Eastlund, an American physicist, could be considered the father of the HAARP project through his patent N° 4-686 605, filed on August 11, 1987. Lo and behold, in the patent application, I come across a reference to the above-mentioned *New York Times* articles, in which Nikola Tesla discusses his "teleforce."

Here is Tesla's description of the wave from 1915, i.e. right after he patented it: "At 300 miles per second, it can circle the globe in under a minute and a half. The weapon can also be aimed to go *through* the planet." The journalist comments that, according to Tesla's patents, the short-cut through the Earth's crust would take 27 seconds. The interviewee goes on to say that:

> It is perfectly possible to transmit electric energy without wires and to produce destructive effects remotely. I have already built a wireless transmitter that makes that possible. I described it in my technical publications referring to patent number 1-119 732, which was granted

recently, but now is not the time to discuss that sort of thing.[6]

Twenty-five years later, at the start of a new world war and in the same newspaper, "the time," seems to have come:

This "teleforce" is based on an entirely new principle of physics, that "no one has ever dreamed about." This new type of force, Mr. Tesla said, would operate through a beam one-hundred-millionth of a square centimeter in diameter, and could be generated from a special plant that would cost no more than $2,000,000 and would take only about three months to construct.

The beam, he states, involves four new inventions, two of which have already been tested. One of these is a method and apparatus for producing rays "and other manifestations of energy" in free air, eliminating the need for a high vacuum. A second is a process for producing a "very great electrical force." A third is a method of amplifying this force. The fourth is a new method for producing "a tremendous repelling electrical force." This would be the projector or the gun of the system. The voltage for propelling the beam to its objective, according to the inventor, will attain a potential of 50,000,000 volts. With this enormous voltage, he said, microscopic electrical particles of matter will be catapulted on their mission of defensive destruction.[7]

A year before the United States entered the war, the interview made commentators—who still saw the situation as humorous—chuckle. Several famous radio announcers compared the ageing inventor's "babbling" to Einstein's "pranks." Paramount asked Max Fleischer's studio to have Superman neutralize "Tesla the Terrorist." The cartoon permanently destroyed the octogenarian's credibility in the eyes of the general public. He was almost literally destroyed, too. In young people's eyes, he had become a fictional character, which made it that much easier to "disappear" him from physics books and science manuals after his death.

By referring to the interviews that the father of HAARP included in his patent application as both a reference and a tribute, the posthumous memory claiming to be Tesla seems to be expressing remorse, but is his inadvertent responsibility real or illusory? Are his discoveries really the basis for the technological nightmare many believe has been established in Alaska?

A name and address close the message: Paula Randol-Smith / P.O. Box 91 665 / Pasadena, CA 91109-1655. They lead me to an article, from the

April 1998 issue of *Exotic Research Report*, about producer Paula Randol-Smith's crusade against the HAARP project. To my surprise, I realize the details provided by my informer correspond essentially to an advertisement. The address appears on the order form included with Ms. Randol-Smith's documentary *Holes in Heaven*.

My readers should feel free to follow up on that information if they so desire. As for me, I will close this extremely sensitive chapter by copying out the message's conclusion: "Someone may be suddenly overcome by a wave of sadness. They might look for a reason in their own minds, when they might have noticed that it was caused simply by a cloud blocking out the sun."

The poetic resonance with the meteo-psychological ravages attributed to the Alaskan antennae seems obvious, and yet in this case, the presumptive Tesla is quoting himself. I came across the phrase a few days later in *My Inventions*. At the time he wrote it, just after the end of World War I, the engineer wasn't referring to climate manipulation, but rather to the therapeutic benefits of neutrinos radiating from the sun.

1. www.jp-petit.org
2. i-Télé, January 2, 2008.
3. A4 report– 0005/99 on the Environment, Security and Foreign Policy, January 14, 1999.
4. Jeane Manning and Nick Begich, *Les anges ne jouent pas de cette HAARP (Angels Don't Play This HAARP)*, Louise Courteau, 2003.
5. Report by Jean-Luc Mampaey, Peace and Security Research and Information Group, Brussels.
6. Nikola Tesla interview, *The New York Times*, December 8, 1915.
7. Idem, December 22, 1940.

20

The handprint

New clarification from the Teslan avatar on April 23, 2016:
Anything that you can see or touch, all those things are algebraically coded beyond the visible world. There is something very mysterious in the universe, something that governs the fate of everything that exists, from the smallest elementary particle to the vast cluster of the galaxies. $S = k \log W$.

When I show the formula to the theoretical physicist Dr. Christophe Galfard, he is jubilant. "It's the most beautiful formula of all! It's called Boltzmann's equation, and it's engraved on his tombstone in Vienna. It conjoins disorder and the number of possible states in which a system can be found."

To illustrate what he means, he points to the chairs around us in the café where we have met. Within each empty chair, he explains, there exists the number and weight of the people likely to sit on it. The equation is fabulous, he insists, because it unifies different theories. For instance, the state of warmth I feel depends on the number of atoms striking my skin. It's not the Theory of Everything, but it's pretty close.

"Unfortunately, he committed suicide because nobody believed in atoms, whose existence he had been trying to prove. He hanged himself in 1906, just before experimental physics proved him right."

That may be the precise moment at which I felt that we were in contact with Tesla's soul: that way he had of introducing me to a fellow misunderstood soul through a simple formula, one that had left its mark on a man's life and might have even have contributed to his death. It's typical of the sense I get of Nikola's character, both from his own writings and from those about him, let alone from the feeling that some of his messages communicate to me directly.

"S = k log W," Galfard concludes, "represents abstraction becoming reality."

The problem is that the medium who has been receiving these formulas is fed up with abstraction. She wants a sign, good news, sweet nothings, something to give her hope—she wants her man. The next day, when she summons up the courage to ask her night visitor if he has been in touch with Michel Delpech, the hologram replies with a smile. "Here is particle X. Followed by 45... then masses, a myriad. Proof that your universe is worth two. That your world is worth two."

Hoping to soothe the widow's distress by discovering the hidden symbolic meaning in those hermetic words, I google, "Particle X/45" and come across an ad for a device called a DuÒ. It's a sort of hard-core paper shredder that reduces documents to particles of 4 x 45 mm.

Busy with the upcoming publication of my novel, *On dirait nous* (*You'd Think It Was Us*), I don't have time to look any further. Just two days later, however, I happen to catch part of a program called "Science publique," on France Culture radio. Just as I'm getting into a cab, the newscaster, Michel Alberganti, is announcing:

Thanks to the new power of the LHC—the CERN particle accelerator near Geneva—physicists have detected a mysterious signal that, if it is confirmed, would be the signature of a new particle christened X... Its existence would challenge the standard model that has defined subatomic physics for the past 40 years.

In the rear-view mirror, I can see the cabbie wondering why I'm so excited by the news. After galactic-energy halos and gravitational waves, it looks like my ectoplasmic informer has offered me yet another scoop. All I have to do now is to wait for the official announcement.

Unfortunately, a short time later, in early May, the particle accelerator breaks down because a rodent gnawed through a power cable. It looks like I'll have to wait a little longer for particle X's existence to be confirmed, let alone the 45 unknown fellow particles promised by my source. "Proof that your universe is worth two," he had specified.

What exactly am I supposed to make of that last phrase? Does it validate Jean-Pierre Garnier Malet's doubling theory? I'd sent him the first equations I'd received without realizing they might contain an element able to confirm his astrophysics model. As it was, considering his triumphant reaction to the detection of gravitational waves, I wondered about the role played by stubborn physicists like him, who clung for decades to the hope that technological advances would finally prove Einstein's predictions. Could it be that scientists' fervent desire—even before the observation proving the reality of a situation, in the quantum sense—can actually influence the emergence of a given phenomenon?

"Probabilities of observing and measuring something are all that exists," starts the reply I get from Tesla's avatar, 48 hours after he alerted me to the imminent discovery of X particles. Then it goes on:

> It isn't until you observe 'something' that it shifts from an indeterminate state to a real one. Nothing physically exists until it is observed. You are still at the very beginning of the search for knowledge and understanding and not, as some people think, nearly at the end. Wendland and Radin. Niels Bohr and Werner Heisenberg."

Nothing very new or exciting for anyone who knows anything about quantum mechanics. Bohr and Heisenberg were the poster boys for it. Wendland and Radin's names, on the other hand, don't ring any bells for me. But googling them sends me to an excerpt from an autobiographical book published in 2015: *The Hand on the Mirror*, by Janis Heaphy Durham. What's the connection? I skim through the text of the book, looking for the pages where the search tool has highlighted the names.

The author, a pragmatic, happily married woman and highly successful newspaper editor in California, was hardly the type to believe in the possibilities of communication with the hereafter. In 2004, when her husband, Max, died of cancer, everything came to a screeching halt for her. Death was the end, and life had no more meaning. Until, that is, the first anniversary of his death, when a print of his right hand appeared on the steamed-up bathroom mirror. Stunned, she took a picture and checked the size, appearance, and shape of the fingers against their home videos—it matched Max's hand precisely, as though he'd stepped out of the shower and placed his hand on the fogged-up mirror.

Deeply shaken, Janis began to research the power of mind over matter. She wrote a book relaying information from scientific studies that she hadn't been aware of prior to that. The keywords from the Teslan message pointed me straight to an excerpt from that book:

> Dr. Wendland, who recently became associated with Dean Radin, Ph. D., Chief Scientist at the Institute of Noetic Sciences (IONS), conducted an experiment, and the results were published in an article

in the journal Physics Essays titled 'Consciousness and the Double-Slit Interference Pattern.'[1]

Richard Feynman, an American theoretical physicist, said of the double-slit interference pattern that it "has in it the heart of quantum mechanics. In reality, it contains the only mystery." Yet the protocol hidden behind that abstruse formulation is very simple really, practically as easy as pie. Cut two slits side-by-side into a sheet of metal and point a beam of light toward the slits so that it shines through both of them. Is it possible that by concentrating on the beam's trajectory, you can get the light to pass through only one of the slits through sheer force of will?

The answer is yes. We have proof of it, now that there are precise-enough instruments of measurement to reveal this effect of *intention* on a law of physics, which, by the same token, must be modified.

There is one condition though: no other witness before you can have observed that particular beam of light passing "naturally" through *those particular slits*. Otherwise, just like in Dr. Peoc'h's retrograde-causality experiments, it will become impossible to change that reality once it has been validated by the first observation and is as good as writ in stone. In other words, our gaze creates the world. The experiments led by Wendland and Radin were directly inspired by a theory called the Copenhagen Interpretation, which was published in 1924 by Niels Bohr and Werner Heisenberg.

Voilà: the four names mentioned in the April 26 message have been united.

At this point in piecing the puzzle together, the elements supplied by Tesla-from-the-hereafter are coming together beautifully. You can start to see where he's headed, how he's guiding and leading us there. Of course, when I share what I've learned with Geneviève, she's most interested in the story of the American woman. Like her, she had lost her husband to cancer and found, within the swirls and eddies of mourning, little-known facets of science. She finds the parallel impressive. But it doesn't stop there.

Geneviève orders Janis Heaphy Durham's book. On the morning of May 5, having barely started reading it, she finds a handprint on her bathroom tiles, even though they're not fogged up. We're talking about a house she just moved into recently, and where she lives alone.

Her immediate reaction? Disappointment. It's not Michel's hand, not even close. It's too big overall: the fingers too thin; the thumb abnormally long. She wipes it off with a sponge. Or rather, she tries to, but the print remains. She goes at it with Ajax, Mr. Clean, and chlorine bleach, but nothing works. The unknown hand turns out to be indelible, so she decides to snap a picture of it with her phone and send it to me.

Wasting no time on far-fetched theories, I go straight to Google images to check out Suspect Number 1. Comparing the size and shape of his fingers, there's no doubt about it: with its distinctively outsized thumb, the hand that left a print on Geneviève's tiles resembles Nikola Tesla's in every particular.

As soon as I text her the results of my expert evaluation, the medium goes back to her bathroom to take a sharper photo, but the print, which had stood up to bleach, has vanished on its own. Our invisible friend's little wink has been understood, so the sign has lost its *raison d'être* and is gone for good.

Once again, having established the inconceivable, questions remain: could Geneviève be, if not the psychic source, at least the vector for the print? Had her unconscious desire for a sign from her deceased husband—like the widow in the story she'd been reading the night before—become the channel for Tesla's intention to the extent that his posthumous consciousness was inspired to leave a print on the tiles? But those questions aren't what matters most to Geneviève. She's hoping that such a potent wink from the other side might be a harbinger, a "first hand" impression heralding her husband's imminent arrival.

Oh well… Michel Delpech's spirit chooses not to manifest itself to his widow through handprints. Instead, it seems to be starting out more impishly, with minor electrical disturbances: ringing the doorbell when nobody's there, opening and shutting the electric gate when there's nothing there to trip the infrared sensor… Over the weeks, other phenomena will appear: automatic writing, his voice becoming audible in her left ear, trans-images reconstituting his face on the screen of her cell phone… But I should bow out here. It's Geneviève's prerogative to recount how their enduring connection was made manifest.[2]

After ten days with no news from the Sky Engineer, and only the briefest of messages from the Light-Beam Rider ("Thanks for everything, I'm occupied elsewhere right now,") it seems that the adventure into which Geneviève's messages drew me is coming to a close—or at least about to leave me enough of a respite to finish writing my account of it. As if to confirm that intuition, as I am writing these lines, a page pops up on my Mac without my having typed or clicked on anything: *Russian Scientists and Nikola Tesla's Tower*.

It's baffling but not surprising. After all, there might be a perfectly plausible technical explanation. About two weeks ago, I ran my cursor over a YouTube banner for the video, thinking I should watch the Next News Network report as soon as I could, and now it has brought itself back to my attention. Is it the result of an algorithm, a minor bug related to my search history? *Or is the information itself trying to attract my attention?* Directly, without bothering to go through one of my human mediums.

Whatever the case may be, two Russian brothers, Leonid and Sergey Plekhanov, graduates of Moscow's Institute of Physics and Technology, decided to build a functioning replica of Tesla's tower, a sort of "Wardenclyffe Tower II," in their own country. Having spent five years carefully studying and modeling Nikola Tesla's patents, these young engineers say they are convinced that with the advantage of modern-day materials and technology, Tesla's system for drawing and transmitting energy from and through the ionosphere should allow for the distribution of clean, unlimited electricity throughout their vast country. They explain:

> The transmitters would be capable of sending millions of gigahertz-frequency volts into the atmosphere in the shape of radio waves. All motorized vehicles could run on zero-pollution electricity. In addition, depending on the number of transmitters and their capacity, one ought to be able to drive one's car across the whole country without needing particularly large batteries. As for people's homes, they would have antennae rather than cables connecting them to the grid.

Moreover, Tesla's Muscovite disciples don't intend to stop there (i.e., at a single tower weighing under two tons, as opposed to Wardenclyffe's 60, and costing $800,000). In their crowdfunding pitch on Indiegogo, they flaunt a boldly planetary ambition: "A 38,000 square-mile solar array in a nice, sunny desert somewhere could provide for all our global power needs," they declare. For a perfectly reasonable sum, if everyone chips in: just $20 trillion. "That's a pretty steep price to pay for free energy," as one visitor to the page quips dryly. Declaring themselves true to Tesla's spirit, the brothers have pledged to "make the results freely available online once the tower has been put into operation."[3]

The only hitch is that the most recent news of their project dates back to the spring of 2015. Have they hit a technical snag, run out of funds, or faced opposition from Russian authorities? Or perhaps the silence is strategic, an information embargo to add to the impact of an upcoming announcement?

It makes you wonder who will win the race for free energy and resolve the energy crises hammering the world. Japan, Malaysia, and Hungary seem to be in the lead in terms of home generators, but India communicates the most on the topic. They have even gone so far as to defend the project being developed by one Dr. Tewari, former Executive Director of the Nuclear Power Corporation of India. "India will not suppress Tewari's free-energy generator, despite threats from the U.K., U.S., and Saudi Arabia," according to an online petition that has already garnered over 10,000 signatures.[4] None of which keeps some sites from insisting it is all just an illusion.

That's where I am in my reflections when a chance letter draws my attention to a different source of "natural" energy. A source to which Tesla devoted years of obsessive work, a source his message of March 24 settled for referring to only briefly, albeit lyrically, but one whose effects he famously reproduced in his lab in Colorado Springs: lightning. Specifically, ball lightning, which he was the first to tame. Who knows, perhaps it will surpass all the fantasies and potential of electricity from the void, establishing itself as the greatest hope for humanity and enabling the as-yet-unattainable grail of nuclear fusion.

Why didn't his presumptive consciousness delve into it more deeply with the mediums? The very moment I formulate that question, I realize that I already know the answer. I didn't need to receive the details through the deceased persons' channel because the living had already informed me. The only hitch is that I didn't pay much attention at the time, and simply set the information aside for later.

It would seem that I had to write an entire book in order to see exactly what it was that my informers might be hoping I would finally realize: the impossible synthesis between the free energy Tesla had dreamed of and "clean and peaceful" nuclear fusion. The one, we can assume, that would represent the only acceptable (to Einstein's conscience) alternative to atomic fission, which, despite his best intentions, led to the bomb over Hiroshima inspired by his famous formula about releasing energy: $E = mc^2$.

1. Janis Heaphy Durham, *The Hand on the Mirror*, Grand Central Publishing, 2015.
2. Geneviève Delpech, *Te retrouver (Finding You Again)*, First, 2017.
3. www.inhabitat.com/russian-physicists-launch-campaign-to-rebuild-teslas-wardenclyffe-tower-and-power-the-world/ and www.pbs.org/newshour/science/russian-physicist-brothers-plan-resurrect-teslas-wardenclyffe-tower
4. http://reflectionofmind.org/india-permits-free-energy-technology-despite-threats-uk-us-saudi-arabia/

21
The next bolt from the blue?

On December 31, 2014, I received a two-page letter—from a perfectly earthbound correspondent, an independent researcher who included his telephone number and postal and e-mail addresses. He hoped I would be interested in hearing about some important discoveries he had made, and that I might include them in a follow-up to my *Dictionary of the Impossible*. Discoveries, he specified, that had been gathering dust on his shelves, since scientific journals had declined to publish his findings. The research in question focused on ball lightning.

At the time, I had found the letter intriguing and had meant to write back to request more details, but then I lost track of it. It has just risen to the surface again, thanks to a sort of landslide of files on my desk. The man's name is Michel Brisset, and here is what he wrote:

Dear Sir,

I am an absolute nobody and that suits me just fine. Please rest assured: the purpose of this letter is not to obtain either fame or fortune for myself (...) It has been granted to me to observe how the energy from two bolts of lightning can be coupled, confined, condensed, and mastered in under three seconds inside a self-engendered 20-cm-diameter magnetic sphere that explodes like a supernova after six or seven seconds.

Contrary to currently accepted theories in both nuclear physics and astrophysics, gravitation does not cause fusion, but the other way around. Fusion is what creates confinement, and very little energy seems to be needed for that. The intensity and guidance of the plasma flux via the coupling of the lightning bolts does it all. Ball lightning behaves like a ball of energy-filled electrons.

In light of the aforementioned principle, it makes perfect sense that despite the tens of billions of euros that have been sunk into it, the international ITER[1] program has been unable to demonstrate the feasibility of a reactor using the principle of nuclear fusion. That principle is diametrically opposed to the Tanaris effect (named after the Celtic god of the sky and of lightning) (...) The plasma state is the most widespread state for matter in the universe, and the Tanaris effect is the overlapping of everything that is capable of organizing and achieving the quantum effect on Earth in a few seconds.

So now you know...

I am offering the information in Michel Brisset's letter to whoever feels concerned by it, as he wished, but as far as lightning goes, he's not the only one on the ball (as it were). Clicking from one site to the next, I soon find that other researchers have freely revealed their secrets for creating lightning balls in labs and even microwave ovens.

Engineer and inventor Jean-Louis Naudin[2] has published a video demonstrating how to produce free energy perfectly legally, but for how much longer, no one knows. Originally sponsored by a Swiss Foundation, Naudin, an exceptionally gifted model-maker, later received a grant from Taser-France. The grant underwrote R&D for a combat drone equipped with a Taser gun, which the company hoped to sell to the national police.[3] Just like in Tesla's time—need I remind everyone that he invented drones?—we can see which one attracts interest and funding from government administrations and powerful private corporations more easily: free energy or new weapons.

Eli Jerby and Vladimir Dikhtyar are research partners at the University of Tel Aviv. When they started using microwaves to manufacture nanoparticles, they were constantly trying to avoid creating the "great balls of fire" that frequently disturbed their experiments and damaged costly equipment. Then they had a light-bulb moment, realizing they would be much better off (both conceptually and financially) studying how the balls of fire were made. If you can't beat them, learn to create them instead, like the lightning tamer from Colorado Springs.[4]

Tesla's balls of lightning lasted a full minute as opposed to a few thousandths of second for the Israelis'. Nevertheless, it's a safe bet to say he is grateful for their dogged perseverance. "Don't stop at what I find," he used to remind his assistants in New York and Colorado Springs. "Keep on searching. Search elsewhere. Never stop searching. I need other insights besides my own."

*

That's how Tesla was, and that may well be how he still is: intent on inspiring, admiring, shedding light on, and honoring all those who pursue his wild bursts of creativity. His memory is reactivated through the methodical obstinacy of obscure researchers and the actions of those—dead or alive—who periodically stick up for him and whom he has asked me to salute in his name. From young Marco Metrovic to unlucky Ludwig Boltzmann, via John Searl, Bruce De Palma, Shiuji Inomata, Thomas Moray, Ettore Majorana, Tom Bearden, and Bleuette Diot, let alone all the pyro-technicians who have been drawn into the slipstream of his bolts of artificial lightning.

What else can we do for him? He has always been allergic to both pointless tributes and partisan proselytizing. His memory mustn't be reduced to the closing credits. He has repeatedly made it clear to me over the past six months that he hasn't turned his back on the living yet. When he asked to be "left alone" on January 9, 2016, he was referring to people exploiting his ashes. Not of his lightning.

Thus, on June 2, he answers my question about the best way to tame and reproduce energy from lightning via his two mediums: "For the ball of lightning, consider sand. Silicon, calcium, iron, nitrogen, and oxygen."

There. I've shared the recipe. No patents filed.

Nevertheless, urged on by a combination of professional integrity and curiosity, I google the terms. Lo and behold, an article from the *New Scientist*, a perfectly respectable journal, pops up, along with a French review of it by Marc Mennessier in *Le Figaro's* science pages. That's how I learn that certain ingredients from the recipe I just received have already been used with great success by a team led by Antonio Pavão and Gerson Paiva, at the Federal University of Pernambuco (Brazil).[5]

They based their experiment on one of Tesla's theories that has been revived by John Abrahamson (University of Canterbury, Christchurch, New Zealand). The article, which I knew nothing about, explains:

Abrahamson surmised that when lightning hits the ground, the sudden, intense heat can vaporize silicon oxide in the dirt, and a shockwave blows the gas up into the air. If there's also carbon in the soil, perhaps from dead leaves or tree roots, it will steal oxygen from the silicon oxide, leaving a bundle of pure silicon vapor. But the planet's oxygen-rich atmosphere rapidly re-oxidizes the hot ball of gas, and this reaction makes the orb glow briefly.[6]

In 2007, Pavão and Paiva placed 320-micron-thick slices of silicon between two electrodes to which they applied a current of more than 140 amperes. After a few seconds, they slowly moved the electrodes apart, producing an electric arc to vaporize the silicon. In their video, you can see very bright fireballs a few centimeters in diameter, rolling and bouncing on the ground briefly before they go out. Their temperature has been estimated at over 1,700° C (3,000° F).

It's not bad, but it doesn't hold a candle to what Tesla achieved in front of a large audience in New York, in May 1899. Mark Twain, one of Tesla's staunchest fans, was sitting in the front row, as was the English reporter Chauncey McGovern.[7] The latter described the astounding experience witnessed by those in attendance:

> Fancy yourself seated in a large, well-lighted room, with mountains of curious-looking machinery on all sides. A tall, thin, young man walks up to you, and by merely snapping his fingers, creates instantaneously a ball of leaping red flame, and holds it calmly in his hands. As you gaze, you are surprised to see it does not burn his fingers. He lets it fall upon his clothing, on his hair, into your lap, and, finally puts the ball of flame into a wooden box.

By producing that fireball which, according to his definition, "burned without consuming matter or without the slightest chemical reaction," Tesla actually "pre-invented" plasma physics in the late 19th century. The scientific community of the day refused to see it as anything other than a conjuring trick. And that's where things stood until 1978, when Engineer Robert Golka was able to reproduce Tesla's feat in front of a roomful of officers on Wendover Air Force Base in Utah.

What might the balls' practical purpose be? Well, a plasmoid—the scientific name for ball lightning—is a huge vortex of self-confined electrical energy. So the future belongs to whoever can work out how to prevent plasmoids from vanishing after a few seconds, or at least can harvest their incredible energy potential to use for controlled fusion.

When asked about progress in that field, our pyro-technician from the hereafter remains silent. Which means what? He's not actually sure? She's not receiving him? Or perhaps he's staying mum because someone has just found the answer, and any indiscretion on my informer's part could lead to that person being robbed—as Tesla was—of the patent of the century.

*

Is there a link between lightning and parallel universes? Might the former be a means of accessing the latter? In a sense, for Tesla, the answer would have to be yes. While he was still alive, after nearly being killed more than once from electric shocks or getting hit by lightning, he left somewhat fuzzy notes on the subject. Four days after providing the recipe for fireballs, he had Geneviève Delpech draw a very bushy oak tree with many ramifications. The caption dictated said, "The tree of life—branches of the future," and he added, "Dr. Ranga Chary. Very interesting."

Here we go again. When I google the name, which I have never come across before, the search engine points me to a page from *Paris Match* of November 6, 2015: "Multiverses: Proof at Last?", about an article originally published in the *New Scientist*.[8] Ranga-Ram Chary, an American astrophysicist and researcher at the Planck Telescope Data Center, has captured traces left by a 13-billion-year-old collision between our universe and a parallel one shortly after the Big Bang. "While trying to establish a map of the famous Cosmic Microwave Background (CMB, the electromagnetic waves issued from the Big Bang) Ranga-Ram Chary revealed an 'eerie glow.' More precisely: patches in the cosmos that are 4,500 times brighter than calculations had predicted."

In his published findings,[9] Chary defends the hypothesis that the glow may have been caused by a brush with another universe bumping up against our own. According to that theory, the bright patches formed a few hundred thousand years after the Big Bang, "when electrons and protons first joined forces to create hydrogen, which emits light in a limited range of colors." During that process, a certain number of those protons and electrons seem to have come into contact with another universe, and the recombination made their light burn a lot brighter.

The theory is appealing, but naturally, it has not been unanimously accepted. David Spergel, an astrophysicist at Princeton, has commented dryly that, "I suspect that it would be worth looking into alternative possibilities," before pointing to parallel universes. Chary himself recognizes that "Unusual claims like evidence for alternate universes require a very high burden of proof." But he's working on it—under the watchful eye of a benevolent Tesla, it would seem.

Though to be fair, our hologram Tesla seems to approve of the idea as a valid avenue of research, rather than acknowledging it as an established theory. "Very interesting," is all he says. I may well be interpreting—after all, only Geneviève Delpech knows what the tone of his voice in her left ear was—but I think I perceive a certain indulgent pleasure in her correspondent's judgment.

Why would he have wanted me to promote the astrophysicist's data when it had attracted such surprisingly little attention in France? I get the feeling that even the dead aren't all-knowing. Assuming an entity that pursues scientific activities in the hereafter can only continue its research through colleagues in the here and now, it would have to do so *at their pace*, drawing on their trial and error, intuitions, and hypotheses as much as on the irrefutable proof they sometimes uncover.

If it is confirmed, the irruption into our world of matter from a parallel universe could be the first concrete step enabling us to "follow that path," to penetrate, other than through a random bolt out of the blue (whether literally or figuratively) one of those worlds that until now has been the fruit of theoretical models only. Patience is a virtue. We've only just, thanks to gravitational waves, obtained concrete proof of the actual existence of black holes. The adventure is ongoing—as we were told on April 26: this is just the beginning.

But what about Einstein in all of this?

There's no news; he's out surfing space-time waves with his three children, I suppose.

His first wife and first love—the mother of Lieserl, Hans-Albert, and Eduard—interrupted Geneviève's nap one day, arriving during a previously unoccupied time slot (3:30 p.m.) to fill in for her ex-husband. Here's how Geneviève described the encounter:

> She was in her thirties, wearing a black dress buttoned up the front with a high collar of off-white lace. Her thick hair had been pulled back in a bun, and she seemed very sweet. She told me her name was Mileva, then she said that you should get in touch with Nicomède Pokowski in Toruń, that the existence of parallel universes—including one stuck to ours at the other end of black holes—was correct, and that it explained the phenomenon of the expansion of the universe despite gravitational force. She also said those bright, powerful explosions or eruptions of gamma rays that no one understands yet take place when matter and energy leaking from black and white holes from parent universes come into contact. She added that Albert Einstein had been right.

It's hard to know what to think of this message from the presumptive first

Mrs. Einstein, aside from that she's clearly not a spiteful person.

Who was Mileva Maric? A young physicist who fell in love and dedicated herself to supporting Albert's genius rather than developing her own talent; a mother devastated by the death of her first child and the schizophrenia of the third; a wife cut to the quick by her husband's endless affairs with lesser women; the companion whose disgust and hatred he did his utmost to incite... in hopes of a divorce that would allow him to marry his first cousin, Elsa.

In 1913, Albert concocted a set of "conditions" for their continued cohabitation that will hardly go down in history as his most inspired text:

A. You will make sure:
> 1. that my clothes and laundry are kept in good order;
> 2. that I will receive my three meals regularly in my room;
> 3. that my bedroom and study are kept neat, and especially that my desk is left for my use only.

B. You will renounce all personal relations with me insofar as they are not completely necessary for social reasons. Specifically, you will forego:
> 1. my sitting at home with you;
> 2. my going out or traveling with you.[10]

And that's just an excerpt. Even without the conjugal particulars, the end of the message from that talented scientist who has been relegated to her husband's shadow—"Albert Einstein had been right"—takes on a disconcerting resonance. I hope it really was Mileva Maric's autonomous spirit and not some declination sent as a sort of post-scriptum by Einstein's redemptive sense of humor, unique conception of guilt, or an expanding desire for reconciliation.

Nevertheless, her comment about gamma eruptions does make one wonder. She's referring to explosions of colossal emissions of photons, known as "gamma-ray bursts." They generate more energy in seconds than the sun has or will in 10 billion years. Although they were discovered 50 years ago, the bursts' origins are still disputed. Are they the collapse of high-mass stars leading to the formation of hyper-massive black holes, "simply" the effect of quantum gravitation on smaller black holes, or is there some other explanation?

Wherever they come from, the gamma rays are believed to have been responsible for the five major extinctions of biodiversity our planet has known. On the other hand, they may also play a role in the possible existence of life on other planets. Aside from the connection to parallel universes her message implies, they are also related to the galactic-energy halos that might emit them, to gravitational waves, and to neutrinos from the scalar waves that transmit most of their energy,[11] as well as to the fireballs used as miniature models of the phenomenon.[12]

In a way, it's as though the spectral Mileva Maric has synthesized, in just a few words, the themes raised in all of the messages from both Einstein and Tesla I'd received to that point. If this were a novel, it would make the perfect ending: the whole thing was the generous, open-minded "payback" of a brilliant woman overshadowed by her husband's aura. It would have been she who scripted and staged his posthumous image, memories, joys, and remorse; she who thought to include the figure of his overlooked peer, Tesla, who needed to be brought back into the limelight.

Laurent Seksik pays tribute to Mileva in his book,[13] but I am pleased to be able to salute her here in my own way. As for Nicomède Pokowski from Toruń, whom she suggested I get in touch with, I can find no trace of him online, and I don't have time to search for him elsewhere. As Swejen Salter, communications director for the planet Marduk would say, "Here's the ball—I'm happy to toss it to whoever wants to run with it."

1. International Thermonuclear Experimental reactor: an experimental nuclear fusion reactor being built next to the Cadarache facility in southern France. The project aims to master nuclear fusion, but for the moment is consuming infinitely more electricity than it is capable of producing.
2. www.jlnlabs.online.fr
3. *Ouest France*, 8 February 2008.
4. www.scienceinschool.org
5. www.lefigaro.fr, 16 January 2007
6. www.newscientist.com/article/dn24886-natural-ball-lightning-probed-for-the-first-time/
7. Chauncey McGovern, "The New Wizard of the West," *Pearson's Magazine*, London, May, 1899.
8. https://www.newscientist.com/article/2063204-mystery-bright-spots-could-be-first-glimpse-of-another-universe/
9. Ranga-Ram Chary, "Spectral variations of the Sky: Constraints on Alternate universes" *The New Scientist*, November 2015.
10. *Lettres de rupture. Petite histoire de la séparation amoureuse à travers les plus belles lettres de personnages célèbres (Dear John Letters: A Brief History of Breaking Up As Seen through the Loveliest Letters by Famous People)*, presented by Agnès Pierron, Le Robert, 2015.
11. *L'Astronomie*, issue 62, June 2013.
12. *Gamma-ray bursts*, Wikipedia.
13. Laurent Seksik, *Le Cas Éduard Einstein*, op. cit.

22
Finishing touches

June 2016. What with the train strikes, and worse, the acts of terrorism, France is having a miserable spring. As for me, I'm re-reading, correcting, completing, pruning and refining. At some point, I am going to have to write the words "The End." But for the moment, I'm still hesitating. Will the Sky Engineer's messages stop for good once I've finished my task, and written the last word of this book? Geneviève dreads that possibility. Fortunately, more and more of her time is being taken up by her late husband, whose thoughts now flow through her fingers in writing that is sometimes automatic, sometimes not. Although the longed-for reunion is an unfettered joy for her, she would still like to continue her relationship with Nikola. He hasn't shown up for two weeks now. The last time, he was only there for a flash. Sounding polite but distracted, he barely had time to say, "I'll be back."

She misses him. More than the flamboyant Albert, who only ever showed her his sunny side. She has grown quite attached to the ascetic penitent, the companion in loneliness who gave her all sorts of grief, but who also touched her with his sensitivity, his wounded humanity, and his sadness brightened only by the occasional fleeting smile. The surges of hope he shared with her when scientists served all of humankind by discovering new ways of deciphering the visible or invisible world in order to disarm obtuse materialism and rein in fundamentalist absurdities. But he came unbidden, and it's unlikely he'd stick around against his will if one were to try to hold him back.

Unlike Geneviève, Marie-France has grown immune to the nocturnal absences without a by-your-leave: "When they have something vital to say they find a way to get through to us, but when they stop answering, it means they have better things to do." That, in a nutshell, is her sole philosophy as a medium.

As for me, I don't know what I will be writing tomorrow, and that uncertainty suits me just fine. These past few months of writing under the inspiring pressure of energies that insisted on being transmitted have been enthralling, but it is time for me to move on. I'm dying—no pun intended—to get my autonomy back. I'm longing to be guided by nothing more than my own imagination and free will.

In retrospect, the contradictory signs, occasional elements of proof, and predictions—some that came true and others we're still waiting on, as well as the concrete data I received, deciphered and checked now seem to me to be both extraordinary and already obsolete. I may have needed them to lend credence to the messages I was being asked to disseminate; but I have no more use for them now.

Deep inside me, some instinct (for freedom or self-preservation... or is it just pride?) is starting to rebel against the "mission" as an interface or intermediary that I accepted willingly until recently. I'm hoping Einstein will go back to being a semi-fictional character of my imagination, and that the indelible yet self-erasing print on the tiles will be the last time Tesla's energy leaves its mark on my everyday life. I find it reassuring just to formulate those thoughts. If I'm hoping my life will go back to the way it was before, it means that despite all these notions, I'm still the same person I always was.

When all is said and done, what should I retain from this experience, which I wrote as it was taking place, in a high-pressure space-time in which incessant, unforeseen developments were at loggerheads with the perspective needed to put things into words properly? I think this amazing adventure, in which I could have lost my footing, actually wound up making me feel more stable, rather than less. It strengthened my convictions on several fronts: my acceptance of phenomena beyond our ken, my belief that it's best to "consume" them with moderation, and my intuition that they can never be summarized in a single hypothesis.

What Marie-France, Geneviève, and I lived through was absolutely, undeniably authentic; yet that doesn't mean it was necessarily *real*. What I mean by that is that we can't know if the *real* Einstein, the *real* Tesla, or the *real* Delpech actually came, in person, to intrude on the mediums' daily lives. Even the photos we obtained are not edifying proof. We do know that we didn't doctor them, but we still don't know where they came from. Are the deceased—famous deceased people in particular—the only ones able to access their own images, or have those images fallen into a sort of "public domain" in which their appearance and aptitudes can be freely used in their best interests or to the advantage of whatever entity has managed to take possession of them?

Let's take the hypothesis of the post-conjugal "misappropriation" a little further. One can legitimately wonder if Albert Einstein's energy, amplified by an ever-more glorious posterity, might have constituted a kind of independent egregore.

Might Nikola Tesla, who had so much stolen from him in his lifetime, not have lost the rights to his posthumous image as well? Was he actually in control of those messages, or was he letting franchisers, or even counterfeiters, speak for him? Has he been so corroded by the oblivion into which he has fallen that he is not even aware of what is being done in his name, and with his appearance?

If that were the case, then the "Tesla consciousness" and its equivalent labeled Einstein would be nothing more than empty shells, casings, modular vehicles from Luxembourg (both a tax haven and a spirit one), the planet Marduk, God-knows-what parallel universe, or simply our own psychic energy—vehicles that adapt themselves to each "client's" needs and tastes in order to transmit the information that suits them best. So are we in the presence of just a few more spiritual holograms among so many others, combinations of memories, perceptions, and intentions drawn from an infinite virtual library of them that has been accruing since the beginning of time?

Some people call that reservoir of knowledge the Akashic records, a sort of natural iCloud. The trick is knowing if the information comes *to* us or *from* us. Are we subjected to it, or do we create it through our desire to believe?

With the passing of time, my doubts have begun to get the upper hand over the sense of normalcy with which the mediums, scientists, and my nearest and dearest and I all accepted the whole crazy situation. But doubts don't prove anything in and of themselves. I remain Cartesian through thick and thin. Unlike what many people seem to think, according to Descartes, the truest, most profound doubt consists in doubting everything—including the validity of the doubt itself. You won't necessarily see any more clearly, but you're less like to be blinded by false beliefs.

And so I wind up back at the crucial question: were those *really* the ghosts

244 | TESLA AND ME

of Einstein and Tesla that appeared to the two mediums? And was that a real revenant that let itself be immortalized, or was it the mental image the person taking the photograph associated with him that imprinted itself on her phone, like the psycho-photographs produced by Ted Serios in the lab?

The fact that Geneviève Delpech hadn't the slightest idea who Nikola Tesla was nor what he looked like before December 19, 2015 pleads against the latter. I was the one who suggested the hologram's identity to her when she first described the stranger who had popped up at the foot of her bed. I could, of course, be accused or suspected of some sort of telepathic projection. But, unlike Einstein, with whom I've been obsessed for years, when Tesla first appeared to her, he was nowhere in my thoughts.

Having said that, it is also true that a few months earlier, I had briefly pondered the idea of doing something about him someday. But it had been only a vague notion that hadn't taken shape yet. If one chooses to take that expression literally, then perhaps I am the unconscious source of the three successive ghostly apparitions: my father, Einstein, and Tesla—two people about whom I had already written, and one who was raring to be next.

Were the mediums unwittingly led to borrow images and visuals from my unconsciousness so as to deactivate my skepticism in order to be able to "pass on" the information meant for me? I truly don't know. And I have to admit that ignorance can be bliss. I like for anything to be possible. I'm always suspicious of what seems obvious.

At the end of the day, neither the spectacular manifestations, nor the inexplicable photos, nor the incredibly precise contents of certain messages, nor the weight of doubts alternating with the incredible buoyancy of the amazing is what strikes me most about the adventure. More than anything, it is the overall climate of emotion and humor in which it all unfurled. The disconcerting surprise that "someone" gave me by inserting a situation drawn from my imagination—perhaps even inspired and modeled by it—into my real life.

Then there is the incredible range of sentiments I felt—admiration, distrust, discomfort, compassion, doubt, enthusiasm, confusion about what to do— for Nikola Tesla, whose life I would never have explored with such passion if he hadn't seemed to be making such an effort to attract my attention. Those sentiments also amplified and refined the ones that Einstein, who fascinates me all the more—now that I can see him through the prism of that inverted double shedding light on his dark side—already inspired in me.

Could that emotional enrichment have been the point of the whole thing? The idea, even if it is fanciful, that I may have helped Einstein get some "closure" simply by visualizing a reconciliation scene with his children is, in and of itself, a lovely gift. I also find it most touching, and flattering, too, that someone as totally unlike me as Tesla was—in terms of his character, options, fate, phobias, and refusal of all things carnal—might ask me for help. It fills me with a swaggering modesty that is fairly typical of me. Although in all honesty, the only true comfort I can bring him is by acting as a loudspeaker (which he invented in 1881) for him, in the face of the silence the industrial and military lobbies have doggedly attempted to dissolve him into.

What will come out of the recently announced or imminent discoveries the avatars of Einstein and Tesla shared with us? Without a doubt, gravitational waves are going to stand our knowledge of the universe and its origins on its head. Jostled by that swelling wave, time and space will never look the same again.

And what about parallel universes? Once a theoretical concept, they seem to have started "releasing matter" into our dimension. Will they eventually share all their secrets? Will free energy—whether harnessed from the air or extracted from tamed lightning—ever live up to its promises? If we do achieve it, will it tip the global economy into a fatal crisis or succeed at reducing poverty, pollution, war, and the fanaticism fed by petroleum and gas money? Will the heralded discoveries about our origins and multiple universes, in addition to the true nature of space-time, hold back the fundamentalist hijacking of religion and the eternal short-term thinking that leads us to suicide?

We shall see. Or not. Like Einstein—but with even less luck or appreciation—Tesla was always ahead of his time. He is ahead of ours, too, and I'm not sure a flesh-and-blood "I" will ever witness widespread distribution of free electricity drawn from the air or the void. Having said that, I'm not worried about Tesla. They pulled the plug on his dreams, but he has never given up on switching them back on. Assuming his personality is still active and autonomous, time is on his side… As long as he can occasionally refresh his memory by plugging into the living, renewing his energy via the very act of transmitting it.

*

Wednesday, July 13, 2016: I send the manuscript to my editor. Having cloistered myself with the final revisions, I haven't been in touch with either medium for two weeks. So they have no idea where I am in the process. The next day, I receive two messages. A quick, "You're done, but not quite," from Einstein via Marie-France; and a long text from Geneviève informing me that her Tesla has dropped in:

> I've come to say farewell. It is time for me to work elsewhere. My last message is to remind your friend to look into the tree of life that I had you draw, as well as Einstein's relationship to the sacred texts. As for me, let me inform you that the universe is God's hardware. It is an organic entity of which you are the minuscule cells. You are both the Gods of your cells and the neurons of God, but your universe is not unique, and is only one fragment of God. Millions of others exist. There is intention, intelligence, and consciousness in the universe for the conception of life. Thank you, and good-bye.

The phone rings. My editor has read the manuscript and thinks I should reinstate some personal passages about Tesla, Einstein, and myself that I had cut at the last minute for the sake of impartiality. That's lucky—I was already starting to regret the cuts.

The tree of life and the sacred texts will have to wait.

*

This morning, I took the train with my revised manuscript under one arm and the most important elements of my documentation under the other. I can't go anywhere without them at this stage, not even for a quick day trip that has been planned for quite some time. There's a sentence stuck in my head: "I'll be back." I don't know why, but ever since I woke up this morning, I've been haunted by those words spoken by the entity formerly known as Tesla, the announcement made last month and later rendered obsolete by his adieus on July 14.

Having decided last night how I would conclude this book, I am flipping through the dog-eared pages of *Man Out of Time*, Margaret Cheney's imposing biography of Tesla, in search of the letter Mark Twain wrote to him in 1898. I eventually come up with it:

> Dear Mr. Tesla,
>
> Here in the hotel the other night when some interested men were discussing means to persuade the nations to join with the Czar & disarm, I advised them to seek something more sure than disarmament by perishable paper-contract – invite the great inventors to contrive something against which fleets and armies would be helpless, & thus make war thenceforth impossible. I did not suspect that you were already attending to that, & getting ready to introduce into the earth

permanent peace & disarmament in a practical & mandatory way."[1]

I raise my eyes. The documents and first-person accounts we now dispose of imply that, contrary to the calumnies spread by his enemies for decades, the idol of New York's pigeons did indeed have the wherewithal to achieve his dream: imposing universal peace on all nations by equipping each of them with both an absolute weapon and infallible protection from it—a directed-energy ray and its scalar shield. If Tesla hadn't been kept from preventing mankind's folly, we might have been spared two World Wars. On the other hand, if we're interested, it seems that he is still at our service.

But my task ends here. Other work demands my time. I have done, at my own risk, what I could to pass on the information transmitted to me. Now I'm passing the baton on to investigative journalists, scientists, and concerned citizens. It is up to them to follow Tesla's path to the "eco-responsible" discoveries we have been deprived of until now. It's up to them, if they so choose, to do what they can to break through the lies of the past and build a better future.

As the rising sun warms the window of the high-speed train, I re-read the notes I've scribbled in the margins of Margaret Cheney's book, which I'm holding in front of my face. The cover shows the famous photo of Tesla that acquired my impossible reflection a month ago. A little girl coming back from the café compartment with her mother tosses out a cheerful greeting as she passes me.

"Do you know him?" her mother asks, smiling at me.

"Yes," the child answers, "I've seen him before." But it wasn't me she was looking at.

---

1. Letter from Mark Twain to Nikola Tesla, November 17, 1898, Library of Congress.

Acknowledgements

To the scientists who assisted me with both their knowledge and their open-mindedness: Dr. Gaston Ciais, Dr. Jean-Jacques Charbonier; the physicists Jean-Pierre Garnier Malet, Christophe Galfard, and Thibault Damour; the astrophysicists Trinh Xuan Thuan and Jean-Pierre Luminet.

To my explorers of the invisible: Marie-France Cazeaux, Geneviève Delpech and Yaguel Didier, as well as Michèle Blaise and Martine Le Coz.

Made in the USA
San Bernardino, CA
06 January 2019